CULTURE AND IDENTITY IN EUROPE

LIVERPOOL
JOHN MOORES UNIVERSIT.
TRUEMAN STREET LIBRARY
15-21 WEBSTER STREET
LIVERPOOL L3 2ET
TEL. 051 231 4022/4023

For Jacky, with our thanks

Culture and Identity in Europe

Perceptions of divergence and unity in past and present

Edited by

MICHAEL WINTLE
Department of European Studies
University of Hull

Avebury

Aldershot · Brookfield USA · Hong Kong · Singapore · Sydney

Published by
Avebury
Ashgate Publishing Ltd
Gower House
Croft Road
Aldershot
Hants GU11 3HR
England

Ashgate Publishing Company
Old Post Road
Brookfield
Vermont 05036
USA

British Library Cataloguing in Publication Data

Culture and Identity in Europe:
    Perceptions of Divergence and Unity in
    Past and Present. - (Perspectives on
    Europe Series)
    I. Wintle, M. J. II. Series
    306.094

Library of Congress Catalog Card Number: 95-83287

ISBN 1 85972 135 4

Camera ready copy prepared by
Rachel Al-Azzawi
School of Geography
University of Oxford
Oxford OX1 3TB

Printed in Great Britain by
Antony Rowe Ltd, Chippenham, Wiltshire

Contents

Figures and tables

Acknowledgements

These essays do not arise from a symposium or conference, but from the informal research discussions of a small academic department. Of the seven authors, Philip Morgan, David Willis, Xiudian Dai, and Michael Wintle are on the lecturing staff of the Department of European Studies at the University of Hull (U.K.), while Vian Bakir is a Graduate Teaching Assistant in the same Department. The other two authors, M. Spiering and Bram Boxhoorn, work in the Department of European Studies at the University of Amsterdam, with which Hull's Department has a long history of close association and exchange. About eighteen months ago, it was decided to formalize some of our seminar and coffee-room discussions about our current research interests at Hull into a collection of essays centred on the theme of identity in Europe, with an emphasis on the discrepancies between perception and reality. This book is the result of that initiative, and I am grateful to the authors, and the very helpful publishing staff at the Avebury Press, for enabling it to come to fruition.

I am happy to acknowledge permission to reproduce the illustrative material in this book. I am grateful to the Bodleian Library Oxford (Fig. 4.8), The Royal Geographical Society (Figs 4.1-4.3), The British Library (Figs 4.4, 4.6, 4.7, 4.9, 4.14, 4.15), Edinburgh University Press (Fig. 4.5), Harper Collins Publishers (Fig. 4.10), The Strahov Monastery Library in Prague (Fig. 4.12), Max Niemeyer Verlag in Tübingen (Fig. 4.11), and Viking Penguin (Fig. 5.1). I am also more than happy to acknowledge my own debt, in Chapter 4, to both the text and plates of Peter Whitfield's wonderfully illustrated *The image of the world*, published by The British Library in 1994.

Finally, our thanks are due to Rachel Al-Azzawi, of the University of Oxford, for converting the text into camera-ready copy, and to Sarah Anthony, desk editor at Avebury.

Michael Wintle
University of Hull
October 1995

1 Introduction: Cultural diversity and identity in Europe

Michael Wintle

The essays commissioned for this volume all address the idea of Europe. Most refer to the problem in terms of identity; all are concerned with European culture and with what the concept of Europe means, both in the minds of Europeans, and in terms of objective reality. Indeed the contrast between those two is one of the book's themes. The issues are approached from several disciplinary directions. Historians examine the evidence for the existence of a common European experience and culture through the centuries, the history of attempts and schemes to unify Europe, and the graphic portrayal of Europe from the earliest times down to today, all in attempts to uncover what the 'essence' or 'identity' of this Europe might be. The disciplines of anthropology, social psychology, international relations, and cultural and literary studies are scoured for insights into the juxtaposition of national identity with unity and identity at the European level. Another historian undertakes a study of what the European Commission has meant by the word identity, and political economists put the notion of Europe under the microscope from the point of view of the re-integration of East and West since 1989, of the role to be played by the news media in cultivating a European identity, and of whether it is possible to have an EU policy on technical standards in a rapidly changing industry. These attempts to isolate and define European identity or essence make clear that it is elusive and equivocal, that identity is complex and made up of many layers interacting at different and changing levels, that to manipulate it is by no means impossible but unpredictable and potentially even dangerous, and that identity at European level is weak compared with national identity. All the authors agree that it is a mistake to view past instances of common European experience and shared culture, the building blocks of identity, as some sort of pre-history of the EU.

The collection opens with an examination of the concept of cultural identity itself, and of its application to Europe as an entity. That European cultural identity is not easy to locate and define, although several shared experiences, from the Roman Empire through to industrialization, are shown to have had a formative influence. Theories of state- and nation-formation are applied to Europe: significant and important elements of those processes are found to have occurred already in Europe. Identity is usually multiple and potentially integrational, so there is no ostensible reason why a European identity should not exist alongside a national one, in the same way that nation already exists alongside gender, race, age, and all the other aspects of identity which we have. The mistake, perhaps, is to link the concept of a European cultural identity with the relatively brief post-war history of the present European project.

Philip Morgan undertakes a selective survey of some of the schemes for European unity which have unfolded since the Middle Ages, and asks in somewhat sceptical vein whether political projects for European unity right up to today have been anything more than well concealed attempts to promote national interests. His conclusion is that a preoccupation with the idea of Europe can seriously impede an analysis of the history of attempts to achieve a degree of political unity in Europe. From the thirteenth century onwards, the only schemes for integration in Europe which have gained any foothold in political reality at all have been attempts to promote the interests of nation-states. Coudenhove-Kalergi may have been a disinterested idealist in favour of a united Europe, but Briand was simply seeking a way of Europeanizing France's German problem. The EEC and now the EU, Morgan concludes, have very little to do with a European cultural identity, but have essentially provided an arena where national states can promote their own interests.

In his essay on visual representations of Europe, Michael Wintle tackles the question of 'What is Europe?' by asking, 'What does Europe look like?' The chapter examines what people think of when they talk of Europe, how big they think it is, where its boundaries are, and how it has been personified. After surveying the various fragments of European unity in the past, in which discontinuity is emphasized, the study moves to a consideration of maps as a projection of the image of Europe, and also examines allegorical portrayals of the continent in decorations, cartoons, paintings, and in the marginalia of the maps themselves. From early traditions of Europa and the bull, Japheth, and Europe's place in God's universe, the Renaissance unleashed a more triumphant and even predatory image of the continent as a whole, presented as a unity with common characteristics and indeed identity: it self-consciously represented the best in the world, and increasingly dominated it. The unity in the graphic portrayals of Europe was only halted by the onset of nationalism and imperialism in the nineteenth century, which fragmented the image into myriad and often inimical nationalisms. The image, then, reflected the reality.

M. Spiering, a specialist in the analysis of images of national identity through literary and other texts, takes the concept of national identity and interrogates it for applicability to the European (EU) level. He agrees with Morgan that much of the apparent unity of Europe since the war has been based on the national interests of the member states, rather than on any higher ideals. He handles in turn the notions of state, nation, and nationalism, employing some

2

of the concepts and methodology of social psychology to illuminate these complicated issues. Having cleared the ground, he moves on to weigh the issue of national identity. Is it nature or nurture? Is it in-born and natural to mankind, not because man was born to be nationalist but because he was born to have identity, and therefore national identity? Or is national identity constructed, learned, and nurtured? Both probably play a role, and the resulting strength of national identity is a considerable obstacle to the achievement of a 'reinforced European identity', in the words of the *Treaty on European Union*. Spiering sees all manner of problems at the European level: to achieve a genuine EU-level identity analogous to national identity would probably require widespread violence (as did the founding of most nation-states), an alternative image of alien alterity, and a strong ideology of Europeanness, and none of these is either likely or desirable. A gentle, well-meaning, benevolent pan-Europeanism is all well and good, but it amounts to little more than idealism.

Bram Boxhoorn focuses on what is actually meant, in spite of all the rhetoric, by European 'identity' as expressed in the legal documents of the European Union. Building on an earlier study by B. de Witte,[1] Boxhoorn examines the text of various treaties and declarations issued over the last twenty years, and analyses the use of the concept of identity. It was first employed in these documents in the 1970s, when 'identity' was seen as a panacea for the problems besetting the EC at the time. The concept was employed in two ways: externally and internally. External identity appears to consist, for those who draw up these documents, of a common approach amongst the member-states to their foreign relations. Internally, identity refers to more cohesion and integration, and a great number of words were spent on 'unity in diversity', a Citizen's Europe, and the People's Europe. The duality in the use of the term continued through the 1980s, but in the 1990s, notably in the Maastricht Treaty, while the external form continued to refer to a search for a common foreign and defence policy, internal identity was radically scaled down, in favour of subsidiarity.

Political claims for the importance of identity have often been viewed with suspicion, which is not to deny the power of identity politics in Central Europe, where, especially since 1989, there has been such a drive to dissociate national identity from 'Eastern' or Soviet-dominated Europe. David Willis, a political economist who professionally distrusts the analysis of politics without economics, or vice versa, poses the question of whether this apparent shift to the West, embracing Western liberal values in economics and politics, is merely another episode in the attempts of politicians to fabricate myths, or whether it has actually contributed to a shift in perspectives and ideas of what Europe is, and what European integration might be. Is the promotion of the idea of a convergence on the part of the states of Eastern and Central Europe on Western values any more than a greater emphasis on 'marketization'? By means of examining the concepts of a 'pax Europeana' sponsored by the EU, of Fortress Europe, and the strength of ethnic nationalism, Willis comes to the conclusion that, even were it possible to construct a new identity for Eastern Europe in the image of the West, the EU is hardly the appropriate vehicle to achieve it. The idea of imposing - for the best of ostensible reasons - a liberal free-market economy on Central and Eastern Europe through the agency of the EU may, it seems, not only fail in economic terms, but might succeed in driving out much of that diversity of cultural identity and accommodation which is the socio-political concomitant of Western (European) liberalism.

Vian Bakir's essay approaches the question of European identity from the viewpoint of the news media. She investigates the evolution of the EC's desire to encourage the emergence of a European identity, what that could mean, and whether it could co-exist with national identities. There have been high expectations of the media in its ability to assist, or even lead from the front, in the nurturing of such a transnational identity: Bakir examines the reality, taking as a case-study the media's role in using the UK monarchy to bolster a national identity. The conclusion is that such attempts have been problematic and by no means successful, and that, given a number of structural problems in the European media, it is unlikely that it will be able to assist the EU at the European level in creating an identity there.

Xiudian Dai's chapter examines the nuts and bolts of the capacity of Europe - in the form of the EU - to deliver a coherent policy on technical standards in the television industry. He looks at the issue of technical convergence which is assumed to be taking place, and asks what the EU has done and might do to facilitate convergence in the sector of information and communications technologies (ICT). Could a harmonized standard EU policy replace the diversified regimes which exist in the member states, and should indeed the EU attempt it? And what would be the costs of creating such a policy identity? Dai's survey of this highly topical field reveals that Europe has had a much harder time trying to bring its industry together than, for example, have the United States and Japan, and the ability of the European Commission to make itself a 'government' in that sense is questionable. In the end, Dai characterizes European (EU) attempts at standardization as 'parochialist', and recommends immediate progression to concentrating on the global level.

Unity in diversity?

What are we to make of Europe? Has it an identity? Has it a culture? Has it a unity? The essays here, in their different methodological and disciplinary approaches, seem to indicate that, while there are and have been in the past elements of all these things, the diversity in Europe is just as strong as its unity. Is this, then, an endorsement of the European Commission's official dictum of 'unity in diversity'?

The idea or conceit of 'unity in diversity' stems from the work of Guizot and his contemporaries in the nineteenth century, with their Romantic nationalism combined with an idealistic pan-Europeanism. From the 1970s onwards the need to make the EC 'more interesting than the price of butter' led to a Commission campaign to give the EC more 'soul', which eventually resulted in the adoption of the slogan of 'unity in diversity'. What does that mean? Logically, it means very little: it is empty rhetoric.[2] However, it is not entirely to be dismissed. Simply put, Europe is certainly very diverse, but there is also some kind of common quality, if not unity, in Europe. And the connection between the two is that, on a good day (and let no-one forget that there have been plenty of very bad ones), one of the distinctive features of Europe - even of a European identity - is a recognition of and accommodation of diversity.[3]

There can be no doubt of the diversity: indeed it is the problem of the EU authorities that European culture is far more complicated than the EU, and cannot be harnessed as a rallying cry for the Union.[4] On the other hand, the diversity can be portrayed as one of Europe's particular strengths: it has promoted cross-fertilization of ideas, and has provided a 'succulent seed-bed' for evolution and development.[5] An analysis of recent opinion polls (in *Eurobaromètre*) seems to indicate that

> European identity is becoming increasingly identified with a capacity to tolerate considerable cultural diversity - at least of those values that European citizens consider to be most worth preserving.[6]

There are problems here, of course: this is an image of tolerance that Europeans have of themselves, it concerns only those values of which they approve, most opinion polls suffer from methodological defects, and in any case tolerance is no substitute for genuine freedom. Nonetheless, there is a real sense in which Europe does prize pluralism, democracy, and civil society. The reality does not always match the ideal, but the very perception and recognition of the ideal is at least a step in the right direction towards the protection and nurturing of minorities within Europe, whether they be cultural, political, ethnic, or social.[7]

The identity of Europe is contested, and its culture, although occasionally and partially shared, can never be defined into a single coherent dominant. To sloganize that into 'unity in diversity' is perhaps to cheapen it; to try to press it into the service of the present European project is perhaps futile. But to prize that accommodation of diversity, and value it, is no bad starting point.

The image of identity

Identity is about images, rather than realities, and this collection is a study of images. One of the most comprehensive essays in its coverage, on national and European identity by M. Spiering, puts the whole debate into the context of 'image studies' or 'imagology', the study of the interaction of projections of national and other identity through 'texts', whether literary or more popular. Identity is now generally seen, in its dynamic sense, not as a set of essential characteristics, but as the ascribed or recognized characteristics which a person or group is agreed to possess. These characteristics may be ascribed to itself by the group, but just as importantly ascribed to the group by others. In other words, we are dealing with perception, rather than reality. Furthermore, although we can often agree about our group identity vis-à-vis outsiders, or the alterity, we seldom concur on our representation of the group towards ourselves, or our self-representation. The same applies to culture, as well as to identity. In the words of P. Odermatt,

> used in its symbolically charged form, the term 'culture' implies that there is such a thing as a homogeneous group, even though there need be no consensus throughout that group as to the actual content of that culture.[8]

Images of identity, of culture, and unity, and their relationship to actual events, form one of the themes which run through the essays in this collection. Maps and other two-dimensional cultural statements are examined for what they try to project about contemporary ideas of the nature of Europe. Schemes of European unity are checked for their nation-driven content. Protestations about the re-integration of Eastern and Western Europe are scrutinized in the light of the agendas of the protagonists: at the very least there is a disjunction between the rhetoric of liberalization and the reality of protectionism. Treaties and declarations are studied for what they actually mean by such things as 'European identity'. The news media's role of spin-doctor is analysed for its contribution to images of unity, identity and culture. And the viability of a single pro-active EU public policy in industrial standards is challenged and found wanting. Europe is contested; no-one can agree on precisely what it means, even geographically. To study Europe in terms of the EU and its history is worthy and important, but only part of the subject. Even in the limited context of Western Europe or the EU, the same debates about identity and culture are conducted. The events of 1989 formed a watershed for European culture and identity:[9] certainly it is no longer possible for the EU to imagine that it has any kind of monopoly on European identity. What European cultural identity has been, is now, and will become in the future is not an objective reality but a set of aspirations and images; one of the conclusions of this book is that the more inclusive and accommodating of diversity that cultural projection, the better.

Notes

1. De Witte, 'Building Europe's image'.

2. Leerssen & Van Montfrans, eds, *Borders and territories*, 1-2: 'ramshackle'.

3. García, ed., *European identity*, 132.

4. J. Keane's essay in Nelson, ed., *The idea of Europe*, 56-7.

5. Hay, 'Europe revisited: 1979', 5.

6. K. Reif, in García, ed., *European identity*, 131.

7. Nelson, ed., *The idea of Europe*, 5; Shelley, ed., *Aspects of European cultural diversity*, 171.

8. Odermatt, 'The use of symbols', 219.

9. Nelson, ed., *The idea of Europe*, 9-11.

References

García, S., ed., *European identity and the search for legitimacy* (London, Pinter, 1993).

Hay, D., 'Europe revisited: 1979', *History of European Ideas*, 1(1980), 1-6.

Leerssen, J.T & M van Montfrans, eds, *Borders and territories, Yearbook of European Studies*, 6 (Amsterdam, Rodopi, 1993).

Nelson, B., et al., ed., *The idea of Europe: problems of national and transnational identity* (Oxford, Berg, 1992).

Odermatt, P., 'The use of symbols in the drive for European integration', *Yearbook of European Studies*, 4(1991), 217-40.

Shelley, M., et al., ed., *Aspects of European cultural diversity*, revised edition, What is Europe? 2 (London, Routledge, 1995).

Witte, B. de, 'Building Europe's image and identity', in A. Rijksbaron et al., eds, *Europe from a cultural perspective: historiography and perceptions* (The Hague, 1987), 132-9.

2 Cultural identity in Europe: Shared experience

Michael Wintle

European cultural identity: first reactions

Is there such a thing as a European cultural identity? Or is there simply so much diversity that any talk of 'sameness', let alone 'identity', within Europe is rendered meaningless? What do the terms 'Europe', 'culture', and 'identity' mean anyway? These questions are presently very much at issue, and words have flowed from the pens of scholars in all disciplines for at least the last quarter-century. The reason for that must have something to do with the progress of institutional unification in Western Europe in the form of the ECSC, the EEC, the EC, and now the EU. The sporadic progress towards union of a part of Europe on the economic and political fronts has led to questions being posed about the 'essence' behind the unification, if indeed there is one. In the words of J. Cuisenier in 1979:

> Indeed, how can a European community or something alike be established without examining the supranationalism of its institutions, ... a detailed knowledge of the regions, ... the mechanisms at the root of their cultural identity and their basic principles?[1]

The question of whether there is such a thing as a European cultural identity commands a number of possible summary answers. A recent study of the whole issue, by H.J. Kleinsteuber *et al.*, focusing particularly on the regulation of the media in the EU, rejects the concept of cultural identity in Europe out of hand, and insists on substituting cultural diversity as far more meaningful.[2] A second and more frequent response is to see the whole issue as part of an almost underhand agenda, advanced by Euro-enthusiasts to strengthen the movement towards European union. From the early 1970s on, so the reasoning runs, and especially in the 1980s, with the discussions leading to the establishment of the Single European Market, and then Maastricht, it was deemed necessary to try to generate a broad political will in support of the economic and political unification process.[3] In the words of Hugh Seton-Watson, writing just before his death in 1985, there was a 'need ... for something more exciting than the price of butter ... a need for a European *mystique*', in order to galvanize popular support for the EC.[4] Concern was and is expressed at the 'democratic deficit' in the EU, in that while unification continues to move ahead, driven by enthusiastic politicians, bureaucrats and intellectuals, there is a distinct lack of heartfelt support from ordinary Western Europeans.[5] From the early 1970s onwards it was seen to be necessary to rejuvenate the general concepts which had previously underpinned the EC, and 'identity' was seized upon as the solution to the problems. In 1973 the EC Foreign Ministers adopted in Copenhagen a 'Declaration concerning European Identity', which was followed in 1976 by Leo Tindemans' *Report on European Union*, introducing the concept of 'a Citizen's Europe', and in 1983 by the Stuttgart 'Solemn Declaration on European Union'. B. de Witte has examined these key official texts on EC 'identity' up to the mid-1980s,[6] and Bram Boxhoorn's essay in this volume does the same for the more recent official statements. In the 1980s, there were official attempts to develop the trappings and symbols of a European identity, like a flag, and even an anthem.[7] The enthusiasts aside, these attempts to construct artificially a European popular 'soul' to bolster up less popular economic and political union seem contrived and shallow, and are fertile ground for cynicism, even from people who would not count themselves as Euro-sceptics. As De Witte put it,

> The impression therefore prevails that the policy of promoting European identity is no more than an effort to spread a more favourable image of Europe, without any substance backing it. Such a pretence is of dubious value.[8]

An equally important point, if seldom made, is that all these considerations of European identity - cultural or otherwise - are focused on the European Communities or Union, which for nearly all its existence has represented only a very small minority of the states, nations and people who would describe themselves as 'European'.

A third answer to the question of whether or not there is such a thing as a European cultural identity is that it consists simply of 'modernity'. Some commentators have taken this to be the 'essence' of European civilization, insofar as that constitutes identity. The post-modernist debate, with its rejection of Eurocentrism,[9] criticizes the association of Europe with modernization and modernism, but in doing so actually focuses attention on that same association. This approach to the cultural identity of Europe certainly has the advantage of being applicable - in varying degrees - to the whole of Europe, and moreover it puts culture first - in an anti-Marxist sense - by assuming that the modernization of Europe somehow grew out of its essential identity or

10

quintessential qualities, rather the 'culture' and 'identity' being artificially constructed in the wake of economic convergence, in the manner of the attempts of the EU protagonists.[10]

Some authors have made an explicit connection, or 'identity' in the sense of 'sameness', between Europe, Modernism, and the West in general; Agnes Heller asserts that 'European culture *is* modernity', and by 'modernity' she means concepts of relentless cumulative progress in knowledge, technology and wealth, and a politics based on the nation-state with ideals of freedom and equality.[11] In his study of Eurocentrism, Samir Amin links the 'construction of a European culture' with a 'culture of capitalism'.[12] More often, however, the association of Europe with things modern is made more by assumption and insinuation rather than worked out theoretically, and it is indeed the unthinking assumption and blinkered thoughtlessness which critics like Edward Said have most wished to undermine. The assumption under attack is that Europe has been the cradle of civilization from the beginning of recorded history, and that European civilization stretches in an unbroken line from the ancient Greeks (with the Egyptians often co-opted as honorary Europeans) right down to the present day; that unbroken line represents the nurturing and gradual refinement of the most important institutions, values, ethics, and culture which the world has today. As this 'modernization' process has continued, its fruits (according to this astonishingly ubiquitous approach) have been exported to other parts of the world, so that 'European civilization' has become virtually synonymous with 'Western civilization'. Countless textbooks on the history of art bear witness to these assumptions of progression and improvement, or 'modernization', and very many history books from previous generations do precisely the same, trumpeting the glories of a European 'tradition' as it progresses regally from the ancients through to the EC, picking up refinements here and there along the way and instructing the world.[13]

This offensive view of Europe, as the fount of wisdom and educator of the world through 'modern' and 'western' civilization, has of course been heavily criticized, not least at a conceptual level by the post-modernists and opponents of Eurocentrism. It has also been taken to pieces from within, as it were, by European scholars demonstrating that the long, unbroken development of any sort of civilization in Europe is a nonsense, or at best a myth. The whole issue of linking Greek civilization with later developments in western Europe was of course central to Renaissance Humanism, but is shot through with problems. It wrenches Greek history out of its Middle Eastern and oriental context, and has been the subject of considerable academic sophistry.[14] A much stronger case can be made for the 'torch of the ancients' being taken over and then Christianized by the Orthodox civilization of Eastern Europe, rather than by *Latin* Christian *Western* Europe, and indeed Byzantium has much better claims to being the cradle of European civilization and culture for at least a thousand years after the fall of the Roman Empire.[15] Moreover, such criticisms of the notion of a European continuity from Homer to the ECSC have been by no

11

means confined to the era of post-modernism: Arnold Toynbee was derisive in his dismissal of the notion of 'this mirage of a "European civilization"'. It was, he exclaimed, just 'another hallucination', and a 'thorough-going misinterpretation of the history of Mankind', leading to all sorts of dangerous exclusions from 'civilization', despite the fact that Asian and other inputs had always been crucial to what has become known as 'European' civilization or culture.[16] The same arguments were robustly articulated by Geoffrey Barraclough, who showed that the myth of the continuity of a European tradition was a nineteenth-century invention, that the classical tradition was dead by the third century AD, and that when the Turks conquered Constantinople in 1453 the traditions of ancient Rome, such as they were, passed to Russia, and not to the West. He also made the cogent point that the myth of European 'civilization' conveniently ignored the messier parts, as well as being offensively exclusive (to Asia and China, for example), and absurdly teleological.[17] Thus, answers to questions about European cultural identity in terms of a continuing European 'civilization', and the progress and modernization which that implies, tend to founder on the rocks of empirical verification: they are myths, with some highly misleading and negatively provocative qualities.

Shared heritage: European culture?

And yet. There is *something*, recognized by many commentators, past and present, idealistic and sceptical, which brings Europeans together, even if only partially. Most have found it hard to put their finger on it. For Seton-Watson, it was only 'a belief among thinking men and women that they belong to a single, even if diverse, European cultural community.' He identified some common values, and acknowledged the importance of classical Humanism and of Christianity as influences, but in the end he could only identify it vaguely: 'There still is a European culture ... it exists, but it comprehends only those who can see and feel it ... it is simply the end-product of 3,000 years ... it is a heritage.'[18] For the Indian philosopher Radhakrishnan, the roots of European civilization are their Greek-derived thinking, their Judaeo-Christian sense of being a chosen people, and their Roman talents for statecraft and expansion.[19] Indeed, ideas have been the key to Europe's uniqueness in the eyes of many a commentator, for example S. Papcke:

> Nowhere else have the ideas of personality, democracy, tolerance, social justice, liberty, human rights and so on been defined.[20]

Even someone like Barraclough, who vehemently rejected the continuity of European civilization, could not deny that there was something unique about it, talking in almost ecstatic terms about 'the incomparable soaring of the human spirit'.[21] With his feet more firmly on the ground, he pointed to the importance of such formative influences as the partial survival of Roman structures, the influence of the invaders from the East, and the long-standing effects of Christianity. This did not - for Barraclough - result in a single European civilization or culture, but there was a shared heritage.[22] More recently, J.B. Duroselle has echoed similar cautious sentiments in his history of Europe semi-sponsored by the EC: there is no single European civilization or culture, but there are shared experiences, embodied for example in the more-or-less Europe-wide influence of the Celts, the Romans, the Germanic peoples, Judaeo-Christianity, and (more selectively) the Vikings and the Arabs of Spain.[23]

A pattern is emerging. To talk in terms of a quintessential or single European culture, civilization, or identity leads quickly to unsustainable generalization, and to all manner of heady and evidently false claims for one's own continent. Nonetheless, if the triumphalism can be left to one side, there is a long history of shared influences and experiences, a heritage, which has not touched all parts of Europe or all Europeans equally, and which is therefore hard and perhaps dangerous to define in single sentences or even paragraphs, but which is felt and experienced in varying ways and degrees by those whose home is Europe, and which is recognized - whether approvingly or disapprovingly - by many from outside. Let us examine those shared influences and experiences in more detail.

A good shortlist of them was provided, more than a quarter-century ago, by James Joll, who focused on the Roman Empire, Christianity, the Enlightenment, and industrialization as key influences on the European experience.[24] To that list might be added the influence of the geological and geographical environment, and the issue of languages.

The Roman Empire is really a shorthand for certain values of the Ancients, including especially the Greeks and the Roman Republic. The Roman rule of law survived from the end of the Empire in small pockets, but was rediscovered, together with much of the rest of Ancient civilization, through the Renaissance. Greek ideas of art, philosophy and politics were transmitted through the Roman experience, together with the more specifically Roman legacy of military, bureaucratic and infrastructural organization.

Christianity has had no exclusive hold on Europe, and certainly does not hold one now. There have always been important Christian presences outside Europe. There is no doubt that Christianity has been the direct cause of appalling infighting, bigotry, misery, war, torture, and attempted genocide over the centuries. Nevertheless, it has been the majority religion of the continent for nearly two millenia, and at times the geographical extent of *Roman* Christianity has closely approximated to the boundaries of what was called 'Europe'. For example, in the late eighth and ninth centuries, the Carolingian empire was identified with both concepts (Latin Christianity and 'Europe'). Charlemagne himself was hailed as 'regnum Europae', 'rex pater Europae', and 'apex Europae', and in 870 Pope John VIII was called 'Rector Europae'.[25] One of the great scholars of the history of the idea of Europe, Denys Hay, has established the virtual identity (in the sense of sameness) of the terms 'Europe' and 'Christendom' for more than two hundred years from the end of the thirteenth century.[26] And despite the fact that the Reformation seemed to tear the unity of both (Latin) Christendom and Europe to pieces,[27] not a few prominent Europeans, led enthusiastically by Hugo Grotius, dreamed that peace in Europe might allow the way to open for the reunification of Christendom.[28] Furthermore, few Europeans would deny the importance of Judaeo-Christian ethics in European civilization today, and the strength of Christian-Democrat centre parties in European countries and indeed the EU parliament are further testaments to the lasting influence of Latin Christianity on Europe.

Joll includes the Enlightenment in his list of formative European experiences.[29] With the proviso that it was not strictly limited to Europe, but was a critical influence elsewhere, especially in North America, it would be hard to deny that in the eighteenth century there was a Europe-wide change in thinking, building on the influences of the Renaissance and the seventeenth-century scientific revolution, which we call the Enlightenment. It was confined in the main to the elite, and did not affect all parts of Europe equally, but it was a genuinely multinational and international intellectual movement with profound consequences. It was linked, moreover, with a fundamental sense of 'Europeanness', aptly encapsulated in Edmund Burke's exclamation that 'no European can be a complete exile in any part of Europe'.[30] The *philosophes* (of all countries) were international and cosmopolitan, but (in the phrase of J. Lively) they 'could reconcile their cosmopolitanism with a sense of a distinct European identity'.[31] The scientific and sceptical spirit of the Enlightenment felt Europe to be superior to the other continents (as will become abundantly clear in the chapter below on visual representations of Europe), and Voltaire could praise Europe as 'a great republic, embracing several states' with the same religion, the same law, and the same political ideas.[32] 'Europe' in the Enlightenment sense meant more than Christianity; it embraced a certainty of the superiority of the 'civilization' of Europe as a platform on which to build the future.[33] By the eighteenth century, intellectual Europe had a clear self-image, which was to release a torrent of '*Europabild*' literature;[34] the Enlightenment was both a shared influence in Europe of deep significance, and the occasion when the consciousness of Europe attained new heights.

Moving to a consideration of industrialization as a common European experience, we are dealing with something which is clearly no longer confined to Europe - indeed, Europe has long been overtaken. But the early experience of industrialization was critical for the kind of self-image which Europe was to acquire from the late eighteenth century onwards, and which it has retained in the late twentieth century (whether justifiably or not). There has been extensive discussion about the reasons for Europe's early pre-eminence in this respect, one of the most engaging studies being E.L. Jones's attribution of Europe's comparative advantages to environmental factors.[35] Whatever the reasons, that head-start generated the wealth, the technology and the military power which put Europe in a world-dominating position for one and a half of our two most recent centuries, and that, like it or not, must be one of the most formative influences on the people and nations of Europe, as well as on those in other parts of the world. Some would argue further that early industrialization in Europe has generated a unique social evolution, in terms of demographic structures, employment patterns, welfare provisions and industrial relations.[36] In leading to imperialism, it certainly contributed to 'them/us' feelings, and sentiments of superiority. There can be little doubt, then, that the kind of economic development shared in varying degrees by Europeans from roughly 1750 onwards has been a critically important shared experience, contributing directly to feelings - however vague and uneven - of European 'specialness'.

So much for Joll's list; two additional shared European experiences are language and environment. Language is problematic. To begin with, there are a very large number of different languages in a relatively small space: some forty-three, in three different alphabets.[37] Many of Europe's languages clearly have Latin or Germanic roots; the claim that ancient Greek is directly linked to an Indo-European family of languages, which is strictly differentiated from Semitic languages, has been called an artificially constructed myth.[38] Whatever the theoretical linguistic technicalities, there do appear to be empirical links between most European languages (with the notable exceptions of Finnish, Hungarian, Estonian and Basque) which most of us notice. As for single languages, or *linguae francae*, Greek had a claim to that function under the Roman Empire, and Latin served the same purpose for the highly educated in the Middle Ages until about 1600; in the sixteenth century it was challenged by Italian, and then French.[39] English - often American English - has tended to become the universal means of communication in Europe in the media-saturated later twentieth century. The issues are not clear about Europe's shared linguistic heritage, and there is certainly still enormous diversity, but it is true to say that now, as for many centuries, most Europeans understand more of each others' languages than they do of non-European ones.

Finally, there are the environmental or ecological influences. Certainly it is the case that, from the earliest times, Europeans have identified their continent as having a particular climate which differentiated it from other parts of the world. In about 400 BC, the physician Hippocrates accounted for differentials in warlike valour between the Europeans and the Asians by the difference in their climates.[40] Strabo, in his *Geography* of c. 10 AD, stressed Europe's variety of micro-climates and agricultural products as being superior.[41] These authors were influential once again in the Renaissance, but before then, in AD 1095, we have none other than the Pope, Urban II, preaching the first crusade at Clermont in terms of the superiority of Europe's climate and civilization.[42] The identification of the advantages of the European environment continued in the

15

Renaissance, with Sebastian Münster praising Europe's climate, terrain and population as the best in the world, in his *Cosmographia Universalia* of 1544.[43] In political thought, these tendencies to derive personal qualities such as bravery, cunning and political skill from local environmental factors were present from Machiavelli onwards, and reached their zenith in the eighteenth century, especially in the work of Montesquieu, whose views amounted virtually to environmental determinism, and he articulated them especially concerning Europe, as opposed to Asia.[44] There is little doubt, then, that the environment of Europe has been recognized as distinctive by individual observers since ancient times, a view which had become part of mainstream thought by the eighteenth century. In geological terms it is true that, West of a line running approximately from the Baltic to the Black Sea, there is a rich complexity and variety which is not found to the East; there is in the West a relatively wide variety in soil types, and the proximity to the Atlantic and other expanses of water means that much of Europe to the West of that line has an oceanic rather than a continental climate. The relatively deep penetration of the sea to most areas of Europe is an environmental factor in itself of considerable influence. The strength of these statements is evident in the fact that modern scholars, and not only the Enlightenment followers of Montesquieu, have seen the environment as the determining factor in Europe's achievements: we have already observed the historian E.L. Jones's selection of environment as the prime mover in the *European Miracle*, and the geographer W.H. Parker would not disagree. Europe's physical geography, he claims, made it defensible against the Eastern hordes, led to healthy rivalry, material progress, and civilization: 'Europe became culturally distinct because it was geographically different.'[45]

Parker speaks of 'cultural distinction', which brings us back to a point quite close to our scene of departure, cultural identity. We have seen that, despite justifiable scepticism about attempts in Brussels to manufacture a latter-day EU identity, about portraying Europe as the spirit of modernization, and about a myth of continuity in European civilization, there are nonetheless significant shared experiences and influences which amount to a heritage. The question remains, what has that to do with cultural identity? And why is the question of cultural identity important to the shared experience of Europe?

State-formation and nation-building

The concept of collective identity has become especially important to political scientists and historians (as well as to psychologists and anthropologists) in recent years, mainly because of the growth of the debate on state-formation and nation-building. In many senses the debate about European unity and European collective and cultural identity is derived from the concepts evolved in the literature about nations and states. Therefore it will be useful to determine what

16

is meant by cultural identity in the context of nations and states, and then apply it to the European case.

It is as well to begin by remembering the distinction between state-formation and nation-formation.[46] The former is to do with structures in international and national law, constitutions, and infrastructure; the second, nation-building, is more to do with culture and consciousness, with sentiment and perception. A.D. Smith, following K.W. Deutsch, defines a nation as

> a named human population sharing an historical territory, common myths and historical memories, a mass, public culture, a common economy and common legal rights and duties for all members.[47]

States, on the other hand, are a matter of public institutions, with a monopoly on coercive force, and in the early 1970s it was estimated that only some 10 per cent of states were truly nation-states.[48] The fortunes of nations and states are obviously intertwined and interdependent, and 'reciprocally influence and condition each other';[49] nonetheless the distinction is an indispensable one. The formation of the *state* is often dependent on external circumstances, most notably on relations with other states or groups of states. Once the structure of the state is externally determined, attempts are made to realise the new structure internally as well as externally. There tend to be considerable reactions against the imposition of a centralized state unity, and so successive governments find it necessary to penetrate society by reforms in administration, law, finance, infrastructure, and defence. In order to make these reforms which intrude upon local positions acceptable and permanent, governments also pursue 'a *nation*-building policy through education, use of a national language, an Erastian church policy, control of the press, army recruitment, and patronage'.[50] These strategies have not always worked: one only has to look at the former Soviet Union to see that neither state nor empire is likely to be imposed *permanently* if there is no successful campaign of persuasion that the imposed values are acceptable and bear some relationship to reality.[51] State-formation, then, requires some attempt at nation-building.

The progress of *nation*-formation, however, involves more than that; it is a largely internal and cultural process, on the road to a common perception of the nation, and is only incidentally in tune with the expansion of the apparatus of the state. To arrive at this stage of affairs, and its further refinement, the cultural community is moulded both by 'top-down' initiatives from the centre, and by more-or-less spontaneous 'bottom-up' movements and developments from the disparate communities - in both geographical and ideological senses - in the 'nation'.[52] Thus there have been central attempts to impose what Ernest Gellner calls a 'universal high culture',[53] assisted by an army of willing civilizers anxious to create a uniform language and spelling, an improved and standardized education, and generally shared concepts of cultural behaviour.

17

These are powerful 'civilization offensives'. At the same time, however, and inextricably linked to the top-down initiatives, local movements towards national identity and consciousness have taken place, with more and more previously uninvolved ordinary people taking part in the celebration of the nation, and moving towards a definition of their own community, class or ideology group in terms of the national past, present, and future. This could take the form of Eric Hobsbawm's 'invention of tradition',[54] or what the Dutch cultural historian Jan Bank has called the 'monumentalization' of the past.[55]

This framework allows us to place a number of developments in the history of a nation or a state (and, potentially, of Europe) in the context of nation- and state-building, and to locate particular aspects on which we wish to focus in the framework of the nation-building process as a whole. Important strands in that framework at the level of nation and state, which might also be applied at European level, are constitutional definitions of the state by both internal and external authorities, the centralization or unification of the state carried out after the imposition of a generalized unitary constitutional order, and the introduction of a national political system, with gradually increasing participation on a uniform basis across the country. At the same time, there are the distinct elements of a cultural acceptance of this burgeoning unity, reinforced by changes in education, metrology, and currency, with keen proselytizers spreading the bourgeois message through the civil society and charity networks. In addition, many diverse groups assist in the process by discovering their own identity in national terms. For example, certain religious groups have formed institutions and pressure-groups to strengthen their group identities and their places in the nation and in the national traditions. Other secular groups have followed the same route, for example representatives of labour, women, and immigrants, all seeking and locating their position within the framework of the national identity.[56]

To recapitulate the relevant parts of the state-and-nation debate: states are formal constitutional structures imposed from outside and from above; nations are cultural concepts of collective heritage, immensely complex in origin and variety, which only occasionally coincide with states, and which are by definition myth and imagination rather than empirically verifiable fact.[57] Interest in national 'character' and national 'genius' arose from the eighteenth century onwards, and indeed A.D. Smith argues that, at least with European nations, this 'pre-modern identity' is often a 'baseline' for explaining how modern nations emerged.[58] The emphasis in any model must be on two things: the reciprocal inter-reaction between the imposition of a unity by the state on the one hand, and the acceptance and conditioning of that unity by (increasing) numbers of the state's subjects on the other. Secondly, a model must allow for and explain the *varieties* of national feeling which go to make up the integrated whole. Cultural identity has evidently been crucial to these processes in the context of the nation and the state; is this a suitable matrix of analysis at the European level?

In general the pundits have been pessimistic about the prospect of applying the state-and-nation analysis to Europe. W.H. Roobol pointed to Europe's weak ideology, the persistent particularism of its parts, and the fact that its ethics and ideals are more-or-less universal; he concluded that Western Europe's chances of following the path of nation-state formation were rather remote.[59] A.D. Smith, in a chapter entitled 'Beyond National Identity', reviews the field of supra-nationalisms, and concludes:

> There is ... little prospect of a European 'super-nation' until the majority of each European nation's population becomes infused with a genuinely European consciousness.

We must, he decides, await the

> rise of a sense of specifically 'European' heritage and ... the growth of an accepted 'European mythology'.[60]

These are persuasive arguments; nonetheless, in some ways they are over-dismissive, on two grounds. First, they assume that the object in view is a EU super-state, a United States of (Western) Europe, with sovereign powers and functioning like a Western (so-called) nation-state; second, both complain that what is lacking is an ideology, a mythology, a heritage. These things may be weak, as Roobol suggests, but we have seen above they certainly exist, and since we have already concluded that they are always subjective myths rather than objective reality, it is more a question of how strongly they are promoted and believed, than of any inherent strength they may or may not have. A deeper problem is that these evaluations look at 'Europe' in terms of the debate on nation-state formation, but in doing so only adopt selected parts of the model outlined above, rather than the whole matrix. By applying the nation/state model in its totality, by not pinning the issue to the fortunes of the present-day European Union, and by taking a more historical perspective, it becomes apparent there are some grounds for cautious and qualified optimism, especially with regard to a European cultural identity.

A nation can - and frequently does - exist independently of a state, and it is another myth that, in order to be fulfilled, nations must form exclusive states. In practice, few do. State-formation, as defined above, would in the European case involve heavy pressure from outside - in the form of inter-bloc rivalry and possibly even war, and would result in structures in law such as constitutions, and the monopoly of coercion (even if it were delegated to regions). Attempts have been made in this direction in the past, from the Romans onwards, many of them with some degree of successs, though none of them permanent. But what is permanent? Our so-called European nation-states can hardly be described as such, with their few hundred years of existence; they have so far lasted little longer than the power of Rome. As for the future, the present drift towards integration, in the form of the EU, has certainly created some structures, especially in the economic sphere. In state-formation and in the moulding of identities generally, 'alterity' is crucial, and the identity is partly defined by the counter-identity. France cannot be France without the presence of Germany, and Europe needs (in this sense) a common enemy.[61] It has always had its external threats, from the ancient Persians and the Eastern invaders, to the Arabs and Turks of the Middle Ages, to the Communist threat in the twentieth century. In the age of exploration and colonialism, Said and others have shown how Europe used its perceptions of other parts of the globe, like 'the Orient', to refine its own identity.[62] Nowadays there are still plenty of external pressures to aid or even enforce the process of state-formation: the cultural threat from America and the military danger from the Middle East are among many other perceived common enemies, like terrorism, pollution, drugs, crime, immigration, and Islam.[63] All in all, elements of the *state*-formation process are clearly underway, and have been so for some time.

But what of the European *nation*? That is to say, what of the process of *nation*-formation, transposed to a European level? We have distinguished between 'top-down' and 'bottom-up' initiatives in nation-building. Some of the part played by the government or elite in the EU in top-down nation-construction is what we have already seen to be viewed so cynically. This is the alleged artificiality and contrivance on the part of the Commission, with its rhetoric of 'European identity' and its transparent popularizing of the Euro-flag and Euro-anthem. Nevertheless, these and other initiatives are part of the serious business of nation-building. A.D. Smith doubts whether the EU leaders have the power and capability to lay on a 'memoryless' artificial culture.[64] In the terms of our matrix, however, this is precisely what Gellner calls the 'universal high culture', and the achievements of the European elite over the centuries have been by no means meagre. In 'nation-states' this would include language standardization, control of the media, religious policy, control of the army, education policies, and standardization of taxation. Religion is not the issue it was, but historically the Papacy did a persistent if variable job of bringing the continent together, and ecumenical movements continue to do so now. Education standards and syllabi are creeping slowly towards convergences, and the EU higher education policies have been an outstanding success in creating a European consciousness; the Socrates programme is likely to further that even more. With varying degrees of success, there have been European initiatives to bring together the continent (or parts of it) with regard to defence (with the EDF, NATO, etc.) and the media (with regulation and mergers). In the modern period a variety of attempts has been made to integrate Europe's economy and finances, by means of all manner of trade agreements and currency exchange mechanisms from tariff treaties and the Gold Standard onwards, right down to the EU's present initiatives. Even language has been the subject of attention, at least at elite level, with Greek, Latin, diplomatic French, American English, and even Esperanto; EU translation services are also regularizing and minimizing the language barriers in the continent. The present efforts of the EU should be seen in a long historical context, some of it successful and some less so; there has always been top-down activity of one sort or another, and it is by no means simply a question of anthems and flags.

Much of this 'top-down' activity can contribute to the formation of an 'identity', but a European identity cannot be constructed solely from above.[65] It is also necessary to have grass-roots or 'bottom-up' initiatives to complement the actions of government and elite, and external forces. These, as we have seen, tend to be generated by local movements, minority groups, and newcomers to politics and public life of all sorts, engaged in a process of building their own identity by locating it within a larger perceived identity. It consists of the creation of a niche, which provides a location or identity within a larger group. In the national and state context, the examples are legion: for instance, Catholics undergoing emancipation in northern Europe in the nineteenth century 'located' or 'identified' themselves through rediscovering, inventing, or monumentalizing their past, reviving forgotten saints, festivals and rituals which emphasized both the Catholic and national-patriotic nature of their identity.[66] At the European level, the EC initiative of the 'Europe of the Regions' encouraged regional groupings, like the Basques, the Welsh and the Walloons to realise their identity in a European framework, with considerable success: as local Catholics embraced the nation in their search for a way round the Protestant local elite, Scots have looked to Europe to strengthen their identity in the face of Westminster's intransigence. Any number of 'European' organizations and societies exist, and some have claimed that the key to a European cultural identity lies in building up a Europe-wide 'civil society' of pan-European voluntary associations and pressure groups.[67] Spontaneous 'bottom-up' initiatives, then, clearly do exist, although it is probably the case that they are the weakest of the elements in the model of state- and nation-formation when transposed to a European level.

It would be illuminating to research this matter systematically, by applying such a model to Europe's experience over a sustained period of time, and until that happens, especially for the last two centuries, there must remain an element of speculation. However, for an earlier period, just such a research project has been undertaken, and the results are remarkable. Robert Bartlett is a medieval historian who has applied the theories and models of state-formation to Europe in the high Middle Ages, in his 1993 book *The Making of Europe: conquest, colonization and cultural change 950-1350*.[68] He discovers what he calls the 'Europeanization of Europe', by which he means that in this period Europeans became aware of their European identity. He focuses much attention on external threats and border conflicts in the East, on the Baltic coasts, in Scandinavia, in Wales, Scotland and Ireland, and in southern Spain and southern Italy. Top-down nation-building mechanisms were employed by the leaders - the Frankish monarchs and the popes - who issued standard coins and charters, founded and fostered universities, as well as conquering and imposing

21

the administrative structures of the state. At the same time, and just as importantly, grass-roots initiatives were rife, with 'consortia' of knights, priests, merchants and even peasants identifying themselves in a 'European' framework. By studying such things as proper names and saints' festivals, Bartlett comes to the conclusion that this Latin Christian Europe of the Franks was 'made' not only by conquest, but also by internal changes which provided Europe with 'the ability to maintain cultural identity through legal forms and nurtured attitudes.' 'By 1300 Europe existed as an identifiable cultural identity', based on Latin Christianity and the Carolingian heritage.[69] Here we have an apt case-study of four centuries, set in the past, it is true, which looks at nation-building as well as state-formation, and within the former takes stock of initiatives both from the centre and from the grass roots. It comes to the conclusion that there was indeed a meaningful and significant European cultural identity. How can we dismiss European cultural identity in the twentieth century when the EU has only been in existence since 1957?

Culture, identity, and cultural identity

We have explored the uses, positive and negative, of the models of state- and nation-building as applied to Europe. Definitions of culture, identity, and cultural identity are long overdue. Culture is now generally defined as an ever-changing construct, 'summing up beliefs, norms, institutions and traditional ways of "doing things" in a society'.[70] It has been described as a dialogue or discussion which societies hold on essential themes, or as 'collective mental programming'.[71] We acquire culture by conditioning, both directly from legal systems and formal education, but also by 'secondary socialization' from peer groups and colleagues, in the home and the workplace, and in recreation.[72] Some theorists like Raymond Williams and E.P. Thompson have argued that culture delivers identity, and that people determine their social position or identity by their 'culture'.[73] This brings us neatly to the question of identity - which commands as many definitions as there are academic disciplines which study it, and which only tends to command attention when it is in crisis.[74] Taking it in its modern sense (that is not simply as 'sameness', but in the sense of an image with which one associates and projects oneself), the most essential feature of identity is its multiple nature. It is possible to have a single identity, but it will always be made up of several if not myriad separate identifications or identities, some of which may be contradictory. Some will be stronger than others, and the pattern will change over time. Individuals have identities, as do groups (families, nations, *ethnies*, classes, age-groups, etc.), and it may be that one has rather more choice about one's individual identity than one does over one's group identity. But a single-strand identity is inconceivable, and identities (like cultures) are always changing. The balance between the various strands of an identity, which might consist of associations with gender, region, religion, class, nation, and many other things, will constantly shift. It also means that, within a single (though multiple) identity, allegiances can form with entirely contradictory institutions or concepts; one only has to think of torn loyalties in wartime.[75] If we take the example of *national* identity, there has evidently never been such a thing as single indivisible nationalism, and indeed nationalism is always multi-faceted. Feelings of loyalty and identity are often infinitely varied about the same nation. Perhaps the most remarkable feature of national identity and feeling is that it can unite sometimes wildly different people into powerful alliances, without them even sharing the same ideology. Certainly the beginnings of nationalism are notable for their centrifugal and divergent tendencies rather than for their unifying force. The most distinctive development in national identity has not been the common ideology, but the *integration* of a number of particularist and party-based national identities into an all-embracing national identity and awareness; identity of all kinds is very much to do with that integration process.

That also holds true for cultural identity. It is above all integrative and inclusive, uniting cultural groups which might be otherwise unrelated. It thrives on external cultural threats, and it benefits from at least some means of socio-political expression.[76] Shared memories, shared hopes, and shared continuity (rather than uniformity) are essential; a common subjective perception of the group's history (which may have little to do with fact) is, suggests A.D. Smith, 'a defining element in the concept of cultural identity'.[77] In summary, it is integrational, it is moulded by external forces, and it depends on a set of at least partly shared experiences, hopes and heritage.

European cultural identity

And does Europe have one of these 'cultural identities', so defined? I would contend that it has. Many have dismissed it, like A.D. Smith, who talks witheringly of

> unacceptable historical myths ... [and] a patchwork memoryless
> scientific 'culture' held together solely by the political will and
> economic interest that are so often subject to change.[78]

We should indeed be reminded that 'Europe was, after all, not an altogether untarnished term', and that a European cultural identity was hardly worth the candle by the time the Nazis and other pogrom-leaders had finished with it.[79] J. Bloomfield has called for a jettisoning of the European past, in order to 'take the dialogue on Europe beyond a debate of the deaf', and has ridiculed attempts to correct the 'cultural deficit' by 'creat[ing] a single, binding European cultural identity from above'.[80] The murky parts of Europe's past (and present) should certainly not be whitewashed under any carpets, but the same A.D. Smith offers some hope as well, in the form of a concept he calls a 'family of cultures'. On the premise that identities are multiple, and drawing on research in Nigeria which indicates that 'concentric circles of allegiances' (for example to region, country, and continent) are commonplace, he leaves room in the end for the existence of a European cultural identity. There are all sorts of problems with its languages, its geography, its religion and its alterity, but it does, admits Smith, have a common historical experience, which provides it with a common legal, political and cultural heritage. These shared experiences, some of which we have outlined above,

> together ... constitute not a 'unity in diversity' - the official
> European cultural formula - but a 'family of cultures' made up
> of a syndrome of partially shared historical traditions and
> cultural heritages.[81]

All this is based on the 'common cultural heritage' of a 'unique cultural area'.[82] And we have already noticed that the historian Kaelble has shown how the societies of Europe have been converging for at least the last century in many of their social aspects.[83]

So there is evidence which leads us to be less dismissive than some of the sceptics I have quoted. But let us be very qualified in our enthusiasm. The convergence in European societies which Kaelble documents is specifically not, he insists, some sort of social history of the EU. European cultural identity is one thing; the EU is something entirely different.[84] Smith sees some future for his European 'family of cultures' but it is specifically not the substructure of a Western European super-state, and certainly should not be put to sinister uses such as the cultural exclusion of the Third World; rather he has in mind some kind of over-arching pan-Europeanism, which manages not to conflict with national cultural identities.[85] Neither should the European identity be used as a qualitative yardstick for judging others or indeed for discriminating between various kinds of Europeans, as Hitler and others have been wont to do. And there are certainly very few grounds for trying to export the 'wisdom' of the European experience to other parts of the world; if such a thing exists, it is almost certainly inappropriate for anyone else.[86]

So, in summary: there is indeed a European cultural identity, and it consists mainly of a partially shared historical heritage and experience, in the widest possible sense. It is not, however, some sort of blueprint for the EU, which in terms of the shared heritage is as yet only a flash in the pan, or more correctly, a very short and selective part of that shared experience.

Notes

1. Cuisenier, ed., *Europe as a cultural area*, 3.

2. Shelley, ed., *Aspects of European cultural diversity*, 171.

3. Nelson, ed., *The idea of Europe*, 62; & Shelley, ed., *Aspects of European cultural diversity*, 168-9.

4. Seton-Watson, 'What is Europe, where is Europe?', 13; see also Odermatt, 'The use of symbols', 217.

5. See the essay by Helen Wallace in García, ed., *European identity*, 98ff.

6. In Rijksbaron, et al., ed., *Europe from a cultural perspective*, 132-7.

7. Odermatt, 'The use of symbols', 225-35.

8. In Rijksbaron, et al., ed., *Europe from a cultural perspective*, 137.

9. E.g. Said, *Orientalism*, and Amin, *Eurocentrism*.

10. Amin, *Eurocentrism*, vii & 109. Amin points to but does not agree with this argument.

11. E.g. her essay in Nelson, ed., *The idea of Europe*, p. 22.

12. Amin, *Eurocentrism*, 71-89.

13. A typical (if thoughtful) example is Albrecht-Carrié, *The unity of Europe*.

14. Nelson, ed., *The idea of Europe*, 21-2; Amin, *Eurocentrism*, 89-95.

15. See the essay by H. Ahrweiler in García, ed., *European identity*, especially pp. 38-43.

16. Toynbee, '"Asia" and "Europe"', 725-9.

17. Barraclough, *History in a changing world*, 32-53.

18. Seton-Watson, 'What is Europe, where is Europe?', 9 & 15-17.

19. Cited in Galtung, *Europe in the making*, 11.

20. In Nelson, ed., *The idea of Europe*, 72.

21. Barraclough, *History in a changing world*, 166.

22. Barraclough, *History in a changing world*, 50-3.

23. Duroselle, *Europe: a history of its peoples*, 20-1.

24. Joll, *Europe: a historian's view*.

25. Ullmann, *The Carolingian Renaissance*, especially pp. 135-6 & 165-6.

26. Hay, *Europe; the emergence of an idea*, especially chapters 4,5, & 6.

27. Hay, *Europe; the emergence of an idea*, 96; & Hay, 'Europe revisited: 1979'.

28. Trevor-Roper, 'Hugo Grotius and England'.

29. Joll, *Europe: a historian's view*, 7.

30. Cited in Hay, *Europe; the emergence of an idea*, 123.

31. Lively, 'The Europe of the Enlightenment', 99.

32. Cited in Hazard, *European thought in the eighteenth century*, 463.

33. See Den Boer, et al., *The history of the idea of Europe*, 58-65.

34. Hay, *Europe; the emergence of an idea*, 117.

35. Jones, *The European miracle*. Jones also lays great stress on nation-states and on the balance of power between them.

36. Kaelble, *A social history of Western Europe*, especially pp. 150-4; and on marriage patterns, Hajnal, 'European marriage patterns'.

37. Delouche, ed., *Illustrated history of Europe*, 12-13; according to Shelley, ed., *Aspects of European cultural diversity*, 169, the tally is sixty-seven.

38. Amin, *Eurocentrism*, 93-5.

39. Hale, 'The Renaissance idea of Europe', 56-60.

40. *Influences of atmosphere*, cited in Den Boer, et al., *The history of the idea of Europe*, 16.

41. Cited in Hale, *The civilization of Europe in the Renaissance*, 13-14.

42. As reported by William of Malmesbury; see Hay, *Europe; the emergence of an idea*, 30-3.

43. Published in Basle. See Hay, *Europe; the emergence of an idea*, 105-6.

44. Montesquieu, *The spirit of the laws*, Books XIV-XVIII.

45. Parker, 'Europe: how far?', 292.

46. One of the original seminal texts on state-formation was Tilly, *The formation of national states*; on nation-formation some of the most-cited works are Gellner, *Nations and nationalism*; Anderson, *Imagined communities*; and Smith, *National identity*. I have also benefited from a debate in the learned journals of the Netherlands, in particular Mijnhardt, 'Natievorming in het revolutietijdvak'; Van Sas, 'De mythe Nederland'; Blockmans, 'Beheersen en overtuigen'; & Frijhoff, 'Identiteit en identiteitsbesef'.

47. Smith, *National identity*, 14.

48. Smith, *National identity*, 14-15.

49. Van Sas, 'De mythe Nederland', 8; see also J. Breuilly's essay in Fulbrook, ed., *National histories and European history*, pp. 94-6.

50. From an account of the Netherlands in the early nineteenth century: Tamse & Witte, *Staats- en natievorming in Willem I's koninkrijk*, 16-17. My translation.

51. Blockmans, 'Beheersen en overtuigen', 27.

52. Van Sas, 'De mythe Nederland', 9.

53. Gellner, *Nations and nationalism*, 35-8, 89; & Gellner, *Conditions of liberty*, 111 & 114.

54. Hobsbawm & Ranger, eds, *The invention of tradition*.

55. Bank, *Het roemrijk vaderland*.

56. Smith, *National identity*, 17.

57. Anderson, *Imagined communities*, 15-16; see also the view of the 'imagologists', for whom national attributes are by definition subjective myths about image-stereotypes: Leerssen, 'Over nationale identiteit'.

58. Smith, *National identity*, 70-1 & 84-6.

59. Roobol, 'What is Europe?', 202.

60. Smith, *National identity*, 152.

61. Nelson, ed., *The idea of Europe*, 62-5.

62. Said, *Orientalism*.

63. García, ed., *European identity*, 13-14.

64. Smith, 'National identity and the idea of European unity', 65-6.

65. García, ed., *European identity*, 15.

66. E.g., in the Dutch case, Raedts, 'Katholieken op zoek naar een Nederlandse identiteit'; Bank, *Het roemrijk vaderland*; Van Miert, 'Nationalisme in de lokale politieke cultuur'.

67. See J. Bloomfield's essay in Fulbrook, ed., *National histories and European history*, especially pp. 256-61. See also Gellner, *Conditions of liberty*.

68. Bartlett, *The making of Europe*.

69. Bartlett, *The making of Europe*, 313-4 & 291.

70. Zetterholm, *National cultures and European integration*, 2.

71. Respectively, Frijhoff, 'Identiteit en identiteitsbesef', 634; & Hofstede, G., 'Images of Europe', 67.

72. Shelley, ed., *Aspects of European cultural diversity*, 192.

73. Shelley, ed., *Aspects of European cultural diversity*, 194.

74. Frijhoff, 'Identiteit en identiteitsbesef', 621f; García, ed., *European identity*, 81-2.

75. On the whole question of identity, see Smith, 'National identity and the idea of European unity', 58-9 & passim; & Smith, *National identity*, 4-7; R. Picht's essay in García, ed., *European identity*, pp. 81-93; & Menno Spiering's chapter in this volume.

76. Shelley, ed., *Aspects of European cultural diversity*, 168. See also Kossmann, *De Lage Landen 1780-1980*, vol. 2, p. 380.

77. Smith, 'National identity and the idea of European unity', 58; Smith, *National identity*, 19-25.

78. Smith, 'National identity and the idea of European unity', 74.

79. Rijksbaron, et al., ed., *Europe from a cultural perspective*, 75-7.

80. In Fulbrook, ed., *National histories and European history*, 256 & 266.

81. Smith, 'National identity and the idea of European unity', 67-71. See also Smith, *National identity* 171-5.

82. Smith, *National identity*, 174.

83. Kaelble, *A social history of Western Europe*, 153-7, and passim.

84. Kaelble, *A social history of Western Europe*, 159-60.

85. Smith, 'National identity and the idea of European unity', 75-6; Smith, *National identity*, 174-5.

86. Amin, *Eurocentrism*, 97 & 109.

References

Albrecht-Carrié, R., *The unity of Europe: an historical survey* (London, Secker & Warburg, 1966).

Amin, S., *Eurocentrism* (New York, Monthly Review Press, 1989).

Anderson, B., *Imagined communities: reflections on the origin and spread of nationalism* (London, Verso, 1983).

Bank, J.T.M., *Het roemrijk vaderland: cultureel nationalisme in Nederland in de negentiende eeuw* (The Hague, SDU, 1990).

Barraclough, G., *History in a changing world* (Oxford, Blackwell, 1955).

Bartlett, R., *The making of Europe: conquest, colonization and cultural change 950-1350* (London, Allen Lane, 1993).

Blockmans, W.P., 'Beheersen en overtuigen: reflecties bij nieuwe visies op staatsvorming', *Tijdschrift voor Sociale Geschiedenis*, 16(1990), 18-30.

Boer, P. den, et al., *The history of the idea of Europe*, edited by K. Wilson & J. van der Dussen, What is Europe? 1 (London, Routledge, 1995).

Cuisenier, J., ed., *Europe as a cultural area* (The Hague, Mouton, 1979).

Delouche, F., ed., *Illustrated history of Europe: a unique guide to Europe's common heritage* (London, Weidenfeld & Nicholson, 1993).

Duroselle, J-B., *Europe: a history of its peoples* (London, Viking Penguin, 1990).

Frijhoff, W., 'Identiteit en identiteitsbesef: de historicus en de spanning tussen verbeelding, benoeming en herkenning', *Bijdragen en Mededelingen betreffende de Geschiedenis der Nederlanden*, 107(1992), 614-34.

Fulbrook, M., ed., *National histories and European history* (London, UCL Press, 1993).

Galtung, J., *Europe in the making* (New York, Crane Russak, 1989).

García, S., ed., *European identity and the search for legitimacy* (London, Pinter, 1993).

Gellner, E., *Nations and nationalism* (Oxford, Blackwell, 1983).

Gellner, E., *Conditions of liberty: civil society and its rivals* (London, Hamish Hamilton, 1994).

Hajnal, J., 'European marriage patterns in perspective', in D.V. Glass & D.E.C. Eversley, eds, *Population in history: essays in historical demography* (London, Edward Arnold, 1965), pp. 101-43.

Hale, J., 'The Renaissance idea of Europe', in S. García, ed., *European identity and the search for legitimacy* (London, Pinter, 1993), pp. 46-63.

Hale, J., *The civilization of Europe in the Renaissance* (London, Harper Collins, 1994).

Hay, D., *Europe; the emergence of an idea*, second edition (Edinburgh, Edinburgh University Press, 1968) [first published 1957].

Hay, D., 'Europe revisited: 1979', *History of European Ideas*, 1(1980), 1-6.

Hazard, P., *European thought in the eighteenth century* (Harmondsworth, Penguin, 1965) [originally published 1946].

Hobsbawm, E. & T. Ranger, eds, *The invention of tradition* (Cambridge, C.U.P., 1983).

Hofstede, G., 'Images of Europe', *The Netherlands' Journal of Social Sciences*, 30 no. 1 (Aug. 1994), 63-82.

Joll, J., *Europe: a historian's view* (Leeds, Leeds University Press, 1969).

Jones, E.L., *The European miracle: environments, economies, and geopolitics in the history of Europe and Asia* (Cambridge, CUP, 1981).

Kaelble, H., *A social history of Western Europe 1880-1980* (Dublin, Gill & Mcmillan, 1989).

Kossmann, E.H., *De Lage Landen 1780-1980: twee eeuwen Nederland en België*, 2 vols (Amsterdam, Elsevier, 1986), vol. 2, 1914-1980.

Leerssen, J.T., 'Over nationale identiteit', *Theoretische Geschiedenis*, 15(1988), 417-30.

Lively, J., 'The Europe of the Enlightenment', *History of European Ideas*, 1(1980), 91-102.

Miert, J. van, 'Nationalisme in de lokale politieke cultuur, Tiel 1850-1900', *De Negentiende Eeuw*, 16(1992), 59-85.

Mijnhardt, W.W., 'Natievorming in het revolutietijdvak', *Bijdragen en Mededelingen betreffende de Geschiedenis der Nederlanden*, 104(1989), 546-53.

Montesquieu (C. de Secondat), baron de, *The spirit of the laws*, translated by T. Nugent (New York, Hafner, 1949).

Nelson, B., et al., ed., *The idea of Europe: problems of national and transnational identity* (Oxford, Berg, 1992).

Odermatt, P., 'The use of symbols in the drive for European integration', *Yearbook of European Studies*, 4(1991), 217-40.

Parker, W.H., 'Europe: how far?', *Geographical Journal*, 126 (1960), 278-97.

Raedts, P., 'Katholieken op zoek naar een Nederlandse identiteit 1814-1898', *Bijdragen en Mededelingen betreffende de Geschiedenis der Nederlanden*, 107(1992), 713-25.

Rijksbaron, A., et al., ed., *Europe from a cultural perspective: historiography and perceptions* (Amsterdam, Nijgh & Van Ditmar, 1987).

Roobol, W.H., 'What is Europe?', *Yearbook of European Studies*, 1(1988), 186-204.

Said, E.W., *Orientalism*, revised edition (London, Penguin, 1995).

Sas, N.C.F. van, 'De mythe Nederland', *De Negentiende Eeuw*, 16(1992), 4-22.

Seton-Watson, H., 'What is Europe, where is Europe? From mystique to politique', *Encounter*, 64-65 (July-August 1985), 9-17.

Shelley, M., et al., ed., *Aspects of European cultural diversity*, revised edition, What is Europe? 2 (London, Routledge, 1995).

Smith, A.D., *National identity* (London, Penguin, 1991).

Smith, A.D., 'National identity and the idea of European unity', *International Affairs*, 68 no. 1 (1992), 55-76.

Tamse, C.A. & E. Witte, eds, *Staats- en natievorming in Willem I's koninkrijk* (Brussels, VUB Press, 1992).

Tilly, C., ed., *The formation of national states in Western Europe* (Princeton NJ, Princeton University Press, 1975).

Toynbee, A.J., '"Asia" and "Europe": facts and fantasies', Annex C(I) to *A study of history*, vol. VIII (London, Oxford University Press, 1954), pp. 708-29.

Trevor-Roper, H., 'Hugo Grotius and England', in S. Groenveld & M.J. Wintle, eds, *The exchange of ideas: religion, scholarship and art in Anglo-Dutch relations in the seventeenth century*, Britain and the Netherlands XI (Zutphen, Walburg Pers, 1994), pp. 42-67.

Ullmann, W., *The Carolingian Renaissance and the idea of kingship* (London, Methuen, 1969).

Zetterholm, S., ed., *National cultures and European integration: exploratory essays on cultural diversity and common policies* (Oxford, Berg, 1994).

3 'A vague and puzzling idealism...'[1] Plans for European unity in the era of the modern state

Philip Morgan

This chapter is about the history of the idea of the political unity of Europe, rather than the history of the idea of Europe. The two things are sometimes conflated, as for example, in the title of C.H. Pegg's book, *The evolution of the European idea, 1914-1932*, which is, in fact, a straightforward survey of both practical and visionary schemes for European unity from the First World War to the Great Depression. The conflation is perhaps understandable: the political organization of Europe apparently demands its definition, a decision on who and what is to be included or excluded, and on what grounds. But the connection between the idea of Europe and its political unity is assumed rather than demonstrated. Has there been any necessary and actual reason why a Europe which is thought to 'exist' by virtue of its peoples sharing values, culture and history, should also be politically united? Did the countries constituting the ECSC and the EEC have to partake of a common European civilization, and to be conscious that they did so, in order to create and run these organizations?

Such assumptions often seem to underwrite the view that post-1945 West European integration was the destination of the road to political virtue, the natural and inevitable realization of 'the European idea'. A book like D. Heater's *The idea of European unity*, so careful to contextualize the various schemes for European unity, concludes that a sense of cultural and political identity was required for successful political integration to occur, though later such cultural unities are relegated to the 'settings' for the establishment of a political organization.[2] Both the ideas, of Europe and of European unity, are by now well-trodden paths for historians and political scientists. What is attempted here is a commentary on schemes and projects of European political organization up to and including West European integration in the 1950s, which tests the assumption that the idea of Europe is inseparable from the construction of Europe's political unity.

The starting point is the period from the thirteenth to the seventeenth centuries, when there evolved in Europe a system of what we now call

33

'modern' states. These states, of which the archetypes were the kingdoms of France and England, emerged partly as a result of the long and mutually exhausting rivalry between Papacy and Empire, and in resistance to their universalist pretensions to rule or have authority over Western Christendom. These claims to universal dominion, which was what the idea of political unity of Europe had amounted to in the Middle Ages, persisted long after their proponents had lost the power and authority to sustain them. The princes of Europe gradually extended, consolidated and centralized their sovereign rule over a given demarcated territory, attempting to replace with a single authority, law and administration, the overlapping, multiple and territorially indeterminate obligations of medieval feudal society.

Once sovereign states were emerging, independent of each other and of Pope and Emperor, then the issue of international politics became the ordering or not of relations between them. An international political organization of or between states was one way of managing inter-state relations. As an alternative, it lay somewhere between the two extremes of anarchy and perpetual war, and of empire or dominance by a single state which took away the independence of other states. Dante's *De Monarchia*, published in 1311, was essentially an appeal and an argument for countering the extreme of endemic conflict between states which characterized his own time with a return to the other extreme in the form of a secular universal emperor or monarch keeping the rest in order. His contemporary, Pierre Dubois, like Dante a man of political affairs, was an adviser to the French king, Philip the Fair, and the English king, Edward I, in their disputes with the predatory and universalist Pope Boniface at the turn of the fourteenth century. His proposal, in about 1306, for a Council of Christian princes of Europe ostensibly took account of the reality of emerging states. Their disputes were to be arbitrated by a Council-nominated panel of wise men, whose decisions were to be collectively enforced against any dissenting ruler, if necessary to the point of a war by all against one.

The declared purpose of the league of Christian rulers was to secure peace between them so that united, they could prosecute the holy war against the Turks. This was a constant justification of all proposals for unity into the seventeenth century, for as long as the infidel occupied the Holy Land and later conquered and ruled parts of south-east Europe and threatened to expand further west. But the appeal for political unity, resting on the defence of the common European interest of religion, scarcely disguised Dubois' concern to bring Europe's princes under the leadership of the King of France. In his scheme France, as the strongest kingdom, would dominate the Council and also the final stage of the arbitration process, which was the Pope, then under French control in Avignon. In this situation, what might appear to be collective sanctions against delinquent rulers could very easily be the dominant prince moving to weaken his rivals. Not for the last time, a plan for organized political co-operation between states was really a way of serving the power and interests of one state. Dubois had effectively accepted the reality of separate sovereign states, only in order to reject their right to exist. In a kind of nostalgia for the presumed and only recently lost medieval unity of universal empire, his scheme resolved the conflict of states by establishing the dominance of one of them.

One of the most famous blueprints for a European political organization, the so-called 'Grand Design' of the Duc de Sully, indicated just how much more firmly entrenched the states system was by the early seventeenth century. There was little recall of a universal monarch, if only because the contemporary international situation which Sully addressed was one where the independence of European states and especially that of his own country, France, was threatened by the composite dynastic empire of the Spanish Habsburgs. They ruled over Iberia, the Low Countries, the German Empire, Franche-Comté, and parts of Central Europe and Italy. Although once again the apparent aim of unity was a war of Christian states to expel the Turks from Europe, it was impossible to regard religion as being a source of unity or common purpose. The post-Reformation religious strife between Protestant and Catholic had produced both political and social instability within states, as well as sharpening the conflict between them. It was no wonder that Sully's essentially political scheme was also meant to provide a religious settlement, which would at least allow Protestant and Catholic states to coexist peacefully.

Sully was a minister of the French king, Henry IV, between 1598 and 1611, and probably wrote the 'Grand Design' in the 1620s into a redraft of his memoirs, which were first published in 1638. He fictitiously made his former royal employer the author of the scheme, probably to lend credibility to it. The special pleading on behalf of one state, France, was self-evident: France was the kingdom most at risk from potential Habsburg hegemony over the continent, and Sully's plan called in the other states of Europe to redress the disproportionate power of France's main rival.

If, along with an anti-Turkish crusade, the declared aim of the project was to bring lasting peace between European states, then it could only be secured initially by war. A coalition of states led by France would impose the dismantling of the Habsburg empire. The dynasty's rule would be reduced to Iberia, the Spanish Mediterranean islands, and the overseas empire. Its conquered territories would be distributed among the members of the victorious coalition so as to create a constellation of states in Europe of roughly equal power, whose frontiers would be then fixed for all time. In Sully's confection, this balance of power, or equilibrium, was in itself a guarantee of perpetual peace, since states on a par with each other would apparently lack the will, the incentive and the means to challenge the balance of forces. If more was needed to maintain the balance and therefore the peace, then Sully's proposed standing council or assembly of states' representatives, presided over by the Pope, himself ruling one of the states in balance, would settle disputes between states and rule against any infringement of existing frontiers.

The strikingly static nature of the balance, immobilizing frontiers for good, was in Sully's view what would reconcile states to the arrangement, after the initial inducement to join the coalition in order to carve up the Habsburg lands. But the rigidity of the political and territorial settlement makes the whole scheme implausible. Sully's equilibrium was, after all, to be the product of war and shifting alliances between states, and who could say that a different alignment of states, no less in balance, would not result from other wars and other sets of alliances. In the real world of states, a balance of power was something which was always in the process of being created, always in motion; it was an outcome of conflicts and changing alliances, not a way of preventing such conflicts in the first place, an effect not a cause of peace among states.

Still, Sully's plan did at least take Europe as it was in his day, a grouping of separate states which were often at war with each other, and which clearly had an interest in combining to resist the hegemony of any one state. His solution to the very contemporary problem of inter-state relations, how to bring peace while securing the independence of separate states, avoiding in other words the peace of universal empire, was to impose a balance of power by force and then maintain it through the agency of a permanent organization of states.

Sully's work influenced similar plans over the next 150 years at least, even though it had little resonance among the rulers of countries whose fictitious approval of the scheme was depicted in his memoirs, and least of all in France, which, under Louis XIV in the second half of the seventeenth century, replaced Spain as the potentially hegemonic power against whom the other states had to coalesce in order to protect their independence. The notion of the balance of power, which was not simply Sully's invention but derived from the actual development of relations between states, was to dominate the thinking and practice of international discourse from the late sixteenth century to the late nineteenth century. It was true that Sully excluded the Turks from his 'Grand Design' because they were not Christian, and the Russians because they were the wrong sort of Christians. But his and others' idea of the balance of power had no real moral or cultural basis; if it was a system, then its coherence and rationale came from balancing the interests of states.

The Abbé de Saint-Pierre, who first published his *Project for bringing about everlasting peace in Europe* in 1712-13, had no evident political cause or state interest to promote. A minor intellectual talent of independent means, he had no sustained experience of political affairs. But his work became well known and was widely translated, because he tirelessly circulated his plans to rulers and their ministers, and Rousseau later published an edited version of the work as a vehicle for his own commentary on international relations.

Saint-Pierre modestly acknowledged his intellectual debt to Sully, and offered a rehash of the basic principles and structures of the 'Grand Design' with a dash of Enlightenment certainty and including far greater detail on the procedures for the operation of his 'perpetual alliance' between states. The point of the proposed arrangement, sanctioned in a formal treaty between participating states, was to bring about permanent peace and the economic prosperity which was the considerable side-effect of peace. State frontiers and political systems were to be fixed as established at the most recent treaties between the countries, and the basis of the new constituent treaty of the alliance was the mutual collective guarantee of this international and internal status quo. Here at least was some understanding that treaties were the outcome of wars and gave an agreed form, if only temporarily, to the relative international position of states resulting from war. A permanent assembly of representatives of member states would have the final say in arbitrating on any disputes which occurred, and their majority decision could be collectively enforced. Saint-Pierre clearly expected that the thought of provoking the combined intervention of other states would be sufficient deterrent to any potentially errant state.

Rousseau's devastating critique of Saint-Pierre's scheme was not directed at the aims, principles and structures of his proposed European association of states. He agreed with the diagnosis of a Europe constantly devastated by wars between states, and with the solution of a confederal organization which would keep the peace by limiting the right of states to go to war whenever and against whomever they wished. The scheme was unrealizable because states would never voluntarily and simultaneously agree to its formation in the first place. As Frederik the Great of Prussia sarcastically remarked of the plan, 'the thing is most practicable; for its success all that is lacking is the consent of Europe and a few similar trifles.'[3]

Saint-Pierre had convinced himself, and Rousseau, of the great advantages of lasting peace and economic well-being which would accrue to states once they had joined the association, benefits so self-evident to rulers that they would be reason enough for them to participate. But if, as Saint-Pierre knew and Rousseau understood, states were normally in conflict, what would possibly induce them to co-operate? Certainly not the prospect that they would have to conduct themselves better and give up changing the international status quo. States did not and do not choose the path of virtue for virtue's sake; they did not and do not federate for general principles of peace and common interest, only for compelling and converging reasons of their own interests. To think and expect otherwise was to assume the willingness of states to co-operate which the confederal organization was designed to achieve, to will the end but not the means. Saint-Pierre's scheme, sensible enough in its structures and procedures but unlikely to be realized as long as states behaved like states, exposed the real problem of voluntary federations, namely, how actually to bring them about.

It was during the eighteenth-century Enlightenment that the notion of the balance of power came to be seen as the organizing principle of international relations in Europe. In a much-quoted snatch from Voltaire, Europe was characterized as 'a kind of great Republic divided into several states', sharing the 'same religious foundation ... the same principle of public law and politics',[4] and connected by a sense of a balance of power which both kept them free and independent and limited their conflicts. This passage, and similar ones from Montesquieu and Rousseau, are usually taken as an indication of the growing consciousness of Europe among Europeans. Rousseau, in a more realistic and penetrating view of inter-state relations, rather doubted that they would be determined by sweet reasonableness or that the balance of power would somehow restrain let alone prevent conflict between states.

But although Rousseau, Voltaire and Montesquieu might have expressed an idea of Europe and sense of 'Europeanness' derived from a common historical and cultural experience, this unity did not correspond in any way to a unified political organization of the continent. The glory of Europe, to Montesquieu, was the freedom and independence of separate states, the result of several states balancing each other. Culturally, they might be parts of a whole, but politically their connection ran as far as maintaining a balance of power which kept them separate. From this perspective, the balance of power secured the sovereign freedom of rulers and their peoples; political unity meant empire or the dominance of one state. Rousseau thought that conflict and war between states was inevitable, and that their relations with each other were thus not affected by what unified them, a common culture and history. It was precisely because cultural unity was irrelevant to the political behaviour of states that Rousseau recognized the need for a confederation of states, even though he could not envisage it ever happening.

It was only in the early nineteenth century that European states really started to use the balance of power idea as a device for limiting conflict between themselves in the way idealized by the Enlightenment thinkers. By this time, the balance was a matter for the five Great Powers of the coalition which finally defeated Napoleonic France and determined the political and territorial settlement of Europe in 1815 after more than twenty years of revolutionary wars. The imminent reconstruction of Europe was the immediate incentive for the French positivist philosopher, the Comte de Saint-Simon, to rush out a pamphlet in 1814 on *The reorganization of the European community*, which he clearly hoped would influence the Great Power settlement. It did not and perhaps could not, since his scheme's basic premises for an international organization hardly matched those of the Great Powers.

Saint-Simon rejected the balance of power as the basis of international relations, because it demonstrably led to more rather than less war, and in so doing reworked Sully and Saint-Pierre as conclusively as he isolated himself from Great Power deliberations. But certainly like Saint-Pierre, he regarded his blueprint for a European political organization as a self-evidently sensible proposal, since it corresponded to the new age of democratic government and scientific-industrial economic development. His plan was for a fully fledged European federal organization, with a single European government accountable to a corporately-elected European parliament and responsible for areas of common 'European' concern, including foreign policy, the economy, communications, education, and even religious and ethical matters.

The scale and scope of the reorganization was limited only by the gradualness of its implementation. The process had to start with the basic building block of a general European union, which was the political union of the two leading liberal constitutional and industrial states, France and Britain. The Anglo-French union would stimulate by example the spread of parliamentary government and industrialization in other countries. The gradual convergence of the political and economic systems of European countries would allow the eventual formation of a political and economic union between all states on the same bases.

Saint-Simon's plan most resembles mid-twentieth century federalist schemes, which might explain why he is seen as the 'forerunner' of post-1945 integration, and a man wise before his time. Certainly, the proposal was so out of step with his own time and historical context as to nullify its impact. Like Saint-Pierre's project, it provides no incentive or compelling reason for countries to unite other than its own self-evident rationality. The lynchpin of the scheme, Anglo-French union, was hardly a credible proposition in 1814 or for long after. Saint-Simon argued that the nation-state would cease to be the basic economic and political unit and that a European government would be run by the 'cosmopolitan' technocrats and captains of industry, at a time when the democratic national state and industrialization had yet to appear in much of Europe. His scheme also fed another near-unshakeable twentieth-century assumption that the accelerating scale and pace of transnational technological progress and industrial economic growth made necessary and desirable the creation of political organizations on a similarly large scale.

The balance of power was not only built into the territorial settlement of 1815, which was meant to block the aspiration to hegemony of France or any other Great Power. It was also quite consciously regulated by diplomacy between the Great Powers and international treaties, which were 'the public law of Europe' binding on all signatory states. The 1815 Quadruple Alliance of Austria, Russia, Britain and Prussia committed these powers to 'concert', or act in a co-ordinated way, if a revolutionary government came to power again in France and thereby threatened the security of other states. They also agreed to hold regular meetings, to consider measures necessary to maintain peace within and between states. This provision lay behind the short-lived 'Congress System', which was broken on the British refusal to combine with the conservative Great Powers in using these meetings sanctioned by treaty for authorizing blanket Great Power intervention in the affairs of other states, or acting like a universal government, in other words.

A 'Concert of Europe' survived, however, and worked well into the late nineteenth century. The Great Powers usually though not always co-operated to the extent that any territorial changes were to be agreed multilaterally, and this was often done in and through conferences. Their treaties spoke of a 'system', also of a 'union', but what was meant was not an overarching political organization, nor even a European Secretariat to run the conferences. The 'systematic' nature of their co-operation lay rather in an agreed frame of reference for international relations; the balance of power operated in a way which did not touch the independence of the Great Power states. The irrelevance of cultural definition to the nineteenth-century balance of power mode of political co-operation between states was clear from the other powers' acceptance of Russia as a European Great Power. Politically, Russia was a part of Europe, when conservative Catholic Romantics were excluding her from Europe on cultural-religious grounds.

For the democratic and republican nationalist movements of the first half of the nineteenth century, it was an abuse of terms for the balance of power apologists and practitioners to claim that their 'system' limited inter-state conflict while guaranteeing the sovereign freedom and independence of governments and peoples. Applying the principle of national self-determination, the balance of power kept nations and Europe disunited. In a universal conflagration of kings and states, a Europe of free and democratically run nation-states would emerge and 'naturally' federate in a voluntary union of equals. Why even nation-states should want to unite was not a question to ask. Mazzini and others of the nationalists' international, indeed like Saint-Simon, took the logical leap which Rousseau had refused to make, that states in the international setting could be made to behave like individuals in society. So, by force of analogy, if nothing else, communities of free and equal citizens in nations would form a free and equal community of nations.

Very much in the Mazzinian tradition, the Czech Masaryk and other democratic nationalist leaders after the First World War in Central and Eastern Europe projected a 'New Europe' of federations of free and self-governing nations, as if scarcely a breath needed to be taken between the fulfilment of the principle of national self-determination and that of a European federation. The First World War appeared to indicate that a Europe partly composed of national states was incapable of being at peace with itself. But that same war had liberated the Central and East European nations from the multinational empires, and the new global order of the League of Nations was built on the optimistic nineteenth century premise that nation-states with democratic institutions were more likely to co-operate with each other than not.

The Pan-European union proposed from the early 1920s by that one-man United Nations, Count Richard Coudenhove-Kalergi, took a global perspective of what he saw as Europe's predicament. His conception of pan-Europe was geopolitical and power-political, which helps to explain why neither Britain nor Russia could be included but the African and Far Eastern colonies of continental European Countries were. Britain and her empire-commonwealth, Russia-in-Eurasia, Japan-in-Asia and 'pan-America' were global 'power-fields' in their own right, incipient world federations of considerable political and economic weight. In this light, a Europe newly fragmented into competitive and autarkic nation-states was a pygmy on the world stage. Europe's global decline, already apparent in the emergence of these other inter-continental power blocs, could only be halted by a united European bloc of similar resources and dimensions.

Resolving the problems of Europe's economic and political disunity was thus the way to ensure the continent's survival and strength on the international plane. An internally united Europe would be both cause and effect of peace between European countries, and of a global peace of coexistence between world unions. Pan-European union would deter the immediate threat of a predatory Eurasia, and Coudenhove-Kalergi often melodramatically depicted Europe's current options as being either federal union or Russian conquest. A stage-by-stage cumulative process would take European countries from regular conferences, through a network of arbitration and collective security treaties and a European customs union, to the drafting and signing of a pan-European constitution for a European government.

The plan had its own logic, and, like other earlier plans, addressed real or perceived issues of contemporary Europe. Ideas and concrete schemes for customs unions had a life of their own in the 1920s, and interested businessmen, economists, officials, and politicians saw European disunity as one of the reasons for the decline in both Europe's share of world trade and in intra-European trade. The USA was both an economic rival and a model of the productivity and commercial gains of a vast tariff-free internal market.

Coudenhove-Kalergi's own cosmopolitan background and lack of conventional party-political attachments made it unlikely that he was using Europe as a cover for a nationalist agenda. But he was unable to prevent the pan-Europe movement he founded, which had national sections, from falling under some mutual suspicion of being a double game in both France and Germany. The German section, in particular, had open supporters of *Anschluss* and *Mitteleuropa* in its ranks, who drew Coudenhove's sharp reminder that his movement was pan-European and not pan-German. The German government itself could see the tactical value of trading its revisionist claims in European currency, arousing in turn French concerns that a 'European' resolution of, say, the question of *Anschluss*, would result in a stronger Germany rather than a stronger Europe.

As ever, union could be shown as desirable and beneficial, even as inevitable, but its apparently self-evident advantages were still not necessarily enough to induce the participation of governments even in that proposed first international conference. How was Coudenhove to persuade people to bring about voluntarily what he half-believed was the obvious conclusion to be drawn from world-wide geo-political and economic developments? Whatever his professed commitment to building up a popular pro-Europe movement from below, Coudenhove spent most of his time and energy in lobbying the great and the good, including the French Foreign Minister between 1925 and 1932, Aristide Briand, who became honorary president of Pan-Europe's central council.

Previous plans for European union had bogusly claimed the approval of rulers to give them weight, been hawked around royal courts, heads of government and ministries, and were read by kings and officials. But they remained the unofficial work of individuals which was never acted on by governments. Briand's famous Memorandum of May 1930 to the European states which were members of the League of Nations was significant because it was the first proposal for some kind of European union to be made and considered by governments.

Governments had to respond to Briand's proposal because of its official source, but some of them were clearly either mystified by or suspicious of its contents. The very opacity and tentativeness of the Memorandum contributed to their unease. The document defensively attempted to answer likely objections to the proposals even while it was unveiling them. In its very concern not to offend sensibilities and interests, the Memorandum aroused rather than allayed anxieties as to its real drift and meaning.

The proposals were directed to forming what was variously and vaguely termed 'a kind of federal bond', 'federative organization', 'European association', 'European union', and 'federal European union'. The European bodies which Briand wanted to set up did not amount to much and had no powers of any significance. 'Federal' was a misnomer, since the institutions were quite explicitly not a challenge to the sovereignty and functions of national governments. 'In no case and in no degree can the institution of the federal bond ... affect in any manner the sovereign rights of the states', declared the Memorandum, reinforcing the disclaimer with the statement that 'it is on the basis of absolute sovereignty and of entire political independence that the understanding between European nations ought to be effected.'[5]

The proposed bodies seemed to replicate those of the League of Nations, which was presumably a deliberate attempt to reassure people that nothing extraordinary would be enacted and that the structures of the union would be compatible with those of the League. This amounted to making a rod for one's own back. The British response was that these bodies were either a rival or a duplication of the League, and as such neither desirable nor necessary. A kind of representative European standing Conference or assembly would 'direct' the union. Supported by a Secretariat, there would also be an executive organ of some members of the Conference, the Permanent Political Committee, whose task was to draw up an agenda of issues on which co-operation could proceed, and examine procedures for bringing the union into existence. All these bodies appeared to be merely preparatory to the real thing.

If there was any dynamite in the Memorandum, then it was concealed in the suggested general guide-lines on the essentially exploratory work of the Political Committee. The starting point was the 'general subordination of the economic problem to the political.' Why? Because 'all possibility of progress towards economic union being strictly determined by the question of security and this question being intimately bound up with that of the realizable progress toward political union, it is on the political plane that constructive effort ...

should first be made.' Practically every response homed in on this apparent reversal of priorities, for Briand had earlier publicly declared that economic rather than political matters were the most conducive, concrete and urgent area for likely co-operation.

The British Foreign Office strained every sinew to make itself believe that what Briand meant by this was simply that any process leading towards economic co-operation would be handled by the politicians rather than by the technocrats, because ultimately only political will would bring about tariff reform. This considerable gloss tells us more about the British government's concern to avoid political matters being treated by a European body, than Briand's real intention. It was more plausible to argue that Briand wanted outstanding political issues to be dealt with first, political union before economic union. The Memorandum, in mentioning the kind of political co-operation the Permanent Committee might consider, talked of moves which would provide for the independence and security of each state through collective guarantees of that security and independence. This might well involve, for example, the extension to all of Europe of the international guarantees of the Locarno treaty, thereby creating a general security system in Europe, perhaps backed up by some sort of arbitration machinery.

The cat had been let out of the bag. This was the key passage of the Memorandum, and everybody knew it. The 1925 Locarno agreements involved Britain and Italy as co-guarantors of the frontiers of France with Germany, and therefore apparently provided an international guarantee of French security against Germany. Locarno-style agreements covering the rest of Europe would similarly fix and guarantee European frontiers, including, of course, Germany's eastern frontiers with the 'successor' states.

The responses to the Memorandum were, as a result of this decoding of French intentions, entirely predictable. The German reply, like that of Austria, Hungary and Bulgaria, all states wanting to revise the terms of the post-war peace treaties and thus change frontiers, was that for them the political prerequisite of European co-operation was the restoration of 'full equality of rights', in other words, a reopening rather than a closing down of the question of existing frontiers. Conversely, Poland and France's allies in Eastern Europe, the beneficiaries of the post-war settlement, all replied to the effect that Briand's proposals would lead to a strengthened guarantee of their security.

The interest of the Memorandum lay in its official, governmental nature. The government which proposed it, as much as the governments which had to respond to it, were concerned with the national interest, which was their *raison d'être*. Unsurprisingly, they assessed the proposal for European co-operation in the light of this interest. The underlying reason for Briand's scheme, eventually disclosed in the text of the Memorandum itself, was French security against Germany, the only aim of French foreign policy since 1918. Calling in others to help France keep Germany down had been consistently pursued in various guises, from the abortive Anglo-American guarantee, the strict enforcement of the Treaty of Versailles, the conclusion of treaties with East European states equally fearful of German revisionism, to Locarno itself. It was partly because these efforts were still deemed inadequate for French security that the imaginative step was taken of trying to smother Germany in a general European security system promoted through European institutions.

France might have wanted to 'Europeanize' the German problem, but French motives were not 'European', any more than Germany's were. The German government did not want the kind of European political association which prevented revisionism in Eastern Europe, and pushed hard for Briand's scheme to proceed on the plane of economic co-operation, no less in the national interest. Briand's proposal for European union was conveniently shunted off to a League of Nations Commission of Inquiry, where in 1931 we find the German representative arguing for bilateral and sub-regional economic trading blocs on the lines of the recently mooted Austro-German customs union.

The point about national interest has been made with some emphasis in respect of France and Germany, because the Memorandum was an attempt to address Franco-German conflict, the major reason for post-war international tension in Europe, and its proposals were ultimately broken on that antagonism and mutual suspicion. But the point was generally applicable. Britain worried that a European regional formation, whether political or economic, would upset its more important global relations with the USA, and with the empire and dominions. Most of the governments responding to the Memorandum preferred economic co-operation before any form of political union, however weak. They did so not only because they did not want to be seen rejecting the proposals outright. They wished to avoid high political issues altogether. Matters of foreign policy, defence, and security, touching the most important functions of government in the national interest, were not easily entrusted elsewhere, unless governments wanted to remove the reason for their existence.

There were no villains, here. National governments were bound to behave as national governments. France felt it had a compelling reason to pursue the national interest through a kind of European union; other European states could find no such compelling reason to do the same in the national interest. The Memorandum had lamely stated that Europe's 'geographical situation compels ... solidarity', and that there were 'ethnic affinities and ... community of civilization' drawing states together to consider matters of common concern. These 'affinities' might well be there, but the history of Briand's initiative indicated that the play and interaction of interests, rather than culture, determined the political shape of relations between states.

It has been suggested that whatever the viability of the schemes for some form of European political unity, there has never been any 'natural' inclination of European states to unite. States have not been willing to give up their independence, and have found ways of managing their relations which preserved that independence. The basic problem facing the proponents of unity was getting states to join up in the first place, rather than devising structures of co-operation which would deliver the benefits of unity. There had to be reasons which compelled states to consider political unity, which was not the 'natural' option for sovereign states.

In the post-1945 period, the constraints on the continued independence of the European national states were external. It scarcely needs repeating that the post-war settlement in Europe, simultaneously dividing the continent as a whole while uniting its divided parts, was largely determined by the breakdown of the Allied wartime co-operation and the political and ideological hostility between the USA and the USSR. Although we are obviously dealing with a process the outcome of which was not as certain at the time as it now appears in retrospect, the two 'superpowers' divided Europe because they could not agree on how to reorder it as a whole, both sides apparently applying Stalin's crude maxim that whoever occupies a country imposes on it his own social and political system. If we accept this simplified version of post-war bloc-formation in Europe, then the element of compulsion crucial even for the achievement of voluntary federation was to be found in the combination of the post-war political weakness of European states and the political strength of the two 'superpowers'.

But it is as well to remember that the wartime Allies had effectively decided by 1943 to restore a Europe of national states after they had defeated and dismantled the Nazi Reich. The Allies had discussed with each other, and with the governments in exile, proposals for post-war federation, especially in Eastern Europe. But federation at this point suited neither the USA nor the USSR, and Britain was not prepared to push the issue at the price of endangering Allied co-operation. Stalin feared that any East European federation might well be directed at the Soviet Union, and would get in the way of Russia's own territorial demands in the region. He could also play on the fact that East Europeans themselves were, after all, fighting against Nazi rule to restore national independence, and had exiled governments in waiting to lead their liberated states. Roosevelt thought in turn that European federations might be economically protectionist, cutting across the 'Open Door' free trading approach which would give American business access to global markets. Regional federations also sat uneasily with the US perception of a post-war global international organization, which, like the League of Nations, was to be an association of free and self-governing national states.

The European Resistance movements had anticipated a *tabula rasa* in Europe at the end of the war, with the nation-state discredited by war and defeat and literally erased in the Nazi New Order, which would favour the installation of a European federal system and pre-empt the recovery of the nation-states. Instead, federal aspirations had to come to terms with the rapid reappearance of European states and governments, a reality which inevitably conditioned the kind of European organization which evolved.

There was, evidently, a change in US policy on the shape of post-war Europe, apparent in 1947 with the linked declarations of the Truman Doctrine and the

Marshall Plan. US funds filtered to Western European countries through the European Recovery Programme did not aim solely at the recovery of their economies, but at sustained economic expansion on the American model. The ERP's goals were a high standard of living, full employment and increased production allied to improved productivity These were the premises for a peaceful and stable society which, in the US view, also required 'nothing less than an integration of the Western European economy'.[6]

By the half-way stage of the ERP in late 1949, the USA was making the continuation of Marshall Aid conditional on the West European countries having in place early in 1950 a programme for economic integration. Again, in the American strategy for Western Europe, a free-trading customs union would be the foundation and impetus for political union, a United States of Europe including West Germany. Here, apparently, was the *force majeure* behind Western Europe's first steps in integration.

But if the external pressure to integrate was irresistible, the striking aspect of the process was the extent to which the West European governments were able to influence the kind of integration which occurred. The Americans had quite evidently hoped that the OEEC, the Organization for European Economic Co-operation set up in 1948 to administer Marshall Aid funds, would be the forum where European states could, in the allocation of funds, work out a scheme of economic co-operation. It never materialized; the OEEC was and remained an inter-governmental organization rather than a vehicle for economic integration, almost paralysed by the rounds of trading off national claims for funds. Arguably, something similar happened once the US decided to use the direct leverage of Marshall Aid funds to induce the integration which European governments were reluctant to start on their own account.

American pressure to deliver on economic integration was clearly one of the aspects of that conjuncture which in 1950 resulted in the French Schuman Plan for the organization of the coal and steel industries of France and Germany. This initiative led in turn to the 1951 treaty between these two countries, Italy, and the Benelux countries establishing the ECSC, the European Coal and Steel Community.

The first indication of the European governments' successful resistance to the American grand design was that integration was limited to a single sector, albeit one of the most important, and did not take in the economy as a whole. The choice of sector itself reflected the interplay of the national interests of European states. The French desire for security against Germany was no less pressing in 1945 than it had been in 1918. Initially, they wanted to undermine German economic and political power permanently by dismemberment, a partitioning of the country which would also guarantee French control and access to the coal and coke of the Saar and Ruhr, so essential to France's own plan for post-war reconstruction of the national economy. The strengthening of the French economy was itself an element of French national security against Germany, as much as the recovery of German heavy industrial production was a potential threat to it.

The decision to establish a West German state and for West Germany to play a full part in European economic recovery obliged the French government to pursue the same end of containing Germany through a different strategy. Since some form of economic integration was unavoidable, the Schuman Plan enabled the French government to have some control over West German economic recovery, exercised in a regional framework of co-operation, and continued access to the German resources vital to its own recovery. For its part, the West German government was able to restore the strength of its own national economy, in a way which eased rather than heightened the old fears of her European neighbouring states about the political and economic revival of Germany. Monnet might well have been the closet European federalist he was made out to be, but as the author of the Schuman Plan he was clearly also acting in his capacity as the person in charge of the plan to reconstruct the French economy.

If national interest lay behind this sectoral initiative, it also fed into the form given to the institutions of the ECSC. Its executive arm, the High Authority, responsible for creating and operating common markets in coal and steel, was probably the first supranational European organization to exist. But the scope and impact of supranationalism was diluted by national governments in their insistence that a Council of Ministers, appointed from each participating government, share responsibility for the running of the ECSC with the High Authority.

Whatever the arguments about Monnet's 'functionalism' being federalism by stealth, it is difficult to find any real federalist input or intent, whether European or American, in the way the ECSC was formed. The initiative was limited in scope, and limited to an area which allowed the French government to deal with an impasse in its post-war foreign and economic policies. The ECSC addressed a particular national problem at a particular juncture of time. The proposal came from a national state, was negotiated into existence by political leaders and officials of the national states, and in the institutional balance agreed to by national states, it protected the responsibility of national governments for the economic policies of their own countries. It was conceived as an end, not as a beginning or a first step to something else.

This reading of the origins and significance of the ECSC is perhaps confirmed by the eventual failure of another initiative in sector integration, the European Defence Community, which was launched, again by the French government, in October 1950. Once again, the EDC proposal was a way out of a potential cul-de-sac in French foreign policy. The French government was caught between fears of a reviving Germany, and the USA's insistence that Western Europe make a more significant contribution to its own defence through the rearmament of Germany. The EDC would create a European army incorporating German troops, thereby permitting West Germany to participate in the collective defence of Western Europe without forming a German national army.

Integration was moving onto the high political ground of foreign and defence policy, the core functions and competences of national government which by rights would be the last area for integration. The particular Cold War conjuncture explains its premature entry in 1950, but the prospect frightened away many governments, the British almost immediately. This was especially the case when the draft EDC treaty included provision for a European Political Community, the matter of defence being so important that it necessitated a political authority over it.

The EDC project cannot be seen as the next item of a federalist or even a functionalist agenda. The French government never proposed it as such, and with evident relief the treaty was not ratified by France, which instead agreed to the enlargement of the 1948 Brussels treaty organization in what was called the Western European Union in 1954. The arrangement delivered everything which the French government had wanted to achieve with the EDC scheme, and more. It secured national control over the armed forces, in an inter-governmental rather than supranational framework, it satisfied the US demand for German rearmament, and, since both West Germany and Britain joined the WEU, it counterbalanced German influence with British. The failure of the EDC was only a 'setback' if the ECSC was to be taken as the start of something big.

The reputed 'relance' of West European integration came in 1955, when the Benelux countries took the initiative in proposing to their ECSC partners a full 'European Economic Community', leading to the 1957 Treaty of Rome establishing the EEC. It was an advance on the ECSC, in the sense that it envisaged a generalized customs union as a prelude to economic union. In most other respects, the EEC remained in the mould of the ECSC. It avoided the high political spheres of activity which because they touched the central areas of national sovereignty, were far less susceptible to integration than the economic. In motivation and outcome, the EEC reflected and embodied the play and interaction of national governments pursuing national interests.

As small states, the Benelux countries had always appreciated the economic advantages of involvement in larger economic unions, and equally the political gains of diluting or controlling the power and influence of their larger neighbouring states which could be incorporated with themselves in a single co-operative organization. The French were not the only ones who could seek to handle the problem of potentially over-powerful states by 'Europeanizing' it. The intense Franco-German antagonism seen in the past had probably receded by the mid-1950s. But rising frustration in Germany at the barriers to its export trade by French protectionism were matched by French fears that its economy could not withstand German and European competition. Both concerns were capable of compromise in the EEC's commitment to internal free trade and the eventual shape that was given to a Common Agricultural Policy.

There was not a hint of supranationalism in the 1955 Messina declaration, which launched the two years of negotiation for the EEC. This meant that

Britain had to fall back on its extra-European Commonwealth and imperial ties as its reason for not joining. The Treaty of Rome's preamble talked of laying the foundations of 'an ever closer union among the peoples of Europe', but the EEC bodies replicated those of the ECSC, again with the same intention of halting any charge towards supranational institutions. The Commission shared responsibility with the inter-governmental Council of Ministers, and decision making was skewed towards the latter in both treaty and practice.

Convinced federalists like Altiero Spinelli, the Italian anti-Fascist whose 1941 Ventotene Manifesto provided the European Resistance's blueprint for a federal Europe, were highly critical of what had been done in Western Europe by 1957. Monnet was the man who might have made Europe, but he had made a bad job of it. This kind of disillusionment makes it difficult to say that the West European integration of the 1950s, such as it was, has any real 'precursors' in wartime and early post-war federal plans, or indeed in any of the other plans for European unity.

Some of the politicians and civil servants who actually negotiated the ECSC and the EEC treaties might well have read Briand, or even known about Saint-Pierre and Sully. But there is no evidence that this made any difference, one way or the other, to what they set up and how they went about it. The odd hybrid nature of ECSC and EEC institutions, part supranational, mainly inter-governmental, was not something off the drawing board or a blueprint. Things were too untidy for that. But the hybridity was clearly deliberately conceived. It indicated that organizations were being set up to cope with particular pressures and particular problems, and both to balance and promote the national interests of governments. The only things to which the plans were 'precursors' were the other plans.

If the ECSC and the EEC did not need a history for them to be established or legitimized, then neither did they need a common cultural background or identity, a 'Europeanness', for them to be created. Little, if any, of this appeared in the preambles to the Treaties of Paris and Rome, though there was plenty of it in the declarations and resolutions of the European Movement. The national states, not 'Europe', created the ECSC and the EEC, and for specific national purposes. Whether this is one of the explanations for the so-called 'democratic deficit' of EU institutions, and whether it actually matters, is another story.

Notes

1. British Foreign Office memorandum on Briand's proposal for European union, 30 May 1930, in Woodward & Butler, eds, *Documents on British foreign policy*, 326.

2. Heater, *The idea of European unity*, 186.

3. Quoted in Hinsley, *Power and the pursuit of peace*, 45.

4. Quoted in Hay, *Europe: the emergence of an idea*, 123.

5. The French text and a poor English translation of the Memorandum can be found in *International Conciliation* (1930), 325-53. Briand's speech to the League of Nations Assembly in September 1929, the French text of the Memorandum, the British response, and a summary of other responses, all used in this commentary, are in Woodward and Butler, eds, *Documents on British foreign policy*, 312-53.

6. Paul Hoffman's speech to the OEEC Council, 31 October 1949, in Vaughan, ed., *Post-war integration in Europe*, 47.

References

Arter, D., *The politics of European integration in the twentieth century* (Aldershot, 1993).

Barraclough, G., *European unity in thought and action* (Oxford, 1963).

Beloff, M. et al., eds, *L'Europe du XIXe et XXe siècle*, vol. I (Milan, 1959).

Brugmans, H., *L'idée européenne, 1920-1970*, third edition (Bruges, 1970).

Burke, P., 'Did Europe exist before 1700?', *History of European Ideas*, 1(1980), 21-9.

Chabod, F., *Storia dell'idea d'Europa* (Rome/Bari, 1974).

Forsyth, M., *(Unions of states: the theory and practice of confederation* (Leicester, 1981).

Fuhrmann, M. 'L'Europe - contribution a l'histoire d'une idée culturelle et politique', *History of European Ideas*, 4(1983), 1-15.

García, S., ed., *European identity and the search for legitimacy* (London, 1993).

Hay, D., *Europe: the emergence of an idea*, revised edition (Edinburgh, 1968).

Heater, D., *The idea of European unity* (Leicester/London, 1992).

Hinsley, F.H., *Power and the pursuit of peace: theory and practice in the history of international relations* (Cambridge, 1963).

Joll, J., 'Europe - an historian's view', *History of European Ideas*, 1(1980), 7-19.

Lipgens, W., *A history of European integration* (Oxford, 1982).

Lipgens, W., *Documents on the history of European integration*, 3 vols (Berlin, 1985-88).

Lively, J., 'The Europe of the Enlightenment', *History of European Ideas*, 1(1980), 91-102.

Milward, A., *The reconstruction of Western Europe, 1945-51* (London, 1984).

Pegg, C.H., *Evolution of the European idea, 1914-1932* (Chapel Hill NC/London, 1983).

Rijksbaron, A., et al., eds, *Europe from a cultural perspective: historiography and perceptions* (The Hague, 1987).

Seton-Watson, H., 'What is Europe? Where is Europe? From mystique to politique', *Encounter*, 65(1985), 9-17.

Smith, M.L. & Stirk, P., eds, *Making the new Europe: European unity and the Second World War* (London, 1990).

Stirk, P., ed., *European unity in context: the interwar period* (London, 1989).

Stirk, P. & Willis, D., eds, *Shaping post-war Europe: European unity and disunity* (London, 1991).

Vaughan, R., ed., *Post-war integration in Europe* (London, 1976).

Vaughan, R., *Twentieth-century Europe: paths to unity* (London, 1979).

Wilson, K. & J. van der Dussen, eds, *The history of the idea of Europe* (London, 1993).

Woodward, E.L. & R. Butler, eds, *Documents on British foreign policy, 1919-1939*, second series, vol. I (London, 1946).

4 Europe's image: Visual representations of Europe from the earliest times to the twentieth century

Michael Wintle

Much of the confusion which exists about 'Europe' arises from the fact that the word can be applied in so many different ways. If it is not further qualified, 'Europe' nowadays tends to signify in English 'Brussels', the EU, or the EU Commission. But of course it can mean a great deal more than that, and there lies the ambiguity. Most would agree that Europe is a *geographical* term, being the name of one of the earth's continents. (To that loaded statement we shall return at length.) Then there is European *history*, which also includes such things as 'the expansion of Europe'. There is probably a European *culture*, perhaps a European *identity*, and there are various *economic and political structures* (past and present) associated with Europe (Council of Europe, European Union, ERM, EDF, etc. etc.), which usually encompass only a part of the area embraced by the geographical, historical and cultural definitions.

Not only are there all these different versions of Europe, but they all change incessantly. Even the geography of Europe - contrary to common assumptions - has never been constant: we shall examine its metamorphoses in more detail in this chapter. International borders are no more than 'fictional and ever changing external boundaries' and 'ingenious fabrications', and even the external borders of the continent, especially in the East, amount to little more than a disputed dialogue.[1] Europe has aptly been called 'une notion pseudogéographique'.[2] If the *geography* of Europe is disputed and ever-changing, then that is true in spades of its *history*, its *culture*, and its *politico-economic* manifestations. Even if we could ignore post-modernism, it is clear that there is no such 'thing' as Europe, in the sense of a universally agreed objective reality. Europe is one of those words which means, as Humpty-Dumpty said to Alice, just what you choose it to mean.

Indeed, as Peter Burke has written, 'Europe is not so much a place as an idea.'[3] Certainly the *unity* of Europe is a mental construct, and its identity a 'collective social fabrication over time'.[4] If there is no such thing as Europe, then the only reality is perhaps the 'idea' of Europe, which is certainly real in the sense that it has exercised countless writers, politicians and perhaps large numbers of ordinary people for hundreds of years.[5] And all these ideas of Europe - cultural, political, economic, geographical - can and often do have visual representations, either set down *in concreto* by a draughtsman, cartographer or artist, or in the mind's eye of writers, soldiers, politicians, historians, journalists, and others. It is this visualization of the idea of Europe which is the subject of this chapter. But it is essential to understand from the start that there is no such objective reality as Europe in any sense at all, least of all geographically. Even today's modern maps are two-dimensional representations of a three-dimensional reality which cannot be seen in its entirety, and the conventions for the portrayal of a sphere's surface on a flat piece of paper are even now not yet fully agreed by map-makers. Nonetheless, in every age there are geo-political situations which heavily influence the 'mental maps' of contemporaries.[6] For example, Charlemagne's conquests determined the extent of what his subjects thought was Europe, and in the late twentieth century the maps of the EU which appear incessantly on our television screens have a powerful effect on our mental portrayal of the continent. So we are dealing in the world of intellectual concepts and constructs, mainly as reflected in the work of graphic or plastic artists in an entirely subjective way.

In this chapter two tasks will be tackled. There will be a summary of the changing geo-political situation in Europe down the centuries. We shall examine whether, when, and which people have thought that 'Europe' existed, and how those ideas have changed over time. This will be very much a rapid tour, seen from a distance through a telephoto lens, the prime objective being to notice change between successive images, rather than the detail of individual images. Then in the second and larger part of the chapter, we shall move to a consideration of contemporary visual representations of 'Europe', primarily in maps and drawings, but also in other art-forms. We shall look at the historicity of the various kinds of graphic image used to symbolize the continent, and seek to learn what these images can tell us about how Europeans viewed their continent, why particular images were current in certain periods, and how those views and images changed over time. The emphasis will fall on the period up to 1900, with occasional reference to more recent incidental examples; in the twentieth century the advances of mass media have increased the material to such an extent that any sort of systematic coverage becomes a very large undertaking.

There have certainly been a great number of attempts, since the earliest times, to formulate plans and schemes for a united Europe;[7] however, most of these schemes were dreams, and came to little or nothing. In what sense has 'Europe' existed as a geo-political *reality* in the past? The question can be answered in at least three ways. There have been times when parts of Europe have been politically, intellectually, or culturally united, to the extent that significant parts of its population have identified with the continent; there have been periods of temporary enforced hegemony; and there have been episodes of shared influences. We shall survey all three categories.

Past European unities

Greek political power extended over only a small part of Europe, but the Romans controlled most of it. There is no question of a direct association between the Roman empire and Europe, for the Mediterranean was the 'heart, lungs and breast' of those early civilizations,[8] but in the second century the Romans held sway over all of southern Europe from Portugal in the West to the Black Sea in the East, the whole of France and Belgium, much of Britain, the Netherlands and Germany, and large parts of southern central Europe. Only the north-east, including Scandinavia, lay outside their orbit. The unifying experience of Roman hegemony has always been seen, rightly, as the foundation-layer of successive European civilizations, despite the fact that the Romans were active in other theatres as well, and that much of northern Europe was peripheral to their interests.

It was some time before the next major unifying force began to take effect, but it was to be one of the most pervasive. By the sixth century Latin (as opposed to Byzantine) Christianity stretched from the Middle East to western Spain and northern Britain; by the eleventh century it had spread to much of central, eastern and northern Europe, and Scandinavia as well. But there were deep flaws in this apparent unity: there was the great schism between Latin Christianity and Constantinople, and even in the West, Latin Christianity needed political leadership and will to bring it together. That will and leadership was first in evidence under the Frankish kings.

Charlemagne was certainly called 'the King of Europe' by his courtiers and other sycophants. Geographically, the Frankish empire covered most of France and Germany, the Low Countries and the Alpine states, and much of Italy. Britain, Scandinavia, most of Spain and Portugal, southern Italy, and all of central and south-eastern Europe were not included. Nevertheless, an external threat, that potent catalyst in the formation of group identity, gave Frankish Christian Europe additional cohesion. And the threat came in the shape of Islam, which brought the Frankish monarchy's territories together in an unprecedented way. The papacy, as the centre of Latin Christianity, was an essential player in this first stirring of (partial) European unity and solidarity in the face of an external religious and military threat, for the Europe of the eighth century was 'a wholly religious idea', even if it was enforced by the secular arm of the Frankish kings.[9] When a chronicler called the forces of Charles Martel at the battle of Tours in 732 AD 'the Europeans', he did so in the context of Moslem Arab invasions of the Middle East and North Africa in the seventh century, and of Spain and southern France in the eighth; in 846 Rome itself was sacked. 'Europe' was small, shrinking, and surrounded by the hostile forces of another religion.[10]

'*Christianitas*', or Latin Christendom (as opposed to the eastern variant based in Constantinople) continued to provide the rationale for 'Europe' under a different set of secular princes. As the Seljuk Turks took over in the eleventh century from the Arabs as the main threat from the East, 'Europe' was no longer dominated by a single ruling house, but nonetheless consolidated its unity and identity as civilized, Latin Christian, anti-Turk, anti-Islam. The crusades are the symbol of this unity, but as Robert Bartlett has shown, the sense of European identity went much deeper and further than an appetite for military adventure or fear of danger.[11] 'Europe' and 'Christendom' were interchangeable concepts by the fourteenth century, and remained so until the seventeenth:[12] the last Turkish siege of Vienna was only beaten off in 1683. In the later Middle Ages, then, 'Europe' was held together by faith and religion, set against the threat of the unbeliever. In the high Renaissance, however, the significance of embattled Christendom withered, and a new triumphalist version of Europe emerged.

By the sixteenth century, the idea of Europe as the community of believers threatened by Islam had given way to a much more assertive vision, stoked by overseas explorations and discoveries, and notions of European 'civility' and sophistication.[13] In the words of Charles Tilly, 'the Europe of 1500 had a kind of cultural homogeneity only rivalled, at such a geographic scale, by that of China', and this despite the fact that in the fourteenth century there were probably about one thousand separate states in Europe.[14]

In the seventeenth century a new strand was added to the idea of Europe, alongside the age-old *Christianitas*, and the more recent assertiveness of the expansion of Europe, and that was the idea of resistance to a single dominant political or military force from within.[15] The threat began with the Habsburgs in the sixteenth century, but came of age in the form of Louis XIV in the seventeenth: the campaigns of William III of the United Provinces and then of England were presented in terms of the defence of European freedom against tyranny.[16] It was the beginning of the Enlightenment concept of Europe, of which the essence was a balanced system of sovereign states, with no single dominant force (though claims of modest pre-eminence abounded, especially from France). Voltaire saw Europe as a great Republic, embracing many states;[17] these eighteenth-century elite ideas were of a constellation of equal powers, superior to the rest of the world in maritime, military, cultural, and (increasingly) technological power. These notions matured into the nineteenth century, spawning the heady Romantic ideas of Europe, promoted by such publicists as Saint Simon, Mazzini, and perhaps most of all Victor Hugo, with his extraordinarily high-flown flights of Euro-fantasy, talking of a 'United States of Europe', in which all the 'nations of the continent, without losing your distinctive qualities and your glorious individuality, will forge yourselves into a close and higher unity'.[18] These dreams of Europe, at peace with itself and superior to the rest, were in fact more than dreams, in the sense that they were a mental construct shared by increasing numbers of Europeans from the sixteenth to the nineteenth century, achieving maturity in the Enlightenment and lasting into the age of Romanticism.

They were, however, shattered on the rocks of nationalism and imperialism in the later part of the nineteenth century, despite the fact that all these notions came from almost identical roots. The First World War changed the character of European idealism, with the effect that its dominant feature since then has been the desire for peace and the fear of war - something which has always been present in all the schemes since the Middle Ages,[19] but which has dominated the twentieth century. The relative success of the EU since the 1950s, limited though it is to the richer nations in the west of the continent, is based heavily on perceived practical economic advantage, combined with the negative inducement of binding Germany into peaceful co-existence. The idealistic element is still present, for example in the form of the Federal Union, since 1939,[20] but the achievements on the whole have been pragmatic and limited.

There is an almost natural tendency to see all these episodes or outbreaks of partial European unity in some kind of developmental light, leading teleologically towards our own time, and even towards the present European 'project' or EU. In a recent study, Pim den Boer has reminded us, rightly, that there has been little or no continuity, certainly before the eighteenth century,[21] and these episodes are manifestly not the historical myths and direct antecedents which could turn the present EU into some sort of nation-state.[22]

Imposed hegemonies and shared influences in Europe

Alongside these partial, uneven, and often disjointed experiences of the of unity in Europe, there have also been periods of enforced hegemony, and penetrations of influences from outside which have covered large parts of Europe at once, contributing to its uniformity. The celebrated French historian of Europe, J-B. Duroselle, in his *Europe: a history of its peoples* (1990), has covered most of these hegemonies and influences down the ages; it is convenient to rely on his expertise and summarizing skills.[23]

In pre-historic times from 4000 to 2000 BC, many parts of Europe shared a culture which built megalith structures (like Stonehenge), in the Iberian peninsula, France, Britain, southern Scandinavia and northern Germany;[24] many other cultural features were shared across many parts of Europe, like certain pottery styles, wall-painting techniques and burial customs, indicating some common influences. Then, in the first millenium BC, Celtic civilizations dominated much of western Europe, centred in France, Germany and the British Isles, but extending also into Spain, Italy, and south-eastern Europe. This period saw the widespread introduction of iron to Europe, and great improvements in agricultural practice.

Greek culture, whatever its later influence by transmission through the Romans and the Renaissance, was confined in Europe to the maritime areas of the Mediterranean and Black Seas (as well as extending throughout large parts of the Middle East, Asia and north-eastern Africa). Part of that Greek influence was conveyed to many more parts of Europe by the Romans, as we have noticed above, who by the second century AD had overrun all Europe except the North-East and some of the off-shore islands. These ancient civilizations, along with Arab, Moslem and Jewish influences, locked European culture into a Mediterranean context, which itself had little interest in the Atlantic and looked rather towards the material and cultural riches of the Middle East and Central Asia.

Early Christian influences came from the same source: the Middle East. Christ was not a European, and nor were his disciples, though some of them travelled beyond the Bosphorus. However, as we have seen, the Christian Church in various forms had extended to most parts of Europe by the twelfth century, and indeed Latin Christendom became virtually synonymous with the name of 'Europe'. By the fourteenth century, the Roman Catholic Church held sway over nearly all of Europe, except for southern Spain (Islam), and the Greek Orthodox presence in the East and South-East.

In the early modern period, certain dynasties threatened hegemony over Europe, and one of the earliest and direct threats came from Charles V of Spain. He was born in 1500, son of the Burgundian Duke Philip the Fair, from whom he inherited the Low Countries and Austria, and large estates in France. His maternal grandparents were Ferdinand and Isabella of Spain, which he duly inherited, along with the Spanish possessions in northern Italy, and the New World empire with all its fabulous riches. He was then also elected Holy Roman Emperor, giving him much of the eastern corridor of the old Frankish empire. These massive inheritances united his rivals against him, which in the end prevented real hegemony. In the next century the threat came from Bourbon France, and especially from Louis XIV, who never held title on the scale of the earlier generations of the Habsburg family, but he certainly had dynastic, diplomatic and military pretensions of the same order.

These attempts at hegemony in Europe were unsuccessful - until the French Revolution. The armies of France spread into the Low Countries, Switzerland, Austria and Italy. Napoleon's regime added most of the rest of continental Europe, including the whole of Germany, and client states in Poland and the extreme south-east of Europe. It lasted only from around the time of the battle of Austerlitz in 1805 up to 1813, but its effects were colossal in many areas of western Europe. The Napoleonic legal codes, introduced in most countries occupied by his forces for any length of time, were permanent changes to the system, leading to genuine European convergence in all matters touched by the law, especially public law and administration. No wonder Britain and Russia have continued to be at the periphery of Europe, for they were never affected by Napoleon's civil administration which, like Julius Caesar's in the Roman Republic, was in the end of much more lasting importance than any of the military achievements.

The post-Napoleonic era was the age of the European Concert of Powers, which grew out of the post-Habsburg determination to limit the ambitions of any one power on the continent, honed by its temporary failure with France in the early years of the nineteenth century. It has been called the 'European state system' of balance and counter-check between the major powers.[25] The balance of power mechanism was successfully maintained for the rest of the century, but did not stop two major European wars in the first half of the twentieth century. In the second of those, Nazi Germany achieved - temporarily - what Napoleon had done: hegemony over nearly all of Europe, militarily enforced upon a largely unwilling population. Again, it was a brief hegemony, lasting from 1940 to 1944. The most significant positive effect was a determination that military hegemony would never again unite Europe, and in order to ensure it, that Europe should move towards integration for economic and positive political reasons in the shape - eventually - of the EC and EU. However, somewhat perversely, military hegemony did indeed rear its head again, in the form of NATO's control over the western part of Europe, and the hold of the Soviet Union over the eastern half of the continent. Since 1989, that tension has at least partially defused.

What can we conclude from this canter through some of the common influences and hegemonies which Europe has undergone? That military conquest, even if temporary, has often been of critical importance, just as it was in the process of state-formation;[26] that many cultural influences have extended throughout large swathes of Europe, though seldom throughout the whole of 'geographical' Europe; and that therefore Europe has many shared cultural experiences, though unevenly distributed. The most persistent of those, in the period of recorded history, have undoubtedly been the Roman military and infrastructural control with its value-systems enshrined in its law codes, the western Christian Church with its ethics and hierarchies, and the defensive balance of power between the major nations, originating in the sixteenth century and lasting into the twentieth. These are important historical circumstances, but they should be kept in perspective. Few attempts at hegemony have lasted; few influences have been all-pervasive.

The extent of Europe

There remains the question of the external geographical boundaries of Europe. As has become very clear from the survey of attempts at hegemony and shared influences, there is no sustained cultural geography embracing a consistently defined area called 'Europe'. The cultural boundaries (and the military-political ones, internal and external) are evidently in constant flux. What of the physical ones? We shall look first at the question of the sea and rivers, then at the great debate about the eastern boundary of the continent, and finally, very briefly, at the question of Britain.

The Greeks had little interest in or knowledge of much of the northern part of Europe, although they recognized in a general sense a tripartite division of the known world, the *oecumene*, into the three continents of Europe, Asia and Africa. What was important to them was navigation, and Arnold Toynbee has made a strong case for the origin of the geographical term as a mariner's expression for the land mass which was constantly present to port, as a ship sailed from the Mediterranean and the Aegean, through the Dardanelles into the sea of Marmara, south of Constantinople. This waterway continued, through a second set of straits, the Bosphorus, to emerge into the Black Sea, with still the land to port known as Europe, whereas that to starboard was Asia. Up past the Crimean peninsula sailed the intrepid Greek mariners, through the Straits of Kerch into the Sea of Azov: still Europe lay to the left, and Asia to the right. The River Don (the Tanais) flows into the Sea of Azov from the north, and was navigable to the Greeks; Hippocrates called it the border between Europe and Asia, and in the mariner's sense it was. Further up the river Don the sailors did not penetrate, and the distinction between two land-masses evaporated. As Toynbee put it, beyond the Don there was no division for the Greeks, and the land merged into 'an indivisible Eurasia'.[27] Whether the Greeks had a clear idea of a distinction between northern Europe and northern Asia is uncertain (it will be investigated further in an examination of early maps, below), but it is clear that the waterway running from the Aegean to the Black Sea and the River Don was the boundary between what they called Asia in the East, and Europe in the West. And so it has remained, despite causing many difficulties.

Water has formed the boundary of Europe in the West, North and South as well. Some would argue that one of Europe's most formative influences is the water, from the very earliest times right up to the present. Certainly the penetration of sea arms deep into most areas of Europe, especially in the West and North, has been of significance both environmentally and in producing generation after generation of seafarers. M. Mollat du Jourdin has argued that Europe's special relationship with the sea has been its defining feature. He points to 'merchant Europe', and 'Europe as a community of seamen', to Europe as being culturally unified through its seaports, with *linguae francae* and cultural codes common throughout the continent from the early modern period onwards. The voyages of discovery and the seaborne colonial exploits of the European nations have given Europe its 'alterity', and the sea continues to shape European identity.[28] Mollat du Jourdin's case will not convince everyone, but the sea and water have certainly helped to define the continent, not least in terms of its boundaries.

Except in the East. The question of Europe's eastern frontier shows conclusively how physical geography is as subjective a science as any. Is Russia part of Europe? Or of Asia? Does the answer lie in splitting the country into two parts, as the Victorians did, into Russia-in-Europe and Russia-in-Asia? The same applies to Turkey, with Istambul proper being in Turkey-in-Europe, but

Scutari, a ten-minute boatride across the Bosphorus (or nowadays, a drive across the bridge) is in Asia. At least the Bosphorus is universally agreed to be the *geographical* boundary, even if it is a cultural and political nonsense. North of the Black Sea, even geographical agreement is lacking.

For the Greeks the boundary, as we have seen, was the Sea of Azov and the lower reaches of the Don; beyond that point they lost interest, mainly because of lack of knowledge. We can reconstruct maps from textual geographical descriptions by the Greeks and Romans, but they are extremely vague about the country north of the Black Sea. It seems to be assumed that the Don rises in the Riphaen hills or mountains far in the North, near the external ocean which was thought to surround the known world, and then flow South to the Sea of Azov (see Fig. 4.1).[29]

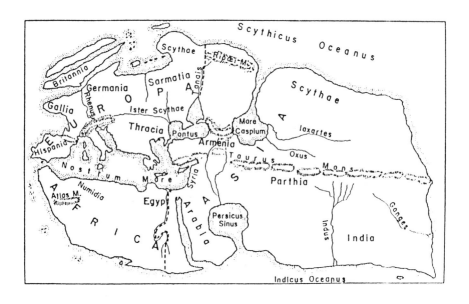

Figure 4.1   **The world according to Pomponius Mela, AD 43**

Source: Parker, *'Europe: how far?'*, 279.

The Romans actually fought to establish frontiers in central Europe, and had very clear ideas of where their own boundaries were, basing them on rivers like the Rhine, the Danube and the Elbe, depending on the success of their campaigns. In the work of the Church Fathers, especially St Augustine, the tripartite division of the world into continents surrounded by an external ocean was maintained, with the Don as the boundary between Europe and Asia. Western Europe continued to see the boundary in those terms for an entire millenium - which W.H. Parker refers to as the 'stagnation of medieval geography'.[30] In the Renaissance reproductions of ancient Greek geographies, the Don continued to be the boundary between the continents in the East, rising in mountains close to the Northern Sea, as the ancients had thought. So far, knowledge had not advanced for 1500 years, since the time of Christ, and the further the maps extended beyond the Black Sea, the more extraordinary they became.

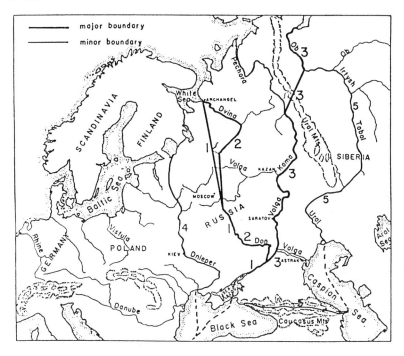

Figure 4.2   Some European boundaries in Russia in the sixteenth and seventeenth centuries
1: Ortelius 1570. 2: Thevet 1575. 3: Cluverius 1616. 4: Sanson 1650. 5: Valck 1680.

Source: Parker, 'Europe: how far?', 282.

Then, in the sixteenth century, Western Europeans began to learn more of Russia. And for the next 500 years there would be an extensive academic and

61

political discussion about where the boundary between the continents should lie.[31] In the thirteenth century it lay at the extent of Roman Catholicism, down the eastern side of Poland, southwards to Turkey; the threat of the Moslem Tartar Khans and the Ottoman Turks after 1453 kept the border there until the end of the seventeenth century, when the danger receded. In the later Renaissance, the boundary of Europe was creeping eastward, but stopping short of Russia; indeed most schemes and maps from about 1300 to the eighteenth century excluded Russia.[32] This frontier united concepts of religion and civilization (versus 'barbarism') in a geographical reality.

In about 1700, however, after an extensive Grand Tour of the West, Peter the Great set about Europeanizing Russia, moving the capital from 'Asian' Moscow to 'European' St Petersburg on the Baltic. His court and the aristocracy took on Western European airs, and Russia became part of Europe. That lasted until the Revolution of 1917, when many of the Europeanized 'White' Russians were killed or driven into exile: H. Seton-Watson maintained that the Europeanization of Russia was only skin-deep and occurred only at elite level, despite the fact that it lasted longer than 200 years, and that in the period of the Cold War Russia was certainly not part of Europe, though its Central and Eastern European satellites were.[33] What intellectual contortions the eastern boundary of Europe has caused! Certainly Russia's part in the defeat of Napoleon, and the participation of Tsarist Russia in the great diplomatic games of Europe throughout the nineteenth century, meant that it was seen as part of Europe, even if it was unclear where the geographical boundary should lie.[34]

In the course of the eighteenth century, geographers gradually moved the inter-continental border eastwards to the Ural Mountains, and then southwards via the Ural river to the Caspian, and across the Caucasus to the Black Sea. The Europeanization of Russia had rendered the Don too westerly a frontier. In 1958 Soviet geographers decided on a line slightly to the East of the Urals, running down to the Caspian and then to the Sea of Azov, but even today the only part of the boundary which is universally agreed and undisputed is the one the ancient Greeks started with - running from the Aegean to the Sea of Azov. Beyond that point there is not yet, after all the debates, any real consensus on geographical delineation, let alone in cultural or political terms. Many geographers would avoid the issue by opting for a mega-continent called Eurasia, with a number of appendages in various directions, like India, China, South-East Asia, and Europe. Where there is no cast-iron physical geographical frontier, like the Bosphorus or the Atlantic coast, politically and culturally difficult as such physical barriers might be, there can be no permanent agreement on the boundary, and the geography is hopelessly affected by politics. Up until 1989 the USSR might be excluded, as W.H. Parker suggested it should be, but the Soviet collapse has thrown the entire question wide open again.[35] The new CIS republics need classification, and the status of the whole of central and eastern Europe has been radically if subtly altered by the end of the Communist hegemony.[36] Europe remains in the mind.

At the other end of Europe, there are such islands as Ireland, Iceland, and Britain. They are not of course part of the land mass of the continent, but in other geographical senses, and in cultural and political terms, there is no reason why they should not be part of Europe, like the Greek islands or Sicily. Let us look very briefly at the case of Britain.

M. Spiering has examined the use of the word 'Europe' in the English language, and has been able to confirm the textbook version of events: while the English had a Norman connection and harboured claims to territory in France, they considered themselves part of the continent; when those claims were extinguished, at the end of the Hundred Years War, then the English lost interest and started using the word 'Europe' to mean something which did not include themselves.[37] As for the view of continental Europe about Britain's position, it varied. It was definitely a part of European Christendom in the High Middle Ages; we have seen that it was not a part of Napoleonic Europe and that therefore it did not receive the Napoleonic codes, and it was not occupied during the Second World War. It was, however, very much a part of the Roman Empire. R. Albrecht-Carrié put Britain and Russia in the same category, as peripheral special cases: they are part of Europe, but borderlands.[38] It seems that Britain can choose. It proves once again that Europe, even in a geographical sense, is not an objective reality, but a state of mind, or a cultural construct.

Visual representations of the continent

In much of the study of history, the visual and perceived spatial elements of human life are largely ignored. Graphic symbolism has always been a powerful political force, and technological refinements of quality and accessibility, like advertising and television, have only increased its potency. In looking at periods before the twentieth century, however, historians tend to refer only sparingly to visual images of collective ideas. Cultural and media historians, historians of *mentalité*, and certain art historians have sometimes formed notable exceptions; and most history dealing with the period after the mass-circulation of newspapers pays some attention to the importance of the visual image in opinion-formation. Generally, however, historians look to the written word rather than the drawn picture for their sources.

Some systematic attention to the visual representation of 'Europe' can have only an enriching effect on the already extensive study of the history of the idea of Europe.[39] In order to make Europe any kind of a political or cultural reality, or even to give it a geographical identity, significant numbers of people need to have a concept of what Europe consists of. Together with such characteristics as language, political systems, religion, physiognomy and skin pigmentation, the actual appearance of the continent itself has been and is important in creating a sense of identity. This is nowadays largely a question of maps: we all have a clear idea of the two-dimensional image of the EU, and of a larger Europe. Cartographic images appear daily on our screens and in our newspapers enforcing the picture. But maps are only part of the story. Before the nineteenth century only certain kinds of maps were thought of as empirically accurate documents; usually they were taken as metaphysical and cultural statements, and as indications of aspiration.[40] Even in modern maps, in which technological enhancements seem to create an objective geographical reality, both the map-maker and the map-reader must interpret the data. Even today, just as with medieval *mappae mundi*, as Peter Whitfield remarks in his book accompanying the exhibition of world maps in the British Museum in 1995, 'the iconographic dimension of the world map is still dominant. The reality, the object as it really is, eludes us.'[41] Earlier, in the Renaissance period for example, an accurate geographical notion of Europe hardly existed, and map-makers struggled to put together an image based on local topographical descriptions and histories. These 'chorographies' were

> the colourful tesserae of regional self-discovery which contributed to the mosaic of a Europe that cartographers were enabling to be imagined as a whole.[42]

In the eighteenth century, increased travelling among the upper classes, in the form of the grand tour, led to the evolution of a clearer mental map of the continent - centred on France, perhaps, and strongly featuring the Low Countries and Italy, but all as a part of Europe.[43]

Maps, however, were not the only visual representations of Europe. Nowadays Europe is constantly portrayed in political cartoons as a bull, or as a girl on a bull; in the past it was often personified as a queen. Writers have also conjured up visual images of Europe in their work, usually to offset their portrayal of a single nation or region. All these evocations of Europe have had powerful effects on defining the identity of Europe at any one time, and it is an influence on the idea of Europe which is often understudied in comparison to those more easily accessible in chronicles, diaries, letters, treaties and the speeches of politicians. The questions to be posed here, then, are the following: how have people thought of Europe in their mind's eye? How have those images changed? Why were particular images of Europe prevalent at particular times? And what effect have those images exercised on political and other socio-cultural events?

Maps of Europe

The first maps we have of Europe or the world date from the seventh century at the earliest. They were based on religious symbolism, with only scant regard for empirical geography; however, the geographical knowledge on which they were based came from the ancients. This knowledge, culminating most famously in the work of Ptolemy in the second century AD, was lost to Western European science after the fall of Rome, though it remained current in Near and Middle Eastern civilizations throughout the European 'Dark Ages'. In the libraries of Constantinople and the Middle East, manuscript geographies (though none of the actual maps) written by Greeks under the Roman Empire survived, and were reintroduced to Western Europe in the fifteenth century, together with the rediscovery of so many of the ancient texts which in a very real sense actually constituted what is known as the Renaissance: the rebirth, the reclaiming of the achievements of ancient learning.

Figure 4.3   **The world according to Hecataeus, c. 500 BC**

Source: Parker, *'Europe: how far?'*, 279.

As far as maps are concerned, this set of circumstances gives us three strands of Western European practice, which of course are only analytically distinguishable, and in fact the various traditions were usually merged in differing measures. Ancient geography before the second century AD was limited by the extent of exploration: for example, the Greeks at the time of Herodotus (fifth century BC) knew virtually nothing of northern or western Europe, though Herodotus himself ridiculed the map-makers of his time for drawing an ocean surrounding the known world. For that is what they did: maps of the time (so far as we can reconstruct them from the surviving accompanying texts), were invariably centred on the eastern Mediterranean, showing the world as a single circular land mass, perforated by inland seas and surrounded by an ocean. The three continents of the known world were separated by the inland seas, the Nile, and the River Don. Herodotus thought that Europe was twice the size of the other continents, and so took up half the map, as in Figure 4.3; others thought that Asia and Europe were the same size.[44]

So at this very early classical stage, Europe was perceived as one of three continents, bounded by the Mediterranean, the waters between the Aegean and the River Don, and the external ocean.[45] By the end of the third century BC, Greek conquest had radically increased empirical knowledge, and thus improved the quality of the geographies. Although Aristotle was fully aware of the idea that the world was a sphere, and though later Greek geographers under the Roman Empire made extraordinarily accurate calculations about the geography of their world, the traditional Greek ideas of a circular flat pancake world, surrounded by ocean and split into three continents, remained popular with the later Romans, as publicized for example by Solinus.[46]

Chronologically the next strand of cartographic representation of Europe was the Ptolemaic. Gradually knowledge of the world increased, and for example Strabo, who was a near contemporary of Christ's, was able to present a much more accurate picture of the world than his predecessors, based on accumulated empirical observation. The height of achievement in this tradition was achieved by Ptolemy, a Greek scientist working in a Roman institution in Alexandria, active during the middle decades of the second century AD. His world map was constructed in about 150 AD, but lost to the West until the Renaissance, when the text was translated into Latin in Florence in 1406, and was actually printed in 1477. Reconstructions of his world map from the text followed rapidly on from that.[47] Ptolemy's achievement was partly mathematical: he succeeded in projecting part of a sphere on a flat piece of paper. More importantly for our purposes, the distances represented were far more accurate than anything previously produced in the ancient world, and certainly in the Middle Ages, and the locations of some 8000 places were marked precisely in a kind of gazetteer. We reproduce here a Ptolemaic map published in Ulm in 1482 (Fig. 4.4).

As far as Europe is concerned, the enormous influence of this later Greek geography, lost with the end of the Roman Empire and resurfacing in the Renaissance, is accuracy. There are strange features on the Ptolemaic map, but concerning Europe its accuracy surpassed all that went before, and provided a new empirical basis for representing the continent in men's minds. On this map, for the first time, Europe was shown as a realistically small part of the known world. This improved accuracy of the later ancients was the second kind of map of Europe.

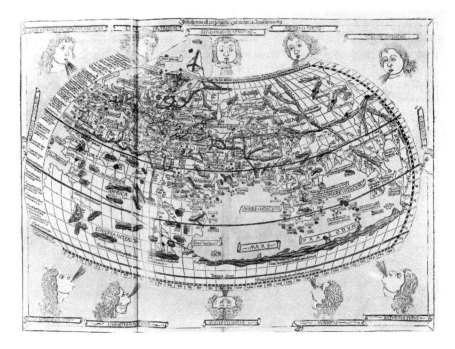

Figure 4.4   Ptolemy's world map, c. 150 AD, republished in 1482

Source: Whitfield, *The image of the world*, 8-9.[48]

The third tradition of map-making which portrays Europe is the medieval Christian one. These maps owe a create deal to the work of St Augustine, transmitted through such later scholars as Alcuin and Bede.[49] These are post-Roman maps, but which take the older concepts of early Greek maps of the inhabited world, circular and surrounded by ocean, ignoring the empirical accuracy of the later Greeks and Romans, and linking that simple circular shape with biblical concepts. The result is not in any way an attempt at an accurate geographical representation; it is rather a metaphysical statement, and all the more significant for that. A mere and unimportant modicum of geographical knowledge is adapted and entirely subjected to theological notions, not with the object of showing people how to get from A to B or how far they are from their neighbours, but rather that the earthly kingdom is in alignment with the Kingdom of God, and that He rules and adjudicates over all things in heaven and on earth. This simple idea is behind nearly all medieval European mapping, and of the representation of Europe as a part of the earth set in the cosmos. Physical accuracy is not only secondary; it is unimportant. The only object is to show how Europe, and everywhere and everything else, fits into the divine scheme of things. Towards the end of the Middle Ages, and into the Renaissance, fascinating hybrids emerged of religious maps trying to adapt to increasing knowledge and increasing interest in secular empirics and science.

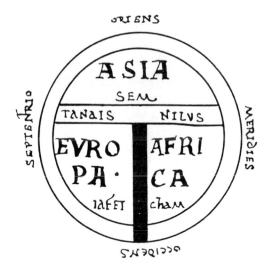

Figure 4.5　　　T-O Map from an eleventh-century copy of Isidore of Seville

Source:　　　Hay, *Europe: the emergence of an idea*, plate 1.

The oldest of these maps of which we have knowledge was by Isidore, Bishop of Seville in the early decades of the seventh century AD. His original manuscript does not survive, but later copies do, together with maps. The one produced below is from an eleventh-century copy of Isidore (Fig. 4.5). Like the map according to Hecataeus of 500 BC in Figure 4.3 above, the world is circular and surrounded by a band of water. The three continents are shown, divided by the Rivers Tanais (Don), and Nile, and by the Mediterranean (the vertical dark stripe). East is at the top. Each continent is labelled, and associated with the names of one of the three sons of Noah: Ham, Shem, and Japheth (we shall return to the Noah legend below). This is the basic image, with only the absolute minimum of geographical intrusion. During the Middle Ages various developments in the technique were refined, and the Beatus map of 1109 AD, shown here in Figure 4.6, displays some of the more interesting ones.

It is a small map, drawn by a Spanish monk obsessed with the Apocalypse. Its features are those of the Isidorean T-O map, but with some differences. There is the surrounding ocean, decorated with fishes, but there is a mysterious fourth continent to the right (south) beyond the vertical stripe of the Red Sea.

The garden of Eden, with Adam, Eve and the serpent, is shown at the top of the map, in the East. The Mediterranean is in the centre, confining Europe to the bottom left hand corner, with its peninsulas like Spain, Italy (Roma), and Macedon clearly marked. It is a feature of the map that an unusually large number of locations are marked, for such a stylized map. The eastern border of Europe is formed by water: the route from the Aegean up to the Sea of Azov, and then the Don, which is shown flowing from the Riphaen Mountains (*Rifrei*) in the north, near the external ocean.

Figure 4.6   Beatus map of the world, AD 1109.

Source: Whitfield, *The image of the world*, 16-17.

What does this map, and other T-O versions, tell us about how contemporaries thought of Europe? Firstly, geography was relatively unimportant: it was interesting to see where places fitted in, but not significant. Europe formed about a quarter of the world, and was bounded by water on all sides - the Don, the Seas and Straits from the Azov to the Mediterranean, and the external ocean. It was often associated with Japheth, son of Noah (see below). But most importantly, it had a fixed and balanced part in the scheme of things. Europe was part of the scheme of creation, heaven, earth and the cosmos, all overseen and held in equilibrium by God. This theological, metaphysical purpose is shown most strikingly in the thirteenth-century psalter map shown in Figure 4.7.

Figure 4.7　　Psalter map, English, c. 1250.

Source:　　Whitfield, *The image of the world*, 19.

Here, Jerusalem is at the centre of the map, and Christ is very obviously presiding over the earth and the cosmos. The T-O shape is clearly preserved, with Europe in the bottom left-hand corner, bounded by the usual waterways and the external ocean; the T-O construction is emphasized in the orb held in Christ's left hand. Considerable geographical detail is included, although it lags heavily behind the knowledge available at the time;[50] the embellishment is undertaken to make a theological statement about the order of things.

These later versions of the earliest schematic T-O religious maps are known as *mappae mundi*, and were something of an English speciality. Probably the most famous one, and certainly the largest and most detailed, is the one held in Hereford Cathedral, in which, as with the Psalter map, Jerusalem is at the centre and Christ presides above. On the Hereford *mappa mundi* (not illustrated here), there is a great deal of encyclopaedic geographical and cultural information included, and the European sector includes the British Isles. Europe's eastern border is formed by rivers which flow clear from the external ocean to the Sea of Azov. The geography is that of the ancients - pre-Ptolemaic. But the extraordinary thing as far as a visual representation of Europe is concerned is that the artist or printer mistakenly reversed - with appalling significance - the names of the continents of Europe and Africa, in the two lower quadrants of the circle. Europe was a part of the scheme of things, and was bounded by certain geographical features, but in this essentially theological vision, it apparently amounted to little more than a label, which could easily be absent-mindedly reversed with that of a virtually unknown dark continent.[51]

We are presented, then, with these three separate traditions in map-making which portrayed Europe: the early Greek, the Ptolemaic, and the medieval Christian, or Augustinian. The Augustinian drew heavily on the empirical knowledge and concepts of the early Greek geographers. Then, in the fifteenth century, as a part of the general intellectual and cultural movement we know as the Renaissance, these three traditions were to come together, intertwine, produce various hybrids, and eventually resolve themselves into a more scientific two-dimensional portrayal of the geography of Europe, but one which would continue to contain all sorts of cultural aspirations and statements, even if they were less religiously metaphysical than in the medieval tradition.

Map-making was subjected, at the end of the Middle Ages, to a number of radical influences. The most obvious was the rediscovery of ancient texts held in Near and Middle Eastern libraries, as we have seen, which revolutionized both the technical drawing of maps especially in terms of projection, and greatly expanded the detail of empirical knowledge. At the same time, new geographical knowledge was also becoming available from contemporary sources, with travels over land and sea revealing new discoveries on almost an annual basis. Meanwhile, Renaissance thought as a whole was beginning to place Man at the centre of the universe, which, while not exactly secularizing the contemporary world view, allowed a gradual releasing of science from the constraints of theology, which had held sway for most of the Middle Ages.

And science itself took new strides, not least in navigation and mathematics. During the fourteenth century new kinds of seafarers' charts evolved, called *portolani*, distinguishable for the layman by the presence of masses of 'windroses' to enable the sailor to calculate direction.[52] A fascinating example of the transition wrought in the portrayal of Europe by the techniques of the *portolani* can be seen in Figure 4.8. A professional cartographer working in Venice, Agnese's two maps both represent the world as it was known in the early sixteenth century, but are drawn employing two completely different sets of concepts and techniques. The top map is an accurate portrayal of navigational data, concentrating on the sea coasts, in the style of the *portolani*.

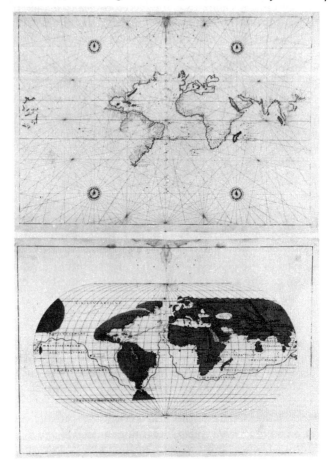

Figure 4.8   **Two world maps by Battista Agnese, c. 1536**

Source: The Bodleian Library, Oxford, MS. Canon. Ital. 144, pp. 16-17 and 18-19.[53]

The lower map is something different: a world picture, relaxing much of the empirical rigour present in the top map, but embodying more of the world view deriving from the Middle Ages. Magellan's trajectory on his circumnavigation is shown, and the oval presentation presents 360 degrees of longitude. But much of the map is fantasy, or rather best-guessing from non-navigational sources. For our purposes the portrayal of Europe in the two maps is very revealing. In the top one, the navigators have a very accurate impression of the Mediterranean, and of the European Atlantic coast up as far as the Low Countries; the portrayal of the British Isles is highly convincing. On the lower, more conceptual map, the shape of Britain is oddly distorted, and the Baltic areas have been filled but are very inaccurate. Most extraordinary is the portrayal of the eastern boundary of the European continent. The sailor's map at the top gives a highly accurate picture of the Black Sea and the Sea of Azov, and makes no attempt to fill in any details to the north of that. But in the lower map, with its late-Medieval traditions, and despite the knowledge visibly available to the same cartographer in the top map, the Sea of Azov is enlarged and distorted in exactly the way the older Greek and Medieval maps had done, with the River Don rising again in those mountains near the northern ocean, and the label 'Europa' placed clearly to the West of it.

The Ptolemaic inheritance, the navigational and other discoveries, the advance of mathematics and technical drawing, the rise of a more anthropocentric view of the world (if not the cosmos); all these things were reflected in the new maps of the early sixteenth century, like those by Martin Waldseemüller, Francesco Rosselli, Albrecht Dürer, and others.[54] Most of them continued to distinguish Europe from Asia with the River Don, rising in the northern mountains, and flowing into a greatly expanded Sea of Azov. In the second half of the sixteenth century, the centre of European map-making was moving from Italy and Spain northwards to the Low Countries, reflecting the rise of the Dutch Republic as a world sea-power, and Gerard Mercator's achievements symbolize that shift, alongside the work of others like Jodocus Hondius. These increasingly accurate and competently drawn world maps anchored a visual representation of the world in the minds of men, and of Europe's place within it. During the sixteenth century, as Sir John Hale put it in his monumental study of the Renaissance,

> maps became for the first time a spur to a rationally grasped personal location within a clearly defined continental expanse.[55]

The portrayal of Europe began to be almost triumphalist, and there were few attempts to show internal borders in these maps. Russia was still very indistinct because of lack of geographical knowledge, and although the Don was still used as the line between Europe and Asia, there was evidently some doubt as to whether Russia belonged in Europe or not. Nonetheless, partly by means of these processes in developing cartography, in the course of the sixteenth century, 'Europe passed into the mind'.[56]

The scientific revolution of the seventeenth century brought still more accuracy to maps, a further secularization, and a pretence of scientific objectivity.[57] As far as the portrayal of Europe was concerned, the border with Asia tended to shift to the East, helped by the Europeanizing influence of Peter the Great. A later example is a world map made in England for the use of missionaries in 1822, which replaces the traditional north-south line between the White Sea and the Sea of Azov with one running from the mouth of the Don north-eastwards to follow the Urals up to the Sea of Kara (Fig. 4.9). That part of Russia which falls to the West of the boundary is very clearly labelled, 'Russia in Europe'.

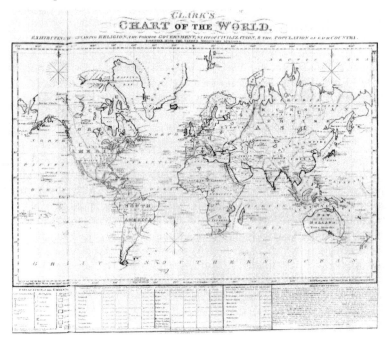

Figure 4.9   **Clark's chart of the world, 1822.**

Source: Whitfield, *The image of the world*, 116-17.

But this is more than just a physical geographical representation: this map too is a cultural statement, celebrating the export of European culture around the world. In the values of the 1990s, it is about as politically incorrect a document as could be imagined. It is a 'thematic' map, purporting to be scientifically objective, but which is in reality highly subjective. It shows not only physical features, but also represents data on religion, forms of government, state of civilization, and population. The most eye-opening indicator is the one depicting the 'state of civilization', which grades various parts of the world as being 'Enlightened' (most of western Europe and parts of the eastern seaboard of North America), 'Civilized' (coastal South America, parts of western North America, southeast Australia), 'Half-Civilized' (north coast of Africa, Middle and Near East, India and China), 'Barbarous' (all the Russian Empire and most of Africa), or 'Savage' (Canada, Siberia, and most of Australia). So the border between Europe and Asia had swung significantly to the East, but the newly Europeanized inhabitants were still classified as barbarous. It is an extraordinary document, which speaks volumes on a spectrum of subjects, not least about the view Europeans held of themselves in the early nineteenth century.

It would be foolish to suggest that maps had been the dominant influence in the shaping of European consciousness and identity. But particularly in the sixteenth century they helped, along with other forms of visual images (which we shall examine below), to create a shared concept of the appearance and nature of the continent, its location in the world, and its borders with other continents.

'Europe' - the imagery of the word

Herodotus assumed that Europe had been named after Europa, a demigoddess in Greek mythology - though he could not imagine why, especially as she never set foot on the continent.[58] We shall return to Europa shortly, but the origin and etymology of the word Europe can cast light on what people have meant by the term and what they visualize it representing. We first hear it as a geographical expression in Hesiod's *Hymn to Apollo* in the eighth century BC, where it was used to mean the northern part of continental Greece, as opposed to the islands and the Peloponnese.[59] Etymologically, it is now thought that the word has Greek origins, meaning 'broad-faced': Toynbee fondly imagined that this might tie in with the bovine features of Europa herself, who was strongly associated with her father's herd of cattle![60] An older hypothesis is that the word Europe derives from Middle-Eastern languages, and means the place where the sun sets - in the West - which accords with notions of Greek mariners giving the name to the land mass to port as they sailed up the straits from the Aegean to the Sea of Azov.[61] Albert Rijksbaron has examined the sources and concludes that originally the Greeks probably used the word to designate the broad river-valleys in the northern part of Greece, but that later the expression was transferred to the plains north of the Black Sea around the mouths of the Danube and the Don, after the Greeks had colonized the area.[62]

There is also a tradition that the word had strong overtones for the Greeks signifying their separateness or alterity from the Persians during their mutual wars; earlier, the words had lent strength to the alterity of Asia Minor, when the Greeks were fighting the Trojans. The origins of the word remains obscure, and the object of academic conjecture. But it is clear that, from the very start, there was a graphic element to the expression - whether to describe physiognomy, landscape features, land masses, or the location of civilizations. From the earliest times, 'Europe' had a strong visual and spatial dimension.

Europa and the bull

The literature of the Ancients, from Herodotus onwards, to the *Odes* of Horace and the *Metamorphoses* of Ovid, refers repeatedly to the myth of the rape of Europa. Europa was a demigod princess, daughter of Agenor, King of Tyre in Phoenicia (where the Lebanon now lies). Zeus, the King of the Gods (Jupiter in the Roman versions), looked down, was besotted with the princess (something that regularly overcame him), and devised a colourful plan to slake his thirst for the maiden. He changed into a magnificent white bull, and swam ashore where she and her attendants were disporting. She was interested enough in this incarnation of male sexuality to get on his back, whereupon he swam off with her to Crete, changed back into his anthropomorphic form and had his way with her, causing her to produce at least three children, named Minos (who built the labyrinth at Crete), and Rhadamanthus and Aeacus (who guarded the gates of Hades). These and others, such as Europa's brother Cadmus, who instituted a long search for her and did great deeds on the way, enliven a subsidiary set of myths.

This is a terrific subject, as Sir John Hale has remarked. It has sex, violence, abduction, dramatic settings, beauty and the beast: how can it fail to have inspired artists throughout the centuries?[63] But on the other hand, no-one actually *believed* the myth, and some have denied that the Europa tale has anything to do with Europe as a continent: Pim den Boer dismisses it as a pleasant story for artists seeking inspiration, 'but it is not the allegorical portrayal of a continent'.[64] This dismissal must, I think, be qualified.

In its original form, the Europa myth almost certainly expressed the rivalry between Greece and Troy, between the opposite sides of the Aegean, later between the Greeks and Persians, and by implication between Europe and Asia. Abduction of the enemy's princesses was almost a commonplace: Io, Medea, and Helen are just some of the more famous of Europa's companion victims in this international and intercontinental rivalry.[65] The myth has been the subject of very extensive scholarship, especially in Germany, into its place in the history of art down the ages,[66] and it is clear that the story has exercised artists of all descriptions since it was coined, although it appears to have been more popular in Byzantine Eastern Europe than in the West during the Middle Ages. In the early Renaissance Ovid's story was moralized into a Christian allegory, with Jove representing Christ, becoming a bull (descending to earth), and carrying mankind (Europa) across the water (to heaven); in the fifteenth century, Europa imagery was all mixed up with the iconography of the Virgin

76

Mary as well. A Florentine poet of the 1470s, one Angelo Poliziano, even ventured that Europa's divinely sired children became the Europeans, and that she was therefore their founding deity. As the Renaissance progressed, the story was divested of its medieval sanctity, and Titian, Veronese and others were able to exploit the subject for all its dramatic potential.[67]

Figure 4.10   Europa seated in triumph on the bull, fresco by Hans Mont in Bucovice (Butschowitz) Castle, c. 1580s

Source: Hale, *The civilization of Europe in the Renaissance*, 12.

The Greek myth probably had a continental dimension, but much of the artistic representation of Europe up to and including the Renaissance - with the exception of Poliziano - can hardly be said to have been intended as the symbolic representation of the geographic continent of Europe, and to that extent we can agree with Den Boer. However, in the later stages of the Renaissance, Europa evolved into a crowned queen, specifically personifying the triumphal continent (see the section below on 'Europe, Queen of the continents'), and the fresco by the Austrian Hans Mont (Fig. 4.10), executed to decorate a Moravian castle in the 1580s, is an excellent example of the transition.

Figure 4.11   Oskar Garvens, Democratic Spring, cartoon in
Kladderadatsch, 14 May 1939.

Source: Guthmüller, '*Europa*', 28.

The lady portrayed is clearly Europa of the legend, complete with bull, but
from her setting and triumphal attitude, she is equally clearly on the verge of

representing the continent as well. Although the myth continued to be used in art in a non-continental context, it has also been used, modestly, for allegorical purposes, arguably by the Greeks in portraying the rivalry between themselves and Asia, in a number of allegorical drawings, prints and woodcuts from the sixteenth century,[68] and on a truly massive scale in the twentieth century. Bodo Guthmüller has collected a number of the images of Europe in the form of Europa and her bull in the twentieth-century media, and there is no doubt that the imagery and symbolism has been common currency since the First World War.[69] The representation in the twentieth century is usually of a girl on a bull, though it can also be just the bull itself; the girl or woman is usually young, attractive, virtuous, humane, vulnerable, sometimes naive and often threatened, for example by war, Fascists, Nazis, or America, who are portrayed as the bull (Fig. 4.11).

In these cartoons, the myth no longer has a significance: it is a mere peg of allegory on which to hang political comment, and in doing so it makes a statement about the nature of the continent. It is still universally used, though less perhaps in Britain than on 'the Continent'. The myth of Europa and the bull has indeed helped to shape men's impression of the continent, modestly until the figure of Europa metamorphosed into Europe crowned in the later Renaissance (see below), but continually, and in our own century, universally.

Japheth

In Genesis 9, the story is told of Noah's drunkenness. Having survived the flood, Noah became drunk and lay naked within his tent; his son Ham saw this, and told his two brothers Shem and Japheth, who covered up their father without looking at him. For this service Noah blessed Shem, saying Ham's children would be his servants, and he blessed Japheth, of whom he pronounced

> God shall enlarge Japheth,
> And he shall dwell in the tents of Shem.[70]

Ham, however, together with his progeny, was roundly cursed by his father; they were destined to become servants. Between these three sons and their offspring, the whole of the earth was settled after the flood. There is no mention of any continents in the Old Testament.

From this story, some of the Church Fathers embroidered a division of the world into continents among the sons of Noah in the course of their commentaries on the scriptures. Josephus, St Augustine, and St Jerome seem to have been the crucial prisms through which the biblical myth was transmuted into a myth of origin for the peoples of each of the three known continents in the ancient and early medieval world. Shem was seen to be the founding father of the Jews and Semitic peoples, and was associated with Asia; Ham's progeny took over Africa; while Japheth's children were the Gentiles, and occupied the continent of Europe. The notion passed from one biblical commentator to the next, being endlessly enriched, until in the seventh century the legend of the apportionment of the continents amongst the sons of Noah had achieved its own momentum. And because most of the commentaries were written by Europeans, there was no doubt in their minds that Japheth had had the best of the settlement.[71]

Japheth, then, was an obvious personification of the continent of Europe from the early Middle Ages onwards. And indeed, the sons of Noah took their place on many of the early T-O maps, for example the Isidorean one illustrated above in Figure 4.5. The symmetry of the arrangement of sharing out the known world of three continents between the three sons of the only family to survive the Great Flood appealed to the medieval mind, and the story remained popular and was reflected in the cartographic representations of the world. Noah continued to be a popular icon in the Middle Ages (though his sons rather less so), and in the Renaissance and the Reformation the story of the apportionment of the continents between Noah's sons gained some additional popularity over the Europa myth for a time because it was seen as rather more respectable. In literature the story lived on well beyond that, in the work of John Donne and Walter Raleigh; the opportunities for metaphysical conceit were very welcome. The Noah-Japheth connection was of course laid to rest effectively by the discovery of further continents beyond the three apportioned to the sons of Noah, but particularly in the Middle Ages, the visual image of a third - the best third - of the world being associated with the virtuous, non-Semitic and non-African descendants of Noah assisted the formation of a self-image amongst some Europeans, especially through the medium of the T-O maps.[72]

Europe, Queen of the continents

In the course of the sixteenth century, and especially towards its end, a new visual image of Europe emerged, that of the crowned queen triumphant. She was no longer being carried off by a bull, or raped by a god, but was a queen in her own right. Slowly she became part of the standard allegorical material used by graphic artists of all kinds, who invested her with certain accoutrements and qualities, which we shall explore briefly below. In doing so, they were expressing the feelings of their contemporaries about the continent in which they found themselves, and about its and their own identity; simultaneously, they were also exercising a powerful formative influence on public opinion on the same matters. Europe the Queen arose in the sixteenth century, which was the age of exploration, the age of European expansion, the later part of the Renaissance, the century of Protestant Reformation, the century of new geography, the century of European ascendancy. Japheth may have been the most favoured son of Noah, and Europa may have been virtuous, but as the Middle Ages finally came to an end and the Modern Age dawned, Europeans needed a more assertive symbol with which to portray themselves.[73]

Figure 4.12   **Europa Prima Pars Terrae in Forma Virginis**

Source: From an original print in the Strahov Monastery Library in Prague, taken from a Czech edition of H. Bunting's *Itinerarium Sacrae Scripturae* (1592), 18-19.

One of the earliest manifestations of the new symbolism (which was of course intimately linked with and evolved from previous emblems) was published in

81

Paris in 1537. Bucius, or Johannes Putsch, who lived from 1516 to 1542, produced an image of a map of Europe arranged to look like a queen in formal dress and regalia.[74] The queen's crowned head was formed by the Iberian peninsula (seat of the Habsburg monarchy), her torso extended over Western and Central Europe, her right arm was Italy, with Sicily as her orb of office, and her skirts extended over Eastern Europe from Lithuania in the North to Bulgaria and Greece in the South. The brilliance of the conceit caught on, and the image was much copied throughout the century, perhaps most famously by Sebastian Münster, in his *Cosmographia*, printed in Basel in 1588.[75] We produce here a slightly later but more unusual version in Figure 4.12.

As in many of these representations, the heart of Europe is portrayed as Bohemia, which is itself depicted as a 'golden groat' suspended on a chain from the Rhineland. The British Isles are portrayed, but not as part of the Queen; in some versions they form the left arm and sceptre, whereas more normally Denmark does, as in this one. The title of the print contains the word 'Virgin': the links with Marian imagery and with Europa and the bull are still strong, and they emphasize the purity, nobility and goodness of the image. Indeed some of these representations actually used the English Virgin Queen, Elizabeth, as their subject.[76] But generally, as the century wore on, the virgin tended to become somewhat older, less vulnerable, and more regal. An unusual example is found on a silver bowl made in 1589, commemorating the Battle of Lepanto of 1571, when the Europeans (Spain, Venice, and the Papal Forces) defeated the Turkish navy. The bowl was made in Nuremburg, which became the heart of Europe in this particular variation.[77]

This personification of Europe is in a highly intricate form, contrived to fit a map. Personification in general was widespread, especially in the Renaissance, and the representation of the continent of Europe as a queen extended far beyond its use on maps, although the Bucius image was one of the earliest forms, and the map was one of the most popular forms of Europe imagery in the sixteenth century. Charles V abdicated in 1556 in favour of his son Philip II, and when the new King visited Antwerp, one of the most important cities of his vast empire, entertainments were arranged for him which included actors dressing up as the different continents of the world, come to pay him homage.[78] This image was immortalized by the painter Frans Francken some eighty years later in 1636, when he painted the scene of Charles V's abdication, with everyone paying homage, including the four continents of the world.[79] With the introduction of Europe personified as a crowned monarch, often alongside other monarchs, artists were able to invest her with all sorts of qualities and attitudes, thus providing us with a clear indication of how contemporaries viewed the continent. In his *Theatrum Orbis Terrarum*, published in Antwerp in 1572, Ortelius used the title page to show the four continents (America had now been added), of which Europe was the only one crowned, seated at the top of the page and obviously the senior figure.[80] In the last quarter of the sixteenth century, 'Europe crowned' was a stock image, made especially famous in the work of Philips Galle, in his *Prosopographia* of 1579.[81]

Figure 4.13 Frontispiece from Jan Commelin, *Horta Medici Amstelodamensis Rariorum Plantarum Historia* (Amsterdam, 1697).

It entered the books of icons intended for the use of artists at the end of the sixteenth and the seventeenth centuries, and once it was listed in such compendia, then it became common knowledge and practice. Cesare Ripa's *Iconologia*, published in Rome in 1593, shows Europe as the only crowned continent, queen and chief of the world, adorned with horns of plenty, crowns to show the power of her princes, weapons and chargers for her military prowess, musical instruments to symbolize the arts, mason's instruments for architects, and, most importantly perhaps, owls and books to signify knowledge and scholarship.[82] Hale points out that this triumphal, superior view of Europe was much influenced by Strabo's geography, and amounted virtually to a 'discovery of Europe' for the late sixteenth century. Europe personified ended up as white, and not Asian, as Europa had been.[83] It was a tradition still established at the end of the seventeenth century, as is shown in the title page of Jan Commelin's catalogue of the Amsterdam botanical gardens, which displays the continents, Europe being the only one crowned, bringing their flora to Amsterdam personified (Fig. 4.13).

The concept of Europe as queen of the continents is also well illustrated in maps of the period, not so much on the maps themselves, but in the embellishing drawings and icons which surrounded nearly all non-nautical maps until relatively recently. We have made the point that a map is a cultural statement often masquerading as an objective scientific document; the marginal drawings allowed the map-maker even more scope to voice his opinions and those of his contemporaries about the phenomena he was representing.

Figure 4.14   Gerard van Keulen, *Paskaart vertonende alle bekende zeekusten en landen op den geheelen aardboodem of werelt* (Amsterdam, c. 1720) (detail).

Source: Whitfield, *The image of the world*, 108-9.

Instances of the portrayal on maps of Queen Europe abound from the seventeenth and eighteenth centuries.[84] The practice became established generally, and the example we display here, in Figure 4.14, is a world map from the early eighteenth century by Gerard van Keulen. Here, at the top left, Europe is crowned, orbed and sceptred, receiving the tribute of the other continents. A charger stands behind her, the icon of martial prowess, while books of wisdom are at her elbow, and the lyre is the icon of European superiority in the arts. Mere materials and riches are brought to her, devotedly, by the other subject continents. What an compact expression of imperialism, especially with the stallion of war waiting threateningly in the bushes, should the persuasions of knowledge and the arts threaten to let Europe down!

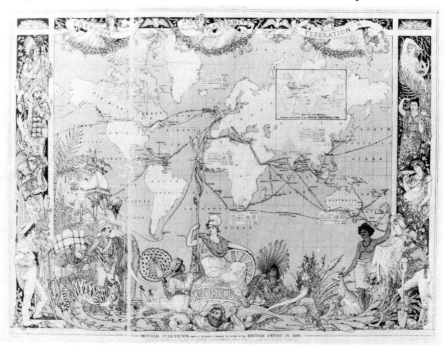

Figure 4.15   Walter Crane, *Map of the World showing the Extent of the British Empire*, 1886.

Source: Whitfield, *The image of the world*, 124-5.

As a footnote to this tradition of representation, we can reproduce another of the maps in Whitfield's collection, this time of the British Empire (Fig. 4.15). By the time of the age of New Imperialism, in the last quarter of the nineteenth century, nationalism had supplanted the European ideal. Britannia now sits as the centre-piece of the marginalia, receiving the tribute of adoring parts of the empire, just as Europe had graciously taken the gifts of the other continents. The 'natives' of the world gaze in wonder at her, as the empire-builders look on with approval. Her iconographical accoutrements are battledress, the Union Jack, and Neptune's trident showing her mastery of the seas. In this immensely powerful image, Britain has taken over the role of Europe in general. And this was published *before* the Scramble for Africa, and so before the struggle between the European powers for dominion of all quarters of the globe had started in earnest!

The image of Europe conveyed by the written word

Europe as a visual image appears in written art, as well as in graphic work. Writers use words to conjure up images, which have just as powerful an impact on our consciousness as does a physical, two-dimensional image; the role left to the imagination can often intensify the strength of the iconography. Here is not the place to examine these literary images of Europe on any systematic scale; rather it is only necessary to indicate that, in the written word, and especially in plays and poems, there were additional sources of visual representation of the continent of Europe.

Guthmüller has drawn our attention to a number of literary uses of the legend of Europa and the bull; in an article entitled 'Europe staged', Ton Hoenselaars has examined English Renaissance drama for images of Europe around the turn of the seventeenth century. In Richard II, Shakespeare shows himself well aware of the European situation and the progress of the Counter-Reformation across the continent's internal boundaries. Shakespeare was not always accurate in his geography - in *The Tempest* he awards Bohemia a coastline - but in the early seventeenth century the dramatists' work reflected the increasing interest in accurate maps, and the wider opportunity for travel in Europe. Denys Hay reports a play by Desmarets de Saint-Sorlin of 1642, called *Europa*, where the nations are cast as separate personified *dramatis personae*, with Richelieu's France of course in the lead role. In a Dutch satirical ballad of 1701, called *Esopus in Europa*, the various countries of the continent are represented by different animals, making up a European menagerie. At the end of the eighteenth century, in William Blake's illustrated poem, *Europe: a prophecy* (1794), 'Europe' signifies a continent, set against other poems in the series about Asia and America, but does not display any particular characteristics beyond being infected with the chaos of Revolutionary France: for Blake, Britain was not in Europe.[85]

Before the twentieth-century explosion of political cartoons, one of the most intriguing was Hadol's print of 1870, shown here in a Dutch version in Figure 4.16. There is no unity in Europe here: it is made up of highly differentiated and potentially inimical nations, with aggression and weakness seldom far

86

below the surface. The image of Russia is chilling, and the way Bismarck's hand rests on the Low Countries, to the obvious concern of France, is an indication of the nationalist upsurge which was to carry Europe into imperialist antagonism and the First World War. In its way it is a reflection of the same disintegration of Europe into feuding nationalism which was marked by the transition on maps of the world from Europe crowned to Britannia imperial (Figs 4.14 & 4.15).

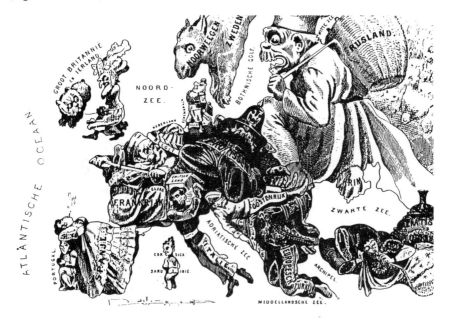

Figure 4.16   **Hadol, Nieuwe kaart van Europa 1870.**

This brief set of allusions to a number of other forms of visual representation of the continent cannot pretend to be systematic, but at the least it tells us that Europe was constantly being portrayed, that geographical accuracy was probably improving in the popular perception of Europe, that nations also played an important role in the public mind, and that after the mid-nineteenth century nationalism probably began to eclipse feelings of loyalty to Europe.

Conclusion

In this article, we have seen Europe change before our very eyes. We have seen constant flux both in cartographic attempts to present the geography of the continent, and in the more fanciful graphic images conjured up by artists of various kinds in order to represent Europe. We began by surveying briefly the fragments of European unity, hegemony and shared influence in the past, and concluded that although there were important aspects of shared experience, it would be misleading to see European unity as evolving or developing over the centuries, contributing teleologically to the European 'project' which we now have in the late twentieth century. The same is true of visual representations of Europe.

Most of Europe's external borders have continually shifted, especially in the East, so that there is even now no agreed version of the geographical extent of Europe, let alone in the past. If we look at maps of Europe, which are themselves a fascinating source for social history and the history of ideas, we see that, before the Renaissance, there were at least three separate (though interrelated) ways of portraying Europe: the early Greek, the Ptolemaic, and the medieval Christian. Then in the high Renaissance, a new form of triumphalist map grew out of these traditions, with Europe dominating the world, which acted as a powerful catalyst in fixing a graphic image of their continent in the minds of Europeans. Only in the nineteenth century did this Europeanism give way to more particularist nationalism.

In the meaning of the word 'Europe' there have also been graphic connotations, constantly changing according to the circumstance of the times. In the myth of Europa and the bull there has been an element of allegorical representation of the continent, especially in modern political cartoons, while the Noah-Japheth story fulfilled that role in the Middle Ages. The portrayal of Europe as queen of the continents, not least in the marginalia of maps, showed a similar trajectory to that of the maps themselves: the sixteenth century saw a celebration of Europe's virtues and power, which grew and lasted into the nineteenth century, before succumbing to the pressures of nationalism and imperialism.

The visual representations of Europe analysed in this article can provide an indication - which is often not available from other sources - about how Europeans have, literally, viewed their continent through the ages. The Greeks accumulated geographic knowledge until, by the second century AD, they had extensive and accurate maps. The early Christians preferred the symmetry of the earlier Greek geographers, and maintained a vision of the continent, associated with the patrimony of Noah's son Japheth, which placed Europe in a rigid and formal relationship with the rest of the universe, held in balance and presided over by God. The Europa legend also had aspects of representing the continent, portraying it as female, virtuous, good, humane, vulnerable, worth fighting for - in fact very like most *national* personification figures. Compared to what came after 1500, however, the medieval period was modest in its concern for representing the continent. The Renaissance and the age of discovery unleashed a new, more geographically realistic, and ultimately triumphant portrayal of the noble continent. Attempts at European hegemony, by the Habsburgs, were reflected in the portrayal of the map of Europe as a virgin queen whose head was Spain and whose heart was in the Holy Roman Empire.[86] In the seventeenth century, dreams of European unity, like those of the Duc de Sully, continued to be reflected in portrayals of a single Europe.[87] Always assured of its own virtue and good qualities (from the time of Strabo on), the presentation of Europe by its graphic artists became more and more assertive and triumphalist as the seventeenth century moved into the Enlightenment, with Europe crowned in glory, receiving the willing tribute of all corners of the earth. As the assertiveness of European chauvinism grew, however, it split into myriad nationalisms in the course of the nineteenth century, caught in Hadol's image of the countries of Europe about to tear each other apart (Fig. 4.16).

Europe's image has constantly changed, and is still changing. There is no objective truth about Europe or Europa, but only the subjective views of successive generations and eras. When Anthony Smith declares that nationalism consists of no more than a series of myths,[88] the same applies at a European level. It is all imagined, ever-changing, all in the mind. We would do well to remember, with Arnold Toynbee, man's 'folly of deifying his own continent'.[89]

Notes

1. See W.H. Roobol's essay in Leerssen & Van Montfrans, eds, *Borders and territories*, 15-33; & Joll, *Europe: a historian's view*, 2-5.

2. Fuhrman, 'L'Europe', 1.

3. Burke, 'Did Europe exist before 1700?', 21.

4. See García, ed., *European identity*, 10 & 31; and Chapter 2 above.

5. See Roobol, 'What is Europe?', 197-8.

6. After popularity in the 1970s, the concept of 'mental maps', or the geography of perception, seems to have attracted little attention from professional geographers. There are few good texts to work with, and none that I know of regarding Europe. An early handbook is Gould & White, *Mental maps*.

7. Heater, *The idea of European unity*, studies a dozen of the better-known schemes from the fourteenth to the eighteenth centuries; Foerster, *Die Idee Europa*, cursorily covers very many more, from about 1300 to 1946.

8. Mollat du Jourdin, *Europe and the sea* , 30.

9. Ullmann, *The Carolingian Renaissance*, 12, 135-9.

10. Hay, *Europe: the emergence of an idea*, 21-5.

11. See Bartlett, *The making of Europe*; and Chapter 2 of this volume.

12. Mollat du Jourdin, *Europe and the sea*, 115-16.

13. Hale, 'The Renaissance idea of Europe', 46 & 52-6. See also Hay, *Europe: the emergence of an idea*, 120-2.

14. Tilly, *The formation of national states*, 18, 76.

15. Burke, 'Did Europe exist before 1700?', 24-6.

16. Schmidt, 'The establishment of "Europe" as a political expression'; see also Hay, *Europe: the emergence of an idea*, 118.

17. Hazard, *European thought in the eighteenth century*, 463.

18. In *Twelve speeches*, 1850, cited in Duroselle, *Europe: a history of its peoples*, 324.

19. Heater, *The idea of European unity*, 189-90.

20. See Mayne, et al., *Federal Union*.

21. Den Boer, et al., *The history of the idea of Europe*, 11-14.

22. See Smith, 'National identity and the idea of European unity', 74; and Chapter 2 above.

23. Duroselle, *Europe: a history of its peoples*, passim, especially the maps found on pp. 27, 42, 55, 62, 71, 103, 147, 193, 260, 272, 371, 385.

24. These dolmen structures are not confined to Europe, however, and are also found, for example, in Africa.

25. See DePorte, *Europe between the superpowers*.

26. See Chapter 2, above.

27. Toynbee, '"Asia" and "Europe"', 710-12; Toynbee's arguments are summarized by B. Smart in Nelson, ed., *The idea of Europe*, 26-8.

28. Mollat du Jourdin, *Europe and the sea*, 115-16, 121-2, 153-76, 227-38, and passim.

29. For this whole discussion, see the seminal article by Parker, 'Europe: how far?'

30. Parker, 'Europe: how far?', 280.

31. This 'Russian Question' is covered well by Toynbee, '"Asia" and "Europe"'; Parker, 'Europe: how far?'; Roobol, 'What is Europe?'; Seton-Watson, 'What is Europe, where is Europe?'; and Waites, et al., *Europe and the wider world*.

32. Hale, *The civilization of Europe in the Renaissance*, 22-6; & Heater, *The idea of European unity*, 181.

33. Seton-Watson, 'What is Europe, where is Europe?', 10, 11, 14 & passim.

34. Hay, *Europe: the emergence of an idea*, 124-6.

35. Parker, 'Europe: how far?', 285-91, 293.

36. See the discussions in 'Eastern Europe ... Central Europe ... Europe'.

37. Spiering, 'Waarom de Britten'.

38. Albrecht-Carrié, *The unity of Europe*, 24-7.

39. Some work has of course been done in this field, and I would like to acknowledge my debt to some of the pioneers, especially the standard work by Hay, *Europe: the emergence of an idea*. I have also relied on Hale, *The civilization of Europe in the Renaissance*; and Parker, 'Europe: how far?' There is a recent useful summary in Den Boer, et al., *The history of the idea of Europe*. Guthmüller, 'Europa', and Whitfield, *The image of the world*, have also proved invaluable.

40. Hay, *Europe: the emergence of an idea*, xxii-xxiii; Whitfield, *The image of the world*, viii & 2.

41. Whitfield, *The image of the world*, 97-8.

42. Hale, *The civilization of Europe in the Renaissance*, 28-31.

43. Hazard, *European thought in the eighteenth century*, 473.

44. Herodotus, *The histories*, 250 & 283-5.

45. Parker, 'Europe: how far?', 278-80.

46. Den Boer, et al., *The history of the idea of Europe*, 18; & Hay, *Europe: the emergence of an idea*, 6-7.

47. Whitfield, *The image of the world*, 7-10 & 36.

48. Whitfield's recent study is a magnigicently illustrated companion to an exhbition of world maps through the ages held in 1995 at the British Museum. I am happy to acknowledge my considerable debt to this book, in both its text and illustrations, several of which are reproduced in this article. I am also grateful to the British Library Publishing Office for kind permission to reproduce some of the illustrations in *The image of the world*. The interest here is primarily in the portrayal of Europe, rather than the global portrayal and the techniques of map-making, which are Whitfield's main concerns.

49. Hay, *Europe: the emergence of an idea*, 37-43; Parker, 'Europe: how far?', 280.

50. Whitfield, *The image of the world*, 17.

51. Hay, *Europe: the emergence of an idea*, 54.

52. Hay, *Europe: the emergence of an idea*, 94-5.

53. Agnese's maps figure in Whitfield, *The image of the world*, 59.

54. See Whitfield, *The image of the world*, 44-59.

55. Hale, *The civilization of Europe in the Renaissance*, 27 & 52. See also Hay, *Europe: the emergence of an idea*, 99-100; Den Boer, et al., *The history of the idea of Europe*, 44-7; Whitfield, *The image of the world*, 66-74.

56. Hale, *The civilization of Europe in the Renaissance*, 22-6; & Hale, 'The Renaissance idea of Europe', 52.

57. Whitfield, *The image of the world*, 96-8.

58. Herodotus, *The histories*, Book 4, p. 285.

59. See Duroselle, *Europe: a history of its peoples*, 19.

60. Toynbee, '"Asia" and "Europe"', 711 note 2.

61. Duroselle, *Europe: a history of its peoples*, 19; Toynbee, '"Asia" and "Europe"' 710-12; Hay, *Europe: the emergence of an idea*, 1.

62. Rijksbaron, 'Wat was Europa, en waarom?'

63. Hale, *The civilization of Europe in the Renaissance*, 9.

64. Den Boer, et al., *The history of the idea of Europe*, 48.

65. Duroselle, *Europe: a history of its peoples*, 19. See also Herodotus, *The histories*, Book 1, p. 42, who explains the Europa myth in the context of woman-stealing being quite a normal practice at the time.

66. For references see Guthmüller, 'Europa', especially pp. 4-9, notes 2-9.

67. Hale, *The civilization of Europe in the Renaissance*, 7-8; Guthmüller, 'Europa', 9; & Hay, *Europe: the emergence of an idea*, 53, 103.

68. See two eloquent examples quoted and illustrated in Guthmüller, 'Europa', 15-18: a Conrad Schnitt drawing of 1520-4, and a painting by Iacopo Palma il Giovane in the Doge's Palace in Venice, from c. 1590, with personifications of Venice fighting alone against Europa.

69. Guthmüller, 'Europa'.

70. Genesis 9, 27.

71. See Hay, *Europe: the emergence of an idea*, 7-14, which gives an authoritative account of this process of myth-construction.

72. Hale, 'The Renaissance idea of Europe', 48; Hale, *The civilization of Europe in the Renaissance*, 9; Hay, *Europe: the emergence of an idea*, 53 & 108-9. The introduction of a Trojan myth of European origin also helped to render the Japheth connection gradually redundant.

73. On this transition generally see Hay, *Europe: the emergence of an idea*, 104; Den Boer, et al., *The history of the idea of Europe*, 48-51; Hale, 'The Renaissance idea of Europe', 49; Hale, *The civilization of Europe in the Renaissance*, 9-13.

74. See T. Hoenselaars' essay in Leerssen & Van Montfrans, eds, *Borders and territories*, 103; & Den Boer, et al., *The history of the idea of Europe*, 52-3.

75. This image is reproduced in Hay, *Europe: the emergence of an idea*, as frontispeice; and in Hale, *The civilization of Europe in the Renaissance*, 11.

76. See a Dutch engraving of 1598 held in the Ashmolean Museum, showing Elizabeth I in anti-papist stance, embodied as a map of Europe, reproduced in Leerssen & Van Montfrans, eds, *Borders and territories*, 107.

77. The plate is illustrated and commented on by Den Boer, et al., *The history of the idea of Europe*, 53-4. It was made for the intended marriage of Rudolph II to the Infante, which never went ahead; the piece is held in the Kunstgewerbemuseum in Berlin.

78. Hale, *The civilization of Europe in the Renaissance*, 12.

79. Den Boer, et al., *The history of the idea of Europe*, 53 & 56; Hay, *Europe: the emergence of an idea*, 104.

80. Hale, *The civilization of Europe in the Renaissance*, 12-13.

81. Illustrated in Hay, *Europe: the emergence of an idea*, plate V and p. 104; see another Galle representation, dated c. 1580, in the Rijksmuseum Amsterdam, illustrated in Den Boer, et al., *The history of the idea of Europe*, 51.

82. Den Boer, et al., *The history of the idea of Europe*, 53 & 55; Hale, 'The Renaissance idea of Europe', 49.

83. Hale, *The civilization of Europe in the Renaissance*, 13-14.

84. An exhibition of world maps at the British Museum allows us to examine the portrayal of Europe in that context, aided by the sumptuously illustrated book accompanying the exhibition, by Peter Whitfield, *The image of the world*. Apart from Fig. 4.14 here, see especially Pieter van den Keere's *Nova Totius Orbis Mappa*, of 1611 (p. 80-1), and Henricus Hondius's *Nova Totius Terrarum Orbis Geographica* of 1630 (p. 75).

85. Respectively: Guthmüller, 'Europa', 34-42; Hoenselaars' essay in Leerssen & Van Montfrans, eds, *Borders and territories*, 85-112, especially pp. 94, 106, & 112; Hay, *Europe: the emergence of an idea*, 118; Burke, 'Did Europe exist before 1700?', 26; & 'Europe' in Blake, *Complete writings*, 237-45.

86. Den Boer, et al., *The history of the idea of Europe*, 48 & 53-4.

87. Hay, *Europe: the emergence of an idea*, 119.

88. Smith, *National identity*, 19.

89. Toynbee, '"Asia" and "Europe"', 729.

References

Albrecht-Carrié, R., *The unity of Europe: an historical survey* (London, Secker & Warburg, 1966).

Bartlett, R., *The making of Europe: conquest, colonization and cultural change 950-1350* (London, Allen Lane, 1993).

Blake, William, *Complete writings with variant readings*, edited by G. Keynes, Oxford Standard Authors (London, OUP, 1966).

Boer, P. den, et al., *The history of the idea of Europe*, edited by K. Wilson & J. van der Dussen, What is Europe? 1 (London, Routledge, 1995).

Burke, P., 'Did Europe exist before 1700?', *History of European Ideas*, 1(1980), 21-29.

DePorte, A.W., *Europe between the superpowers: the enduring balance*, second edition (New Haven, Yale University Press, 1986) [first published 1978].

Duroselle, J-B., *Europe: a history of its peoples* (London, Viking Penguin, 1990).

'Eastern Europe ... Central Europe ... Europe', [special issue of] *Daedalus*, 119 no. 1 (Winter 1990), 1-344.

Foerster, R.H., *Die Idee Europa 1300-1946: Quellen zur Geschichte der poltische Einigung* (s.l., Deutscher Taschenbuch Verlag, s.d. [c. 1970]).

Fuhrman, M., 'L'Europe: contribution à l'historie d'une idée culturelle et politique', *History of European Ideas*, 4(1983), 1-15.

García, S., ed., *European identity and the search for legitimacy* (London, Pinter, 1993).

Gould, P., & R. White, *Mental maps* (Harmondsworth, Penguin, 1974).

Guthmüller, B., 'Europa - Kontinent und antiker Mythos', in *Der Europa-Gedanke*, edited by A. Buck (Tübingen, Niemeyer, 1992), 5-44.

Hale, J., 'The Renaissance idea of Europe', in S. García, ed., *European identity and the search for legitimacy* (London, Pinter, 1993), 46-63.

Hale, J., *The civilization of Europe in the Renaissance* (London, Harper Collins, 1994).

Hay, D., *Europe; the emergence of an idea*, second edition (Edinburgh, Edinburgh University Press, 1968) [first published 1957].

Hay, D., 'Europe revisited: 1979', *History of European Ideas*, 1(1980), 1-6.

Hazard, P., *European thought in the eighteenth century* (Harmondsworth, Penguin, 1965) [originally published 1946].

Heater, D., *The idea of European unity* (London, Leicester University Press, 1992).

Herodotus, *The histories*, translated by A. de Sélincourt, edited by A.R. Burn (Harmondsworth, Penguin, 1954, revised edition 1972).

Joll, J., *Europe: a historian's view* (Leeds, Leeds University Press, 1969).

Leerssen, J.T., & M. van Montfrans, eds, *Borders and territories, Yearbook of European Studies*, 6 (Amsterdam, Rodopi, 1993).

Mayne, R., et al., *Federal Union: the pioneers. A history of Federal Union* (London, Macmillan, 1990).

Mollat du Jourdin, M., *Europe and the sea* (Oxford, Blackwell, 1993).

Nelson, B., et al., ed., *The idea of Europe: problems of national and transnational identity* (Oxford, Berg, 1992).

Parker, W.H., 'Europe: how far?', *Geographical Journal*, 126 (1960), 278-97.

Rijksbaron, A., 'Wat was Europa, en waarom?', in J. Leerssen, et al., eds, *Tussen wetenschap en werkelijkheid: opstellen aangeboden aan Max Weisglas* (Amsterdam, European Cultural Foundation, 1989), 122-29.

Roobol, W.H., 'What is Europe?', *Yearbook of European Studies*, 1(1988), 186-204.

Schmidt, H.D., 'The establishment of "Europe" as a political expression', *Historical Journal*, 9(1966), 172-8.

Seton-Watson, H., 'What is Europe, where is Europe? From mystique to politique', *Encounter*, 64-65 (July-August 1985), 9-17.

Smith, A.D., *National identity* (London, Penguin, 1991).

Smith, A.D., 'National identity and the idea of European unity', *International Affairs*, 68 no. 1 (1992), 55-76.

Spiering, M., 'Waarom de Britten geen Europeanen zijn', *Bulletin Geschiedenis, Kunst, Cultuur*, 3 no 2 (1994), 115-35.

Tilly, C., ed., *The formation of national states in Western Europe* (Princeton NJ, Princeton University Press, 1975).

Toynbee, A.J., '"Asia" and "Europe": facts and fantasies', Annex C(I) to *A study of history*, vol. VIII (London, Oxford University Press, 1954), 708-29.

Ullmann, W., *The Carolingian Renaissance and the idea of kingship* (London, Methuen, 1969).

Waites, B., et al., *Europe and the wider world*, revised edition, What is Europe? 4 (London, Routledge, 1995).

Whitfield, P., *The image of the world: 20 centuries of world maps* (London, British Library, 1994).

5 National identity and European unity

M. Spiering

Worauf man in Europa stolz ist
Dieser Erdteil ist stolz auf sich,
und er kann auch stolz auf sich sein.
Man ist stolz in Europa:

Deutscher zu sein
Franzose zu sein
Engländer zu sein
Kein Deutscher zu sein
Kein Franzose zu sein
Kein Engländer zu sein

Kurt Tucholsky[1]

Studies on post-war Europe tend to focus on the 'E-institutions' which came into being from the late 1940s onwards: the European Council, the European Coal and Steel Community, Euratom, the European Economic Community, the European Union, and so on. This bias in academic scrutiny is understandable. The idea that the Europeans of all regions should somehow co-operate more, or even unite their political institutions, is old. It goes back at least to the sixteenth century and has since surfaced regularly.[2] However, it was not until the post-war period that some of these ideas were put into practice. The E-institutions are unique and deserve the attention they get.

About these institutions two fundamental questions can be asked. The first concerns how they work. To answer this question is important, if only to counter the blatant nonsense which is churned out by the media on an almost daily basis. We read that 'Brussels' has decreed this, that, or the other, or that some practices in (for instance) Britain, have been found to contravene 'European law'. Often these reports refer in fact to rulings of the European Court of Human Rights, a body set up by the Council of Europe to monitor compliance with the European Convention for Human Rights which was signed by fifteen states in 1950. Currently the Council of Europe (not to be confused with the European Council, which is another institution altogether) numbers more than twenty member states.

The public is renowned for its ignorance of the workings of politics, which traditionally gives the manipulators every chance to indulge in scaremongering. But the debate on the question of Europe is too important to be left to 'funny' books such as *Bluff your way in the EEC* (1988), or *The I hate Europe official handbook* (1994), or to be entrusted to the hands of Dr Alan Sked, founder of the U.K. Independence Party, who in a party political broadcast declared that according to European regulations all fishermen are required to carry condoms (a confusion with a directive agreed in 1991 that in fish processing and packaging plants, staff will need to wear some sort of headgear).

This is not to say that 'Euro-sceptics', who can be found in many countries, have no good reason to be critical. It is only to say that a proper understanding of, and education in, exactly how the various European institutions function will make for a better debate.

The second question one might pose about the E-institutions is why they came into being in the first place. Given the respectable age of the idea that 'the Europeans' should somehow join forces, it is surely remarkable that it was only after the Second World War that so many treaties of co-operation were signed, the last one bearing the name, 'Treaty on European Union'. What happened? This question will be briefly examined below. It will appear that the answers rely heavily on the concept and workings of 'the nation-state'. These introductory paragraphs conclude with a statement of the main issues, related to the concept of the nation-state, which this chapter will seek to address.

Post-war Europe and integration

Why did European co-operation began to take on concrete forms after World War II had ended? Two opinions hold the field. According to one school of thought the real players in post-war European developments were a group of idealists who sought to establish a new, integrated Europe, inhabited not by French, Germans or Britons, but by Europeans. Even during the war, so this account runs, many people identified nationalism and the nation-state as the main causes of the disasters which were again sweeping over Europe. Nationalism had proven to be a catastrophic creed. It had claimed, not altogether implausibly, that the people living in Europe, or indeed the world, could be divided up in groups which somehow felt bound by a common descent, culture or history. But then it had proceeded by preaching *apartheid*.

These groups were so unique, so different from one another that they needed to acquire absolute sovereignty. Those who were not memebers of those groups should be destroyed, or at least driven out of the territories that the groups, or nations, claimed as their own and where they sought to organize their own sovereign political powers, or states. Once established, these nation-states engaged in a Darwinian struggle of domination, each claiming to be better than the other and each prepared to kill in order to obtain more of the limited resources the continent had to offer.

Once the latest and most destructive war of the nation-states was finally over, disillusioned individuals voiced their anger, and some united in pressure groups, like the European Movement, founded at a conference in The Hague in 1948. The solution to Europe's woes was clear: unite or be damned. The vicious circle had to be broken. A New Europe had to be created where the nation-states would merge for their common good. Feelings of Europeanness had to be stimulated; loyalties had to be shifted from the smaller nation-states to a greater common European unit. To borrow a term from the parlance of policy-makers and civil servants, this appraisal of post-war events might be dubbed a 'bottom-up' approach. Buoyed up by the groundswell of public opinion, the governments of the European nation-states embarked on a programme of co-operation and dilution of national sovereignty. In 1963, referring to the Congress of 1948 in The Hague, a co-founder of the European Movement declared in a lecture at Geneva University: 'It cannot be said too often that everything else flowed from that Congress.'[3] He and other proponents of this school of thought point to the preambles of the various European treaties, in which it is sonorously declared that the signatories 'intend to lay the foundations of an ever closer union among the peoples of Europe' and that they call 'upon the other peoples of Europe who share their ideal to join in their efforts' (Treaty of Rome, 1957).

A second, opposing, school of thought claims the situation in post-war Europe was - and is - not significantly different from the situation before. The governments of the individual member states play a simple game because, basically, they are still the representatives of that simple structure: the nation-state. The government of a *state* (i.e. the territory where it holds sovereign power) may decide to look after its own interests or the interest of a limited group of individuals. But the brief of the government of a *nation-state* is different. The people who live in such a unit feel 'one'; they feel bound by a common culture and history. Their 'oneness' makes them a force to be reckoned with and therefore their rulers, who, in any case, partake in this feeling of oneness, have no option but to satisfy the needs of their people, their nation, or *the national interest*. In practice this means providing as much affluence for the nation as possible. Hence, the deals which nation-states strike with one another always serve the simple purpose of enriching their own nations. Therefore the post-war European moves towards co-operation and integration were the result not of idealism, but of the old selfish games of nation-states.

Advocates of this school of thought point not to the preambles, but to the explicit articles of the European treaties dealing with the hard business of international bargaining.

It will be clear that these interpretations of post-war European developments rest on simplifications. How influential was the European Movement, if indeed it was a movement, with a clear purpose and agenda? And, on the other hand, what exactly is meant by the 'national interest'? How homogenous are nations? And how true is it that states paternally aim to serve these nations? Some people would argue that the new post-war structures of European co-operation were but the latest ruse of the old elites who owe less allegiance to their nations than to their own pockets.

In practice hardly any study on post-war Europe can be classified as belonging solely to either method of analysis, and the vast majority of commentators draw on several explanations. Europe as it exists today is the result of ideology and selfishness, of fear and greed. It is, however, possible to observe that 'early' studies on post-war Europe tend to include more references to idealism, whereas analyses that have appeared from, roughly, the 1970s onwards tend pay more attention to the member states' hard-nosed pursuit of their individual national interests.

To the 'early' category of commentators who stressed the idealistic background of post-war European developments belong authors such as Denis de Rougemont and the World War II resistance fighter Hendrik Brugmans. They were both very active in the European Movement and were founders, together with Robert Schuman and George Villiers, of the European Cultural Foundation. Blaming the nation-states for the ills of Europe, these visionaries did not, of course, advocate the creation of a new European 'super-nation'.[4] Some form of federation was the answer, and Switzerland was frequently cited as an example. Yet they were convinced that 'the Europeans' could and should unite because they had so much in common. Both authors frequently refer to 'our European culture', 'our spiritual community', 'our heritage', 'our common destiny'. A few pages after De Rougemont's statement that he would not favour the creation of a European nation, he admonishes his audience: 'you don't yet feel as if you belonged to a nation of 335 millions ... Yes, United Europe has not yet been created, and it is imperative to create her.'[5] In other words, the super-nation was awaiting delivery after all, and because it was projected that this European nation was to be loyal to the decisions of a European Assembly, it would appear that a European nation-state was the ultimate goal of these Europeans of the first hour: 'we can tomorrow build the greatest political formation and the greatest economic unit our age has seen', stated a speaker at the Hague Congress.[6]

The idea that there is no such thing as a New Europe, but that the post-war European institutions instead serve to bring as much benefit to the individual nation-states as possible, while keeping them as autonomous as possible, has been vented by various authors, but in particular by Alan Milward. He is convinced that to remain in power national governments have grown more and more dependent on bribing the floating lower-middle-class voter with social provisions and other expensive services. Therefore, economic growth is more important than ever, and so a degree of national sovereignty is surrendered, not out of conviction, but to increase national exports. Thus the national income is raised and the old national states are sustained. In his *The European rescue of the nation-state*, Milward puts every effort into demythologizing the story of the making of the European Communities, and goes to great lengths to unmask the so-called Founding Fathers of the New Europe (Monnet, Schuman, Spaak, Adenauer, De Gasperi) as politicians driven almost solely by domestic motives.

The school of thought of which Milward is such as vocal representative has risen to particular dominance since the 1970s. As to why this should be so, three reasons spring to mind. Firstly, in the field of international relations 'political realism' has traditionally attracted a large number of followers. (Generally speaking political realism holds that states are the main actors on the international stage; that their motives are to retain or enhance their 'power'; that power should be interpreted first and foremost in 'real', that is material terms: capital, troops, weapons, control of resources.) Secondly, scepticism is fashionable in modern, secularized intellectual circles. Influenced by, and themselves influencing movements such as post-structuralism, post-modernism and cultural relativism, many authors feel there is no such thing as idealism, not because man is 'bad' and thus incapable of true morality, but because 'bad' and 'good' are but arbitrary concepts. If the Fathers of the New Europe, such as Monnet, Schuman, Spaak, Adenauer and De Gasperi, were the prophets of European Brotherhood, they were only so to a certain extent and from a certain point of view.

Thirdly, and most importantly, those who would argue that the hopeful talk of the preambles of the various European treaties has not led to any concrete results have found it increasingly easy to present their case. As the years progressed after the signing of the 1957 Rome Treaty, incident after incident has shown that the member states seek to feather their own nests. The 'empty-chair' policy of the French, which introduced the veto in the Council of Ministers in 1966, the refusal to help out the Netherlands when it was hit by an oil boycott in 1973, and many, many other affairs before and since have made it blatantly clear that it is still the nation-state that calls the shots in Europe. Not a sparrow falls onto the ground without the consent of the European Council of National Ministers. The member states allowed the E-institutions to develop because each and every one of them expected that these new developments would result in national gains.

Milward et al. have no difficulty in illustrating their argument: Belgium agreed to the European Coal and Steel Community because it was a way to reorganize its ailing industry, for Germany it meant rehabilitation and economic reconstruction, for the Netherlands more exports, for France it promised reduced economic competition and perhaps a means to inspire parts of the electorate with fresh feelings of *grandeur*. And all saw it as a way to secure American financial support and protect themselves against the European East Bloc. Moreover, opinion polls have consistently revealed that European idealism is hardly a public good. People expect their governments to look after their own nations first and foremost. *Euro-baromètre*, an on-going survey on public opinion organized by the European Commission, demonstrates that 'the emergence of a cosmopolitan European identity within the Community, a European *Zusammengehörigkeitsgefühl*, cannot yet be hailed. If a nation can be defined as a body of people who *feel* they are a nation, then there is little support for the idea of a European nation in the psychological sense.'[7]

This interpretation of events, then, comes with an abundance of documentation. Why did post-war Western Europe witness the creation of a number of unique supranational institutions? Because the new post-war world order prompted the old European nation-states to experiment with new forms of collaboration with a view to retaining as much of their power as possible. This is not to deny that there have been (and still are) genuine idealists who cherish a vision of a European brotherhood of nations and federation of governments. Founded in 1948, the European Movement still has its followers and it might well be that the ideals of this movement at least partly inspired the actions of some post-war European statesmen. But the vast majority of the idealists mentioned in, for instance, Lipgens' study, *Documents on the history of European integration* (1985), never reached influential posts and, in any case, the facts speak for themselves. The European Movement, whose membership is dwindling, has itself more than once declared that the Europe as it exists today is not at all the Europe they had envisaged: 'The EEC is no longer anything more than a co-operative arrangement from which one draws the maximum benefit while making the minimum possible contribution, a cow to be milked by oneself but fed by others.'[8]

If it is so that the new Europe of the E-institutions is the result not of ideology but mainly of collusion between the old nation-states, then this begs the question why the nation-state has proved to be such a preferred and tenacious form of human organization. This chapter will explore this question, paying considerable attention to feelings of national identity, as well as to matters of a more material nature. By way of conclusion a possible answer will be ventured to two other related questions: why has the European Union so far failed to effect a merger of the individual member states à la Brugmans and De Rougemont? And what could or should be done to make such a merger succeed?

The nation-state in Europe

In the preceding paragraphs the terms 'nation', 'state', 'nationalism', and indeed 'Europe', have been only fleetingly examined, and defined in parenthesis.

Before continuing, a round of further definitions is appropriate.

Europe. The word can be interpreted in three ways: geographically, culturally and politically.[9] The political Europe of post-war co-operation is the starting point of this chapter. The paragraphs below will therefore centre on common historical aspects of the European Union member states. The focus will be on what might loosely be called Western Europe.

Nation, state, nationalism, nation-state. Because these terms denote concepts, rather than concrete objects, they have been variously defined by various people at various times. A trawl through the textbooks yields a rich catch of different interpretations of, for instance, nationalism. There is humanitarian nationalism, Jacobin nationalism, traditional or aristocratic nationalism, liberal nationalism, integral nationalism, economic nationalism, Habsburg nationalism, classical-liberal western nationalism, diaspora nationalism, West and East European nationalism.[10]

The history of concepts, or 'ideas', can of course be traced, and the origins and past usages of 'nation' and 'state' are well documented. In Europe, *nation* began to be widely used in an ecclesiastical context in the thirteenth century.[11] Since then there have been significant shifts in the meaning and usage of the term. A common definition today is that a nation refers to a large group of people bound by perceived common descent, history, culture. In 1983 Benedict Anderson coined the now famous phrase 'imagined community' as a synonym for nation, stating that 'the members of even the smallest nation will never know most of their fellow-members, meet them, or even hear of them, yet in the minds of each lives the image of their community.'[12]

Other scholars have argued that nations should be defined also with reference to less subjective phenomena such as domain and political sovereignty. In his *National identity*, Anthony Smith provides a 'check-list' of conditions a group of people should meet in order to qualify as a nation. Amongst others they should share a 'historic territory' and 'a common economy and common legal rights and duties for all members'.[13]

Smith indicates he is well aware that concepts derive their meaning from a personal and cultural context. In fact the idea that territory and political sovereignty are elements of nationhood is heard more frequently in the Anglo-Saxon world than elsewhere. In 1861 John Stuart Mill defined 'a Nationality' as 'a portion of mankind that ... desires to be under the same government, and desires that it should be governed by themselves exclusively.'[14]

In 1983 Ernest Gellner published his *Nations and nationalism*. The book has enjoyed great popularity, not least because it is a slim volume containing definitions of nation, state, and nationalism that are relatively concise and uncontroversial. Building on Max Weber's celebrated pronouncement that the state is that agency within society that possesses the monopoly of legitimate violence, and following similar statements by others, Gellner defines a state as a territorial political unit within the boundaries (or jurisdiction) of which one or various institutions are specifically concerned with the enforcement of order.

'The state exists where specialized order-enforcing agencies, such as police forces and courts, have separated out from the rest of social life. They *are* the state.'[15]

Gellner's definition of *nation* echoes that of Anderson's. He argues that it is possible to define 'nation' in a cultural and/or a voluntaristic sense:

1. Two men are of the same nation if and only if they share the same culture, where culture in turn means a system of ideas and signs and associations and ways of behaving and communicating.
2. Two men are of the same nation if and only if they recognize each other as belonging to the same nation. In other words, *nations maketh man*; nations are the artefacts of men's convictions and loyalties and solidarities.[16]

But Gellner concludes by stating that the definition of nation has been (and is) very much influenced by the varying theories of *nationalism*, i.e. the ideal that desires the world to be divided in *nation-states*, or units in which the borders of nations and states are congruent.[17]

Nationalists, who generally belonged to the intellectual (or at least writing) classes, and who began to be particularly active in Europe in the eighteenth and nineteenth centuries, defined the concept of nation to suit their own purposes and beliefs. Thus for some of the *philosophes* who inspired the ideals of the French Revolution, the nation was primarily a civic concept, a community of people obeying the same laws and institutions. To others, such as for instance the German Romantics Johann Gottfried von Herder and Johann Gottlieb Fichte, the nation represented a mystical entity, a bond of a people, their blood and the earth trodden by their ancestors since time immemorial.

Regarding the nation-state in Europe there is, at least in academic circles, a wide consensus about the following points:

1. The ideal of the nation-state has played an important role in European history for some time. Theories which attempt to explain the past and predict the future without due reference to the nation-state cannot be sustained. The assumption of Marxists that international class loyalties are stronger than feelings of national allegiance have, time and again, been proven wrong. Proletarians have shown more readiness to die for their nation-states than associate with foreigners belonging to the same social class. Social revolution and patriotic sentiment have never been far apart. If the red flag has been hoisted at all, it was in combination with a national one.[18]
2. The ideal of the nation-state is in origin a European phenomenon. It lies at the root of the modern cliché that Europe can only be defined by its diversity (in France they do things the French way, in Britain the British way, etc.). From Europe the ideal of the nation-state was exported to other parts of the world. Now the assumption that mankind consists of separate

nations which deserve to live in their own states is globally accepted. In the nineteenth century the Italian nationalist Guiseppe Mazzini (amongst others) declared that only nations of sufficient size, which were economically viable, could lay claim to their own state. But in 1918 the American President Woodrow Wilson stated that *every* national group deserves self-government.

3. The nation-state, being largely the product of nationalists' aspirations, has not been with us since the beginning. In 1992 the British Liberal-Democrat leader Paddy Ashdown declared, 'I do not believe that the nation-state is anything other than a relatively recent invention. I do not believe that it will always remain.' It was an imprudent statement, for in a party political broadcast in 1994, his Conservative political opponents used it against him by appealing to the sentiments of the electorate. Weren't they proud of Britain's history? Her age-old traditions? Her sovereignty? Her splendid achievements? This is stirring stuff, but it is not validated by history. The idea that Britain is inhabited by Britons who share a sense of identity and feelings of allegiance to a British government, running a British state, began to be generally accepted only in the eighteenth century.[19]

Since these times the doctrine of the nation-state has been so puissant that few people can imagine a differently organized world. Some have come to see the nation-state as sacrosanct: in *Maastricht: a Christian dilemma*, a booklet published in 1993, during the hight of the Maastricht Debate, it is declared that,

> Just as previous theories of the 'brotherhood of man', communism, and socialism, have all failed to produce a real unity between nation-states with mutually exclusive interests, so it must be also for the new Europeans, and the federalists today. Furthermore, these political theories have consistently challenged the three basic institutions ordained by God, namely the nation-state, the church and the family.[20]

4. Given the fact that the nation is largely an idealistic concept, it is evident that true nation-states only exist in theory. That is to say, whereas few people would deny that there is, for example, such a thing as a French state, it is highly improbable that this state serves the interests of *one* nation. Within the borders of France live many people, probably a majority, who would confess to feelings of 'Frenchness', and a shared sense of identity with their compatriots (though every one of these 'Frenchmen' can know only a tiny fraction of the other people living in France - this fact lies at the heart of Anderson's definition of the nation as an 'imagined community'). It remains to be seen, however, whether 'Frenchness' means the same to every Frenchman. Furthermore, France, like every other nation-state, is home to numerous people who feel they belong, or at least *also*

belong, to other nations. The Breton separatist movement forms an obvious example.

5. Like the nation, the state (defined above as a sovereign political unit persisting in time and within certain territorial borders) has not always been with us. There is wide consensus that in Europe the contours of states began to take shape before sentiments of nationhood began to be felt and before nationalist ideals about autonomous nation-states began to be formulated. In Tönnies' oft-quoted terms, *Gemeinschaft* preceded *Gesellschaft*.[21]

Why the nation-state?

The question of when feelings of nationhood and theories about self-ruling nations evolved in Europe is not particularly controversial. There is, however, some disagreement as to *why* the nation-state should have emerged in the first place. Why was this type of human organization embraced by so many? Two basic approaches may be distinguished here. As will be argued in more detail below, it is unusual to encounter either of these in an undiluted form. The following, simplified rendering of the two approaches, therefore, is to some extent a parody: two rudimentary pictures painted in stark colours for the sake of contrast.

Firstly, nations are said to be the result of certain events which changed situation A into situation B. A story of the following kind is often told. Before the fourteenth century or thereabouts, the people of Europe lived in small agricultural communities where everybody knew their place and somehow earned a living. Above these communities stood ruling and ecclesiastical elites who might now be described, somewhat anachronistically, as cosmopolitan. They travelled abroad and mixed and corresponded in their shared second language (Latin) with members of their own class. Then a series of developments caused all this to change, first in England and France, and later elsewhere.

There were, for instance, technical advances. Better roads and improved methods of military organization, administration, and tax collecting made it increasingly possible for rulers not only to possess land and communities in name, but to impose one type of money, a single system of weights and measures, a uniform law, and suchlike on their subjects. The invention of printing was important, because the more books became available, the more people were confronted with the same ideas, formulated in the same language.

Then there was the Reformation. As the efficiency and power of individual secular rulers expanded, anti-Catholic creeds managed to gain a toehold. The Protestant doctrine that every person could and should work towards his own salvation, that people could go their own way and form their own religious communities, meant in practice that rulers were able to demand conformatity

107

to the independent church of their liking or making.

The Enlightenment is said to have played a role in the formation of nations and nationalism. Rational observations of nature seemed to show there was order everywhere. If there was a God, surely He was a God of reason, regularity and laws. And just as 'the earth had brought forth the living creature after his kind', so God had created the different nationalities. According to the theist Henry St. John, Viscount Bolingbroke (1678-1751), God had given these nations two great natural laws: 'the universal law of reason' and 'the particular law or constitution of laws by which every distinct community has chosen to be governed.'[22]

Capitalism played a part as well. More and better forms of transport and banking methods increased trade. The development of a money economy, and the demise of feudalism caused labour specialization, and this in turn caused larger groups of people to be economically interdependent. The growing importance of money, as opposed to birth, resulted in the growth of a large class of people (the middle-classes) with the same aspirations: the stimulation of trade in order to acquire more riches. The last in this series of developments was industrialization, brought about by a combination of capitalism and the invention of mechanized production. Industry demands standardization, in weights and measures, but also in education, habits, customs, and culture.

All these developments resulted in the 'clotting' of sizeable collections of people into homogenized communities, sharing the same law, religion, life-style and often language. Large homogenized societies benefit from economies of scale. Standardization and mass production offer the possibility of the greatest affluence for the largest number of people. It was this reality that made nationalism a viable proposition and gave it mass support. Zealots some nationalists might have been, but underneath their cheering lay the hard fact that nation-states may function as efficient units of production that best serve the material needs, the national interest, of the masses. 'The nation-state is the most beneficial and cohesive type of political unit and ... the sole means of achieving solidarity and collective prosperity.'[23]

The social and cultural homogenization set in motion by the invention of printing, the industrial revolution, etc. - and its perceived benefits for large groups of people - eventually spawned the nationalist appetite for *forced* homogenization and cleared the way for theories about unique national identities that could not tolerate interference by 'others'. Thus the passions and flag-waving that many of us associate with nationalism were a linear consequence of certain historical events that just happen to have happened: 'the rise of modern states that were based on a strong nationalistic sentiment was a logical historical response to the industrial revolution.'[24] Or in the words of another historian: 'the modern age of large-scale production and industrial economy has been prerequisite, in one country after another, and eventually in the world at large, to the ascendancy of nationalism.'[25]

Once it had germinated, the violent creed of nationalism proved a hardy plant. Nationalist wars and revolutions swept over Europe, forcing people to conform to their nations' practices and customs, and, if needs be, die for their nations' unity and purity. Minority groups, who would not conform, or were thought not to conform, were expunged from the nation-state womb to lead a stateless and insecure wandering life. Consequently the building of nation-states frequently also involved nation-destruction.

So much for this simplified version of an often-heard story about nations, the nation-state, nationalism and national identity. The story, or its underlying assumption, is related to the 'realist' school mentioned above. In the last analysis it is primarily about material developments and power: the narrative centres on developments or events that are said to have transferred material affluence, and thus power, from the hands of the few to the hands of the modern national masses. These developments are frequently referred to as 'forces' or 'processes'; they are construed as the prime, external movers that shaped pre-national societies into national ones and eventually implanted sentiments of national uniqueness, or identity, in the peoples of Europe. In the words of Benedict Anderson: these 'were largely unselfconscious processes resulting from the explosive interaction between capitalism and technology'.[26] Anthony Smith puts it as follows: 'nations are products of particular social and historical conditions working upon antecedent ethnic cores.'[27]

A second, alternative view is that the various events referred to above are historically important, but they were not in themselves 'forces' that provoked the birth of nations, nationalism, and the ideal of the nation-state. There is a school of thought which proposes that such phenomena as capitalism, industrialization, and the like could have altered the existing societies of Europe in one or more of several different ways. (Marxists, for example, expected a global class-war.) The fact that many people have embraced nationalism and to this day show great loyalty to their nation-states can but point to one thing: apparently this is what they actually want. Here we enter the realms of psychology, or of social psychology: the field that examines the emotional relations between the individual and the group.

A recurrent psychological argument, for instance, is that the secularizing consequences of the Enlightenment caused a form of spiritual *horror vacui*. Nationalism, therefore, is essentially a religion-substitute. To the question of why commitment to the nation-state remains 'so ubiquitous and pervasive', Anthony Smith eventually formulates the answer:

> Perhaps the most important of its functions is to provide a satisfying answer to the problem of personal oblivion. Identification with the 'nation' in a secular era is the surest way to surmount the finality of death and ensure a measure of personal immortality.[28]

A free rendering of the line of reasoning presented by many of the social psychologists who have philosophized about nation-formation could run as follows: psychoanalysts (amongst whom Sigmund Freud himself) have argued that the human infant, totally unable to look after itself, absorbs into its psyche the behaviour and attitudes of important external figures, primarily parents. This process is usually referred to as 'internalization'. Internalization is an ongoing process. As the child grows up it assimilates the behaviour and attitudes not just of its parents, but of the larger group on which it is dependent for its well-being, even survival. Thus internalization becomes socialization.[29]

Internalization and socialization provide the individual, as well as his group, with a sense of identity, a perception of 'being', of becoming an object to himself, and of sharing a specific culture with his peers and vis-à-vis others. A sense of identity is crucial to psychological well-being. An 'identity crisis' (the term was popularized by the psychoanalyst Erik Erikson in the 1950s) is a form of illness; it leads to personality breakdown, depression and other types of disorder. According to Erikson a clear correlation exists between identity and culture: where culture is threatened, identity is threatened; conversely, an enhancement of culture enhances identity.[30]

Thus there is a psychological need to 'identify'. Individuals, as persons, but also as group-members, have 'a drive to bolster and to defend their identity'.[31] Human beings have always shown strong feelings of loyalty to their group and a parallel propensity to denounce outsiders.

The ongoing process of internalization makes it possible for individuals to identify with several groups, starting at the core-group of the family and branching out to the tribe, village or any other 'identity-securing interpretive system' that might be available (the term is Jurgen Habermas'). 'Through a shared identification, individuals are linked within the same psychological syndrome and will act together to preserve, defend and enhance their common identity.'[32]

In this way, nations were born not because of forces, or 'processes' resulting from 'the explosive interaction between capitalism and technology', but because some of the myriad events that work in and on societies trigger a response, whereas others leave no mark. Printing, for instance, 'caught on' simply because the invention was in tune with the human 'identity dynamic'. In itself it did not prompt the birth of nations; its potential to homogenize, or bind together cultures, merely provided people with an opportunity to pursue yet more forcefully what they had been doing all along: the protection and enhancement of their own and their group's identity. Naturally, enhancement and protection is best pursued in a context of power and sovereignty. Therefore, nations want states. To date, the nation-state is the optimal 'identity-securing interpretive system' which man has created for himself.

This social-psychological school of thought, then, characterizes such things as industrialization merely as environmental factors that precipitated the formation of nations and nation-states. The real 'force' or 'process' is the identity dynamic

110

that resides in the human psyche and continuously motivates groups to fight aggressively for their own niche on earth. Nations are collective mutual admiration societies. 'The psychological need to define oneself in terms of membership in a given political community is at the root of national sentiment.'[33]

In conclusion, both the 'realist' and 'social-psychological' schools agree that nationalism (i.e. the wish for autonomy, self-determination; the drive to establish nation-states) came into being at a certain time in European history, and that it developed into a creed steeped in emotion and violence. For the one, however, the nationalist desire forcibly to homogenize cultures and create a national identity is the by-product of historical developments of a largely material nature ('a logical historical response to the industrial revolution'), while for the other it is a manifestation of an age-old psychological imperative, 'the identity dynamic', that underlies the urge to protect, and where possible, to enhance one's identity.

Taken to extremes, the two answers to the question, 'why the nation-state?', appear to propagate the teachings of determinism and predestination respectively. According to the one, man is a pawn moved about by 'events' following 'events': the invention of better trade and transport methods, printing, and industrial production methods have eventually resulted in the predominance of the nation-state. Other developments could have led to quite different results. According to the other, man's psyche has preordained him to a certain way of life. Through a process akin to natural selection the nation-state has developed, because this system of human organization has so far proven to be the most congenial to people's psychological needs.

Extremism is rare. Realist-determinists will normally give some consideration to psychological factors, and even a dyed-in-the-wool social psychologist will concede that 'the relationship between inner drives and historical circumstances is dialectical.'[34] However, generally people are predisposed towards theories which stress material determinism, while playing down psychological factors. A plausible summary of events, furnished, where possible, with hard material causes that could have led to the predominant position of the nation-state today, tends not to arouse controversy. (Of course, the question of exactly which events and causes are relevant can be hotly debated.) Conversely, theories that appear to point to predestination are usually greeted with unease. Such theories deny 'free will' and seem to declare that we are condemned to live our lives according to fixed patterns.

The nation-state and international relations

Milward demonstrates in his *The European rescue of the nation-state* how the nation-state has endured until this day by showing that the members of what is purportedly a European Union have never ceased to pursue their own, national interests. Relations between the EU states are still very much international.

His book is an example of an analysis that stresses material factors, while playing down psychological ones. He shows in great detail how the member states always manoeuvre with a view to bringing a maximum of affluence to their individual nations. But this desire for profit, which is undoubtedly there, cannot in the end provide the full answer to the question of why the Union is not a union as was envisaged in The Hague in 1948, for the simple point is this: if states were only out to enrich their people or 'nations' (or, even, perhaps only certain cliques within their *supposed* nations) then surely these states must have observed that working with others is always the most lucrative policy. If material conditions stood at the cradle of the nationalist desire for nation-states, and if these nation-states were offered to, and eventually perceived by, the masses as affluence-generating units of production, then the same logic should soon have prompted the conclusion that there is much profit in international integration, more so than in stubbornly defending one's own segment of national uniqueness.

It is all too obvious that this way of thinking does not underly the wheeling and dealing of the European nation-states. Events have shown time and again that nations are prepared to suffer great hardship in order to obtain or defend their independence (their 'states'), rather than tread the profitable road of alliance. In other words, 'the national interest' is not commonly perceived in purely material terms. The European Union and its difficulties cannot be fully understood without due reference to the psychological factors dealt with in the previous section: those feelings of national pride and identity that abound in any nation-state.

Euro-sceptics at times do their best to suggest that the EU harms the national economy, but the point is very hard to prove. The diction used in these 'hard fact' arguments, not to mention the articles, books and cartoons that deal directly with Euro-threats to the national identity, show quite clearly that at the heart of Euro-scepticism lies the demand that others who are different should not be given a say in national affairs:

> In future, Her Majesty will act not on the sole advice of Her ministers but on advice tempered by a qualified majority of the ministers of eleven foreign states. Thus the position of The Queen is impaired by having to accept not the advice of Her own ministers but that of the ministers of a collection of alien states. We have to go back in history before the reign of Henry VIII to find a period where foreign potentates could so interfere in the affairs of Her Majesty's realm.[35]

A passionate conviction that the 'own' national identity is in conflict with the character of 'others' and ought to be protected is not at all, as some might expect, confined to the tabloids and their readerships, though in these circles the noise is undoubtedly loudest: 'We were not told', the *Sunday Express* exclaimed on 21 May 1995, 'that our courts, the bastions of our freedom for 1,000 years, would be overruled by foreigners sitting in Luxembourg.'

Such reactions to the Union are widespread. They are not only heard in Perfidious Albion, nor are they the prerogative of the 'unthinking masses'. At the time of the referendum on whether or not Sweden should join the European Union, the *Nej Till EU* campaign mentioned economic issues, but also argued that saying 'yes' would be tantamount to an assassination of the proud Nordic spirit. And in the Netherlands, usually perceived as European and cosmopolitan to the point of having lost interest in its national identity, a *Comité Buitenlands Cultureel Beleid* (Committee on Foreign Cultural Policy) insisted in 1991 that all European treaties should contain articles safeguarding national cultural autonomy.[36]

That it is not just the tabloid-reading masses that react with fervour to the issue of national identity may be illustrated with another glance at the situation in Britain. In this country it is not difficult to find examples of public figures, politicians (of the right and the left) and 'intellectuals' who argue that protection of the national interest means in the first place protection of the national identity. Alongside John Major's outcry 'I will never, come hell or high water, let our distinctive British identity be lost in a federal Europe!' (Conservative Party Congress, 1993) we can place Tony Benn's comparison of the EU to the dictatorship of the Holy Roman Empire (House of Commons, 23 July 1993), or John Osborn's remark that he is 'sick to death of the Common Supermarket jargon and high-minded greed .... I am prepared to settle for a modest, shabby, poor-but-proud Little England any day.'[37]

Clearly, next to the material advantages for which nation-states undoubtedly compete, feelings of national identity play a major part in international relations. However problematic it might be to talk about emotions in a structured, academic way, the subject cannot be dodged, in particular, it would seem, as far as the European question is concerned. As an article in *The Independent* of 30 March 1994 put it: 'You may not be either a hard Europhile or a hard Eurosceptic. But where you stand between the two will certainly be determined by your own unreasonable sense of national identity.'

What is national identity?

In one sense national identity is real, even tangible. First introduced in Britain after the First World War, passports and similar documents certifying one's nationality were soon referred to as 'identity papers'. Now it is not unusual in many countries for individuals permanently to carry an 'ID', to be shown on demand at all times. It is a piece of paper that attests that one has a personal name and is a citizen of a state. Citizenship gives people rights and duties; it

113

defines them as 'subjects' and thus quite literally provides an identity that is shared with others carrying similar papers. Most people, however, would feel that this 'civic' definition of who we are hardly touches the heart of the matter. The identity of a person, of a group, or of a nation resides in such things as 'behaviour', 'attitude', 'mores', or, in a word, 'culture'. But how should one consider these aspects of identity? Can they be measured? And what might their origins be? As far as *national* identity is concerned (the principal concern of this chapter) both the question of measurement and origins have given rise to some dispute.

Of course one can simply ask people how they view their national identity, and various persons and projects have attempted just that. In the 1950s Geoffrey Gorer sent out questionnaires to a selected group of people living in England, and then in his *Exploring the English character* set out to write 'a study ... to be of use to politicians and political scientists.'[38] Others, like Miles Hewstone (whose book *Understanding attitudes to the European Community* has already been mentioned), opted for more comprehensive studies, making use of the lengthy tables provided by *Euro-baromètre*, containing, amongst others, indexed answers to questions on how people perceive their own and other nations. Something similar, but on a much larger scale, was attempted by UNESCO when, in 1953, it commissioned two researchers to report on *How nations see each other*. Another large-scale project of note is *Het Europese waarden onderzoek* (Inquiry into European values), an ongoing project that was started in 1981 and is co-ordinated at Dutch and Belgian Universities.[39] Finally, some scholars have grappled with 'practical' questions such as how differences in national culture or identity may affect the economic performance of, say, multinational companies.[40]

There is no doubt that statistical measurements of the largely subjective phenomenon 'national identity' can yield valuable data. Equally, it should be understood that this data is itself the product of subjective processes. The manner in which the questions are phrased, the selection of respondents, and the eventual interpretation of the answers all ensure that, at best, this type of study can yield only *a* measurement of national identity. Not all statistical researchers have been equally aware of this, some of them laying themselves wide open to criticism when, on the basis of completed questionnaires, they have happily formulated all sorts of definitive statements about 'the national identity' of the English, the Germans, or the French. Having indexed the answers to his questionnaires Geoffrey Gorer declares that 'the English are certainly among the most peaceful, gentle, courteous and orderly populations that the civilized world has ever seen.'[41]

The question of measurement is so obviously fraught with difficulties that many scholars prefer to approach the issue of national identity from a 'meta' level. National identity, they argue, is an idea and therefore the only useful thing to do is to try to trace the history of that idea. Just how many English people of a particular sex or background would feel, say, that 'love of democracy' is part of their national identity is of lesser importance. Suffice it to conclude that this idea exists (it can be found in various sources), and the next thing to do is to examine who expressed it, where, and in what context, and how was it was passed on, and possibly transformed, *en route*.

In this approach to national identity the term 'image' is often used, underlining, in contrast to 'idea', the unconscious processes involved. Ideas about Englishness, or Germanness, have demonstrably been formulated by various thinkers, but once framed they tend to 'trickle down' in society, providing people through education, literature, and the media with largely unconscious mental representations (images) of what it means to belong to a particular nation. (Of course the 'idea-makers' themselves were, and are, also influenced by such images.) A notorious variation is the cliché, a crude image of ourselves or 'the other', that on a conscious level most people would disown, but that nevertheless forms part of their *baggage intellectuel* (and thus their behaviour and attitudes). The conclusions reached by the secret seminar on 'the Germans' attended by Margaret Thatcher and her Foreign Secretary in 1990 were clearly inspired by stereotypes, rather than genuine analysis. 'We started by talking about the Germans themselves and their characteristics', wrote Charles Powell, the Prime Minister's private secretary, in notes that were subsequently leaked. 'Like other nations, they had certain characteristics which you could identify from the past and expect to find in the future.' Powell then continued to list these characteristics: 'insensitivity to the feelings of others, obsession with themselves, a strong inclination to self-pity, aggressiveness, assertiveness, bullying, egotism, sentimentality'.[42]

So, exactly how one should measure national identity is a moot point, but as a notion it clearly exists. It is the subject of conversations, texts, and, as we have seen, political seminars. And in all these cases very specific national attributes are mentioned. The Germans are aggressive and sentimental, the Italians are corrupt, and so on. How do nations acquire these specific attributes? Broadly speaking, this subject has given rise (once more) to two conflicting schools of thought.

Essentialists

On the one hand, there are what one could call *essentialists*, who argue that national identity is an integral, essential part of 'self'. It is God-given or implanted by nature. This approach accordingly favours terms such as 'national character', 'national temper', or 'national genius'. Reference is frequently made to 'forefathers' (suggesting that national identity is somehow genetically transferred) and to factors such as 'land', food, and climate that are supposed to shape a people's physique as well as mental make-up. In his *L'Esprit des lois* (1748), Montesquieu reflects at length how their 'coarse food' has made the Dutch a strong but dull nation and how the lighter southern foods have caused a Mediterranean character to develop. Rooted as they were in ancient Greek philosophy, Montesquieu's theories were in themselves not new and they have since been echoed by many others.[43] In the 1760s Oliver Goldsmith argued that the English are a moderate people because of their moderate climate, and in the early nineteenth century, in Germany, Johann Gottlieb Fichte argued that groups of people acquire the same language (and thus form a nation) through environmental circumstances such as climate, air, and geographical conditions.[44]

Obviously, the essentialist approach to national identity has now lost appeal and followers since it was taken to extremes in the Nazi philosophy of *Blut und Boden*. However, the school is by no means extinct. In 1943, in his 'The English People', George Orwell explained English society with reference to the country's 'equable climate and pleasantly varied scenery'; in his 1955 Reith Lecture, Nikolaus Pevsner argued that the English language had endowed its speakers with special characteristics; in 1978 Alan Macfarlane in his *The origins of English individualism* stated that this special quality has something to do with the 'Germanic woods' of yore; and in *The Field* of May 1990 the historian A.L. Rowse linked 'the essence of Englishness' with the Anglo-Saxon rites of the sixth century.

Constructivists

The opposing school of thought argues that it is impossible to be born with national characteristics, nor are they the organic consequence of soil and climate. The adherents of this approach prefer to think in terms of ideas and images. They prefer the term national identity to national character and insist that this identity is based on perceptions that are in no way rooted in nature, but are instead the result of 'nurture'. National identity is an 'intellectual artefact' or a 'cultural construct'. Hence, the adherents of this approach could be labelled *constructivists*. Just as essentialism can boast a long pedigree, so the notion that in human affairs nurture plays an eminent role is by no means new. In 1741 David Hume argued that what he termed 'moral causes' (government, education) are the true originators of feelings of national identity.

Old though the underlying idea may be, today constructivists dominate the debate about the meaning and origins of national identity as never before. In 1976 Eugene Weber analysed the making of 'Frenchness' in his *Peasants into Frenchmen*. In Britain, Eric Hobsbawm's *The invention of tradition* set the tone in 1983. Five years later three volumes appeared (edited by Raphael Samuel) under the telling title *Patriotism: the making and unmaking of British national identity*. In 1992 Linda Colley followed with *Britons: forging the nation*.

Constructivists would not normally deny that feelings or images of national identity are 'real' (of course they are: people live and die by them), and they will not attempt to assess the legitimacy of such images. Whether or not

Spaniards are 'insolent' and 'proud' is impossible to prove or refute. Their aim is to show *how* ideas of national identity are assembled. What are their constituent parts; where do they come from? Thus, those who believe that images of national identity are man-made constructs, are often engaged with, to coin a phrase, 'deconstruction'. They take the image apart, not to deride it, not to demonstrate its hollowness, but to understand and explain.

For example, the British imperial system of weights and measures is not infrequently celebrated as an ancient, traditional element of the national heritage. In 1989 Lord Monson declared that inches, pounds and pints are part 'of our cultural identity'. He feared that just as the 'totalitarians of the French Revolution' imposed their system on 'the Continentals', so the European metric system was now being foisted on the British.[45] In 1978 Anthony Burgess went one step further when he argued that the imperial system was a direct reflection of the British character. The Continental, metric system was cold and 'Cartesian', whereas the British system was like the British themselves: human and intuitive. But, unfortunately, it had to go, for 'inches and feet and yards were too much based on thumbs and limbs to be acceptable in a truly rational world.'[46] Similar views are regularly expressed in the media whenever 'Brussels' is seen to impose further regulations on the British way of life.

No doubt these views are deeply felt. It is a worthwhile exercise, though (so constructivists would argue), to isolate the constituent parts and, if possible, trace their origins in history. Such an operation could make one aware that national identity is not based on facts, forever fixed in time and space, but that it consists of images that are subject to change.

Underlying the statements quoted above on the imperial and metric systems there are three images:

a. The British and their national identity are different from the Continentals or the Europeans.
b. The British are 'human'. They prefer common sense to rational, dogmatic, mechanical schemes.
c. Their rulers, therefore, do not impose their will on the people: over the centuries the imperial system of weights and measures has naturally evolved in British society. It is, as the editor of the magazine *This England* once claimed, 'ancient', 'age-old', 'traditional' (Spring, 1995).

Regarding the last point, only some of the names used in the imperial system can be said to be 'old'. However, in the metric system, as it is used in some continental countries, the same 'old' names also occur (there are, for instance, metric pounds and ounces). The imperial system itself is by no means ancient. It was established by law in 1824, came into force in 1826 and in 1834-1835 the use of non-imperial weights and measures was declared illegal. That this imposition caused dismay amongst the population is shown by a letter published in *The Times* in April 1825, claiming that the new-fangled scheme was unnecessary and anti-traditional:

> Sir, - The Proposal in parliament to defer the act for establishing uniformity of weights and measures from the 1st of May next to January, 1826, affords that time for the attention to so important a subject which it has hitherto failed to obtain either in or out of the House. ... a very natural question presents itself - whether the proposed alteration, which deserts every known standard that time has familiarized us with, is the best.

About the point that 'humanness' is part of the British national identity one can remark, firstly, that this image is fostered by many, if not all, groups or nations. Secondly, the image that British 'humanness' manifests itself in a propensity for common sense and intuition, and an attendant abhorrence of rationality and dogma, can be traced back without difficulty to the eighteenth century. In his *The rise of English nationalism* (1987), Gerald Newman shows in detail how, in that century of almost continuous warfare between France and Britain, many books and pamphlets were published in which ideas were 'constructed' and disseminated that aimed to prove that the British were as unlike their opponents as possible. So if, to put it crudely, in France Descartes had established a reputation by reasoning that man was but a machine, then the British were not Cartesian. The image of British common sense and pragmatism (still often evoked today in the debate about the European Union) perhaps finds its starkest expression in Edmund Burke's *Reflections on the revolution in France* (1790), in which he assiduously argues that, unlike the revolutionary and scheming French, the British can boast a manly, moral, regulated sense of liberty.

Finally, the point that 'Britishness' can be opposed to 'Europeanness' is based on an image of national 'self' that can be traced back to the end of the sixteenth century when England had at last given up hope of ever establishing a continental empire and began to sail the seven seas instead. It was in this period that the terms 'Europe' and 'European' began first to acquire the meaning 'not-English' (or 'not-British'), and that Shakespeare composed his famous lines celebrating the special position of England as 'a precious stone', separated from the Continent by a sea 'serving in the office of a wall'.

Images of national identity

Images of national identity and how they 'work' have been the subject of various books, articles and research projects. Some of the scholars who select literature (or, more generally, 'texts') as their main source material refer to their field of study as 'imagology' or 'image-studies'.[47]

As images of national identity typically reach us through texts, it is useful briefly to recount some of the general findings of image studies. For instance, in order to be understood a text has to be 'recognizable'. Therefore, in texts (and perhaps in human discourse in general) recognizability takes precedence over reality. Images of national identity tend to be based on previous images in previous texts. Thus the image evokes what the Germans call an 'aha-experience' (*Aha-Erlebnis*). We respond to it, not because we know it to be true, but simply because it is familiar. Often, however, familiarity is sadly confused with validity. Consequently, the commonplace or stereotype is such a potent image. *Quod latet ignotum est, ignoti nulla cupido.*

Because images of national identity are intertextually related, rather than a reflection of observed reality, they can be said to exist and operate in a world of their own, forming and obeying their separate, independent rules. Images appearing in different texts in different countries tend to follow similar patterns. It has been observed, for instance, that in many countries or regions of Europe, a similar distinction is made between the perceived qualities of 'the north' on the one hand and 'the south' on the other. Northerners are more down-to-earth, prosaic, law-abiding and individualistic, whereas southerners are more sensitive and poetic, but also less honest. 'The fact that the south of Germany is to the north of the north of Italy is a short-circuit which disproves this assumption but has not effaced its existence.'[48]

It is also remarkable that an image of national identity invariably coexists with its own opposite. Shoulder to shoulder with the typical Englishman John Bull (bluff and pugnacious) stands the imperturbable gentleman Bertie Wooster who is deemed equally typical. And the goose-stepping German militarist is nevertheless the brother of the romantic dreamer and typically German Werther. 'The ultimate cliché that can be said of virtually any country is that it is "full of contrasts".'[49] Perhaps this seeming contradiction, which illustrates once again that 'the nation' only exists as an ideal, is the result of class distinctions, Bertie and Werther clearly being the projections of the more genteel elements of their nations. But another, more inherently textual solution is also on offer:

> If one follows the development of an image through literary history, one sees how this ambivalence is often caused by conflicting sources which are brought under the same head. If author A says that the Irish are violent, and author B says that the Irish are sentimental, then author C will reconcile A and B by saying that the Irish are characterized by a 'typical combination of violence and sentimentality'. Which of these two contradictory attributes is then most emphasized, depends on the political attitude of the author, on the point he is trying to make.[50]

This phenomenon of antagonistic pair-forming can also be observed on a supranational level. Just as there is no 'me' without a 'you', there is no image of 'the national self' without an image of 'the other'. There are no protagonists without antagonists, or, in the parlance of image studies, an *auto* image always coexists with a *hetero* image. The mean Scot can only exist because there are supposed to be other nations who are less frugal.

In itself the imagologists' conclusion that an image of identity cannot exist without an attendant image of alterity is not new, and at one level it could even be called trite. Of course, without black, there is no white, without night no day. Nevertheless, notions of national identity are often presented as independent absolutes; we are supposed to accept them as 'true' in their own right. The English are 'a practical people. Not theoretical like the Germans; nor dogmatic like the Russians; nor arrogant like the French.'[51]

These self-images of Englishness (of course the same goes for self-images of Germanness, Frenchness, etc.) undoubtedly spring from genuine and deeply felt convictions, but they are dogmatic; they are unchallengeable and therefore potentially aggressive. The realization that such notions do not spring from careful observations of reality (let alone reflections of essential principles), but are instead the result of the way we order our thoughts, may let some fresh air, as it were, into discussions about national identity. As soon as we name our group and ascribe to it a distinct identity, we must inevitably create an opposite number. No night without day; no Croats without Serbs. In itself the observation is, indeed, almost banal, but an acceptance of its full implications may lead to the, perhaps liberating, realization that images of national identity are neither true nor false. They only have a *significance* that they acquire from a position relative to other such images.

This notion that our knowledge is self-enclosed, that 'a thing' is recognized as 'a thing' not because it has an actuality of its own, but because it can be contrasted to another thing is by no means of recent origin. It achieved, however, some general currency in the early 1920s under the influence of structuralism. Later, in the 1970s, the deconstructionist Jacques Derrida attracted much attention when he stressed that words (or signs) are never meaningful in relation to a 'real world', but only in relation to one another. What counts is diacritical significance, or *différance* (sic).

In its most undiluted form such a relativist position can be condemned as amoral. As Tzvetan Todorov pointed out, 'only within the confined atmosphere of universities, where we tend to forget about the rest of the world, is it possible to flirt with sceptical or relativistic suspension of values.'[52] In image studies, however, the identity/alterity opposition is not seen solely as a textual or linguistic peculiarity. Images of national identity are transmitted through texts and in this medium they acquire their own dynamics, but this is not to say that *context* should be ignored. Identity/alterity images find their way into texts as a result of concrete events and in their turn they affect real-life situations and decisions.

As argued above, many ideas about Englishness find their origin in the eighteenth century, during the 'second hundred years' war' with the French. It was in the novels, plays and drawings of these years that the 'typical' Frenchman (or worse, the Frenchified Englishman) was introduced. The despicable dandy Bellarmine in Henry Fielding's *Joseph Andrews* (1742) was the patriarch of many other such dishonourable characters in a host of subsequent novels, who to this day inspire certain expectations about French behaviour. Asked about the trustworthiness of their fellow Europeans, British respondents to the *Euro-baromètre* questionnaires consistently relegate the French to the bottom of the list.[53]

English readers were familiar with 'the brutal German' long before the great military hostilities of the twentieth century. In 1871, shortly after the Prussian victory over the French, George Chesney published *The Battle of Dorking*, a future-fiction tale (or 'invasion novel') in which well organized but cruel Germans cross the Channel and successfully subdue the English who, by typical identity/alterity contrast, are portrayed as human and freedom-loving. The novel set a trend, and as authors copied and elaborated upon the characters they found in one another's works, the images of Germanness (and Englishness as non-Germanness) acquired ever sharper contours. The genre remains popular, and therefore influential, until this day, the best known example perhaps being Len Deighton's *SS-GB*. The conclusions reached in the Thatcher government's secret seminar about 'the Germans' probably owed as much to these images of Germanness as to the very real atrocities of the two world wars.

The idea that the British/English can be seen as the antithesis of 'the Europeans' from the continent goes back some way, but in the post-war period, as the E-institutions expanded, an image of 'the un-British European' has emerged sporadically in the nation's literature, both with a small and a capital 'l'. In these latter-day invasion tales, Uni-European troops and fraudulent politicians can be seen to wreak havoc in the island, destroying its ancient parliamentary traditions.[54] As the confusion in Britain over EU membership deepens, these identity/alterity images of honest-democratic *versus* corrupt-bureaucratic practices will undoubtedly make their appearance in more and more texts. Influenced by, but also themselves influencing 'real life', the importance of these images in the European debate is set to increase. In the 1993 BBC series *The Downing Street years*, Lady Thatcher declared:

> There is a great strand of equity and fairness in the British people. This is our characteristic. There is no strand of equity and fairness in Europe. They are out to get as much as they can. This is one of those enormous differences.

The Three Races

I

Behold, my child,
    the Nordic Man
And be as like
    him as you can.
His legs are long;
    his mind is slow;
His hair is lank
    and made of tow.

II

And here we have the Alpine Race.
Oh! What a broad and foolish face!

His skin is of a dirty yellow,
He is a most unpleasant fellow.

III

The most degraded of them all
Mediterranean we call.
His hair is crisp, and even curls,

And he is saucy with the girls.

Figure 5.1   Hillaire Belloc, 'The Three Races'

Source: *Selected cautionary verses* (Penguin, 1964), 169-71 [first published 1940].

In conclusion, image studies has revealed some notable principles about the nature and workings of images of national identity in text, the medium through which the vast majority of people receive their opinions about 'self' and 'the other'. Rather than being reflections of observed reality, images tend to be intertextually related. This is not to say, however, as some extreme relativists would have it, that images of national identity float around, remote from the world, in a self-enclosed textual system. There is an interface with reality; the images find their way into texts because of real events and may, sometimes years later, after having solidified in a process of intertextual borrowing, be seen to exert considerable influence in real international relations. The image of the passionate and corrupt European from the south, as contrasted with the more rational, law-abiding northerner, made its appearance in texts after the Reformation had drawn a Catholic/Protestant dividing line across Europe. Since then the image has attached itself to stock characters in literature, and has inspired 'what-if' novels, such as Kingsley Amis' *The alteration* (1978), which presents a nightmare vision of an England firmly integrated in a Catholic Europe. The book describes how Luther travelled to Rome to reconcile himself with the Mother Church and to be crowned as 'a Pope from the North'. As a result there has never been a Reformation. The north of Europe, including the British Isles, has therefore remained rife with Roman cruelty and corruption to the present day.

This image of Protestant/northern morality has played, and still plays, a role in the post-war European debate. 'I can recall from my own student days', a Catholic Englishman once recounted, 'the frequently expressed view that the *Treaty of Rome* was a Roman Catholic plot. No doubt you would find similar views still held in some parts of the United Kingdom today.'[55] In 1991 the historian and columnist Paul Johnson suggested that the south-European disease of corruption was slowly infecting Britain. Therefore, the south should be left to its own devices, while a Protestant Northern Bloc of EC-members with 'traditionally high standards of public probity' should continue to build their open market.[56]

European unity and national identity

In the opening paragraphs of this chapter it was argued that a strong case can be made for the view that, far from a brotherhood driven by idealism, the European Union is an association of convenience between nation-states anxious to preserve their independence. In Europe the nation-state is still prevalent; actions of governments and surveys of public opinion show that protection of 'the national interest' is deemed most important.

As to the question of why the nation-state is capable of drawing so much support, two possible answers have been explored. One school of thought has it that the nation-state developed because of irresistible 'forces' in the real world. Printing, industrialization etc. led to the homogenization of societies into nations. Homogenized, standardized societies offer a prospect of affluence for large groups of people. This is especially true for autonomous nations and thus the notion of the nation-state gained mass support. In due course these processes resulted in the fury of nationalism. Theories about national uniqueness were formed, summoning people to identify with the national cause and demanding loyalty towards co-nationals, whilst denouncing outsiders.

Psychologists and social psychologists, on the other hand, argue that man, motivated by a 'national identity drive', always seeks to live in culturally homogenized societies. The attendant wish to 'enhance and protect' this group identity causes humans to respond to those historical developments that provide the best opportunity to enlarge the group and give it optimal independence. Thus the nation-state is the result of a sort of psychological filtering process. To date, it is the optimal 'identity-securing interpretive system' available. It naturally commands loyalty and inspires group-members to weed out perceived non-nationals and compete with outlanders.

It is rare for either interpretation of the rise and appeal of the nation-state to be expressed in such unequivocal terms. Taken to extremes they are controversial, but the conclusion they share is hard to refute. Whether inspired by external forces or internal drives, cultural homogenization has become an ideal, and this ideal - that one should be loyal to a nation-state and embrace a national identity - has been pursued not only with enthusiasm, but also with considerable force. National majorities have formed because they have coerced minorities. As Raymond Aron put it in his *Peace and war* (1981): 'war is the midwife of nations'. It was Ernest Renan, who in his famous *Qu'est-ce qu'une nation?* (1882), observed that nations, which he defines as large cultural units that share memories about their past, but also a considerable degree of amnesia, are invariably the result of violence and conquests: 'L'unité se fait toujours brutalement; la réunion de la France du Nord et de la France du Midi a été le résultat d'une extermination et d'une terreur continuée pendant près d'un siècle.'[57]

From Renan's supposition it follows that European unity, in the sense it is used by those idealists who envisage a Europe of an 'ever closer union' (or of a 'reinforced European identity', as it is put in the preamble to *The Treaty on European Union*), is unlikely to come about if, as is the case at the moment, methods of coercion are not favoured. The territories of northern America became the United States only after a period of strife and open warfare. In the end one side gained supremacy and after a period of enforced homogenization (which entailed, for instance, compulsory non-segregational education) a feeling of national unity, or national identity, might now be said to have emerged. There is no reason to assume that things would be very different in Europe. A European anthem and a European flag will contribute nothing to European unity.

Experience suggests that the European Union will not automatically develop into something other than a *Zollverein* kept together by expectations of profit on the part of individual member states. Only if an ideology of Europeanism were to develop, as an ideology of nationalism has developed in the past, would it be possible, after a period of conflict and identity destruction, for a sense of a common European identity to come into being. If it comes at all, the birth of the New Europe as envisaged by De Rougemont and Brugmans will not be different from the birth of France as it was described by Renan.

European idealists often cite Switzerland and the Netherlands as living examples of nation-states that have developed out of a voluntary federation of Cantons or Provinces:

> What do we want? Is the overriding priority the 'common good' to be defined and allowed to triumph? Or are we resigned to the conflict of interests which equal each other out? Let Switzerland be our teacher again. To be sure the Swiss do not live in a state of patriotic exultation, for they are practical hard-headed people. No one forgets his own interests. But whenever crisis threatens, they remember their virtues as confederates, their civic duties towards a unit which is greater than the canton. Everyone loves his or her little native canton and all respect those of others. So all are loyal to the country that unites them all. Let Europe see in Switzerland, if not a model to copy at least an example to follow.[58]

The crucial point here is that the Swiss, proudly living in their Cantons, are said to have a overriding common national feeling of Swissness. This may be so, but a mere glance at the history of the Confederation shows that religious civil wars played a major part in the homogenization of Swiss society. Moreover, at the time of the French Revolution and Napoleon, various conflicts between break-away movements (Patriots, Unionists and Federalists) were settled only after blood was shed. Following the 'Swiss example', therefore, would be following a fairly standard European pathway to nation-state creation.

The example set by the forebear of the Kingdom of the Netherlands, the Republic of the Seven United Provinces, is not much different. Clashes between Patriots and Orangists in the late eighteenth and early nineteenth century were preceded by prolonged, and often violent, religious disputes, resulting in endeavours to impose one *national* church upon the people (as at the Synod of Dordrecht in 1618-19).

Even, if by magic, a European nation were to develop peacefully, then its chances of survival would be slim, since the fledgling image of national oneness probably could not be sustained by a contrastive image of alterity. Though Euro-enthusiasts at times argue their case by pointing to presumed antagonist rival nations such as the Japanese, Americans, or Russians, there is

125

no evidence that these groups are collectively perceived as the mirrors in which Europeans see the reflection of their Europeanness. Here, too, one fears, results can only be achieved by force. In *Apocalypse 2000*, a novel published in 1987, a Fascist party (the Europe First Party) succeeds in uniting the Europeans in the 1990s only after vicious propaganda campaigns have imprinted images of unclean, non-European foreigners in the minds of the electorate.

The realization that the ever closer union has so far patently failed to materialize has hardened the resolve of some idealists, while others have stated their intention of becoming less ardent and more 'realistic'. It has also given rise to the idea that a union will only come about when a totally new awareness dawns on the peoples of Europe. The European Union as a nation-state writ large would, indeed, be a much 'closer union', but as history shows that the path to this type of union is paved with acts of violence, the Europeans should, it is argued, respect the multifarious character of their continent and thus find unity in a common acceptance of diversity:

> attempts to persuade Europeans to regard themselves as homogenized *Europeans* ... are bound to fail. Europe cannot exist as such - peacefully and in a civilized mood - unless it reaches explicit agreement with itself that its is riddled with diversity, difference and (potential) conflicts.[59]

Similar sentiments are expressed in numerous books and articles touching on the question of national identity and post-war Europe. In fact, it is almost a stock conclusion. Anthony Smith ends his study of national identity with a call for 'Pan-Europeanism', based on the 'rich, inchoate *mélange* of cultural assumptions, forms and traditions, a cultural heritage that creates sentiments of affinity between the peoples of Europe.'[60] Jürgen Habermas believes that 'in the future a differentiation could occur in a European culture between a common political culture and the branching national traditions of art and literature.' Thus a 'new political self-confidence commensurate with the role of Europe in the twenty-first century' could develop.[61] This listing of hopeful conclusions employing words and phrases such as 'new awareness', 'reform', 'acceptance', 'something beyond the nation-state' and 'unity in diversity' could be added to almost *ad infinitum*. What they share is idealism; an idealism which is perhaps naive, since it does no more than state that if we are all nice and understanding, all will be well. It is this idealism that Milward exposes so easily, and with such relish.

In 1761 Jean-Jacques Rousseau finished an annotated summary of *The project for perpetual peace in Europe* which the Abbé de Saint-Pierre had published in Cologne in 1712. The irritable editor regularly finds it difficult to concur with Saint-Pierre's innocent assumption that the rulers of Europe would gladly join in a confederation, regulated by international law, because peace is more beneficial than conflict and because there is glory in being perceived as peacemakers. Nonetheless, in his concluding remarks Rousseau feels he has to praise the European idealism of the Abbé. One cannot but try, he seems to sigh. Let no man's heart fail because of brutal Goliath. It is not the plans that are fanciful; it is man who so often proves senseless:

> Si, malgré tout cela, ce Projet demeure sans exécution, ce n'est donc pas qu'il soit chimérique, c'est que les hommes sont insensés, & que c'est une sorte de folie d'être sage au milieu des fous.[62]

Notes

1. Tucholsky, *Zwischen Gestern und Morgen*, 25.

2. Surveys are provided by, i.a., Förster, *Europa*; Heater, *The idea of European unity*; Wilson & Van der Dussen, eds, *The history of the idea of Europe*.

3. De Rougemont, *The meaning of Europe*, 82. See also Heater, *The idea of European unity*, 152: 'the influence of convinced individuals was so much more powerful than hitherto'.

4. De Rougemont, *The meaning of Europe*, 64.

5. Ibid., 106.

6. M.P. Kerstens, 'Message to the Europeans', speech at the Congress of Europe, May 1948.

7. Hewstone, *Understanding attitudes to the European Community*, 33.

8. Brugmans, *Europe*, 8.

9. For a discussion of the geographical limits of Europe see Parker, 'Europe: how far?' Many studies have appeared on the various meanings which have been attached to the term Europe over the centuries. Hay, *Europe: the emergence of an idea*, is perhaps the most well known. A concise analysis of the issues involved is in Roobol, 'What is Europe'.

10. The terms are taken from Hayes, *The historical evolution of modern nationalism*; Gellner, *Nations and nationalism*; Smith, *Theories of nationalism*; Kohn, *The idea of nationalism*.

11. Liah Greenfeld, *Nationalism*, 4-5.

12. Anderson, *Imagined communities*, 15.

13. Smith, *National identity*, 40.

14. Mill, *Considerations on representative government*, Chapter XVI.

15. Gellner, *Nations and nationalism*, 4. See also D'Entrèves, *The notion of the state*.

16. Gellner, *Nations and nationalism*, 7.

17. For a full discussion on the usages and misusages of the term nation-state, see Connor, 'A nation is a nation'.

18. See Hobsbawm, *Nations and nationalism*, 146-7.

19. See Colley, *Britons*; and Newman, *The rise of English nationalism*.

20. Wood, *Maastricht*, 25.

21. Tönnies, *Community and society*.

22. As quoted in Hayes, *The historical evolution of modern nationalism*, 19. Also see Carr, *Nationalism and after*, 8.

23. Smith, *National identity*, 151.

24. Coulombis & Wolfe, 'Nation-state and nationalism', 10.

25. Hayes, *The historical evolution of modern nationalism*, 233.

26. Anderson, *Imagined communities*, 48.

27. Smith, *National identity*, 40.

28. Ibid., 161. See also O'Brien, *God's land*.

29. See Habermas, *Legitimation crisis*.

30. Erikson, 'Ego development'.

31. Bloom, *Personal identity*, 37.

32. Ibid., 26.

33. Coulombis & Wolfe, 'Nation-state and nationalism', 7.

34. Bloom, *Personal identity*, 37.

35. Stoddart, 'The erosion of sovereignty', 44.

36. J. de Valk, the Dutch author mentioning this pressure group, ends his article by stating that he will never tolerate 'his Queen' being represented on a European coin or on any other European symbol. 'The emotional aspect of national identity', he argues, 'must not be disregarded.' De Valk, ed., *Nationale identiteit*, 20.

37. *Encounter* (December 1962), 59.

38. Gorer, *Exploring the English character*, 1.

39. See De Moor, 'Globalisering'.

40. E.g. Hofstede, *Culture's consequences*; and Hambden-Turner and Trompenaars, *The seven cultures of capitalism*.

41. Gorer, *Exploring the English character*, 13.

42. *The Independent on Sunday* (15 July 1990).

43. See Meyer Levin, *The political doctrine of Montesquieu*.

44. Quoted in Kedourie, *Nationalism*, 64. See also Zacharasiewicz, *Die Klimattheorie*.

45. *Common Market Watchdog*, 56 (Summer 1989).

46. Burgess, *1985*, 33-34.

47. For introductory works to this subject see Firchow, *The death of the German cousin*, Appendix: 'The nature and usages of imagology'; Boerner, ed., *Concepts of national identity*; Spiering, *Englishness*; Leerssen, *Cultural differences and national images*.

48. Leerssen, 'On national identities', 31.

49. Ibid.

50. Ibid.

51. A.L. Rowse, in *The Field* (May 1990).

52. Todorov, '"Race", writing, and culture', 181.

53. Hewstone, *Understanding attitudes to the European Community*, 32.

54. See, for instance, Angus Wilson, *The old men at the zoo* (1961); Alexander Cordell, *If you believe the soldiers* (1973); Peter Jay and Michael Stewart, *Apocalypse 2000* (1987).

55. Baker-Smith, 'The ghost in the machine', 16.

56. 'Cleansing Europe's Augean stables', *The Sunday Telegraph* (20 October 1991).

57. 'Unity is always achieved in a brutal way. The joining of North and South in France was the result of extermination and a reign of terror which lasted almost a century'. Renan, *Qu'est-ce qu'une nation?*, 8.

58. Brugmans, *Europe*, 9.

59. Keane, 'Questions for Europe', 57.

60. Smith, *National identity*, 174.

61. Habermas, 'Citizenship and national identity', 12.

62. 'If the plan is not put into execution it will not be because it is fanciful; it is because men are senseless, and because it is a kind of folly to be wise in the midst of fools'. Rousseau, *Extrait du projet de paix perpétuelle*, 58.

References

Anderson, Benedict, *Imagined communities: reflections on the origin and spread of nationalism* (London, Verso Editions, 1983).

Baker-Smith, Dominic, 'The ghost in the machine', *Yearbook of European Studies*, 1 (1988), 13-26.

Bloom, William, *Personal identity, national identity and international relations* (Cambridge, CUP, 1990).

Boerner, Peter, ed., *Concepts of national identity: an interdisciplinary dialogue* (Baden Baden, Nomos Verlagsgesellschaft, 1986).

Brugmans, Hendrik, *Europe: a leap in the dark* (Stoke-on-Trent, Trentham Books, 1985).

Burgess, Anthony, *1985* (London, Arrow Books, 1985) [first published 1978].

Carr, E.H., *Nationalism and after* (London, Macmillan, 1945).

Colley, Linda, *Britons: forging the nation 1707-1837* (Yale University Press, 1992).

Connor, Walker, 'A nation is a nation, is a state, is an ethnic group, is a ...', *Ethnic and Racial Studies* 1, no 4 (1978), 378-400.

Coulombis, Theodore A. & Wolfe, James H., 'Nation-state and nationalism', in William Olson, ed., *The theory and practice of international relations* (Englewood Cliffs N.J., Prentice Hall, 1983).

Entrèves, Alexander Passerin d', *The notion of the state: an introduction to political theory* (Oxford, OUP, 1967).

Erikson, Erik H., 'Ego development and historical change', in 'Identity and the life cycle: selected papers', *Psychological Issues* 1, no 1 (1959).

Firchow, Peter, *The death of the German cousin* (London and Toronto, Associated University Presses, 1986).

Förster, R.H., *Europa: Geschichte einer politischen Idee* (München, Nymphenburger Verlagsbuchhandlung, 1967).

Gellner, Ernest, *Nations and nationalism* (Oxford, Blackwell, 1983).

Gorer, Geoffrey, *Exploring the English character* (London, Cresset Press, 1955).

Greenfeld, Liah, *Nationalism: five roads to modernity* (Harvard, 1992).

Habermas, Jürgen, *Legitimation crisis* (London, Heinemann, 1979) [1973].

Habermas, Jürgen, 'Citizenship and national identity: some reflections on the future of Europe', *Praxis International*, 12, no 1 (1992), 1-19.

Hambden-Turner, Charles & Trompenaars, Fons, *The seven cultures of capitalism* (New York, Doubleday, 1993).

Hay, Denys, *Europe: the emergence of an idea* (Edinburgh, Edinburgh UP, 1957).

Hayes, Carlton J.H., *The historical evolution of modern nationalism* (New York, Macmillan, 1931).

Heater, Derek, *The idea of European unity* (London, Leicester UP, 1992).

Hewstone, Miles, *Understanding attitudes to the European Community: a social-psychological study in four member states* (Cambridge, CUP, 1986).

Hobsbawm, Eric J., *Nations and nationalism* (Cambridge, CUP, 1990).

Hofstede, Geert, *Culture's consequences* (Beverly Hills and London, Sage, 1980).

Keane, John, 'Questions for Europe', in B. Nelson, et al., eds, *The idea of Europe: problems of national and transnational identity* (New York, Berg, 1992), 55-60.

Kedourie, Ellie, *Nationalism* (New York, Praeger, 1960).

Kohn, Hans, *The idea of nationalism: a study in its origins and background* (New York, Collier-Macmillan, 1945).

Leerssen, J.T., 'On national identities and how to deal with them', in M. Spiering, ed., *Reader: Britain and Europe* (Amsterdam, University of Amsterdam, 1994), 29-33.

Leerssen, J.T., *Cultural differences and national images* (Amsterdam, Amsterdam UP, forthcoming).

Meyer Levin, Lawrence, *The political doctrine of Montesquieu's* Esprit des lois: *its classical background* (New York, Columbia University, 1936).

Mill, John Stuart, *Considerations on representative government* (London, 1861).

Milward, Alan, *The European rescue of the nation state* (London, Routledge, 1992).

Moor, R.A. de, 'Globalisering van de cultuur en nationale identiteit', in J. de Valk, ed., *Nationale identiteit in Europees perspectief* (Baarn, Ambo, 1993), 21-45.

Newman, Gerald, *The rise of English nationalism: a cultural history* (London, Weidenfeld & Nicolson, 1987).

O'Brien, Conor Cruise, *God's land: reflections on religion and nationalism* (Harvard University Press, 1988).

Parker, W.H., 'Europe: how far?', *Geographical Journal*, 126 (1960), 278-97.

Renan, Ernest, *Qu'est-ce qu'une nation?* (Leiden, Academic Press, 1994) [1882].

Roobol, W.H., 'What is Europe?', *Yearbook of European Studies*, 1 (1988), 187-206.

Rougemont, Denis de, translated by Alan Braley, *The meaning of Europe* (London, Sidgwick & Jackson, 1965) [first published 1963].

Rousseau, J.J., *Extrait du projet de paix perpétuelle de Monsieur l'Abbé de Saint-Pierre* (Amsterdam, 1761).

Smith, Anthony D., *National identity* (London, Penguin Books, 1991).

Smith, Anthony D., *Theories of nationalism* (London, Duckworth, 1971).

Spiering, M., *Englishness* (Amsterdam & Atlanta, Rodopi, 1993).

Stoddart of Swindon, Lord, 'The erosion of sovereignty', in Derek James, ed., *Bound and failing* (London, The Anti-Common Market League, 1987), 43-6.

Todorov, T. '"Race", writing, and culture', in *Critical Inquiry*, 13 (1986), 171-81.

Tönnies, Ferdinand, translated and edited by C.P. Loomis, *Community and society* (London, Routledge, 1955) [first published 1935].

Tucholsky, Kurt, *Zwischen Gestern und Morgen* (Hamburg, Rowohlt, 1952).

Valk, J. de, ed., *Nationale identiteit in Europees perspectief* (Baarn, Ambo, 1993).

Wilson, Kevin, & J. van der Dussen, eds, *The history of the idea of Europe* (London, Routledge, 1995).

Wood, Graham, *Maastricht: a Christian dilemma* (Yorkshire, Campaign for an Independent Britain, 1993).

Zacharasiewicz, Waldamar, *Die Klimattheorie in der englischen Literatur und Literaturkritik* (Stuttgart, Wilhelm Braumüller, 1977).

6 European identity and the process of European unification: Compatible notions?

Bram Boxhoorn

Throughout history the word 'Europe' has been debated and defined time after time. It has been used and - let us not forget - abused by statesmen, politicians, clergymen, and ordinary citizens in order to achieve various goals, and even now the word Europe is used in different meanings and different contexts. Three examples will suffice to make the point. A century ago, Otto von Bismarck remarked of Europe, 'On a tort de parler d'Europe. Notion géographique'; Aristide Briand said in the 1920s on the occasion of the signing of the Treaties of Locarno, 'Nous avons parlé européen'. A more recent use of the expression came from the re-appointed Commissioner for External Relations of the European Union, the Dutchman Hans van den Broek. After the traditional 'night of the long knives' in the autumn of 1994, when the Commissioners decide among themselves the division of labour in the Commission for the new period of government in Brussels, Van den Broek was delighted to have beaten his British rival Leon Brittan. He proudly announced that he would be solely responsible for European international relations, including the question of enlargement, in Eastern Europe. He described this field of activity as a 'future Great-Europe'. Russia's position in this 'Great-Europe', of course, is at yet unclear.

This article focuses on two notions at the centre of the historical and political debate: the process of European unification, and the idea of European identity. European politicians have argued - and some still continue to do so - that a clearly distinct European identity is needed in order to give the European Union a solid socio-intellectual and cultural base. It is often asserted, for example by the former Commission President Jacques Delors, that a Union needs an identity in order to be successful in replacing the European nation-states. In Delors' view (and it is a view shared by many others), this European identity consists of the diversity of cultures in Europe, 'unity in diversity' being the official formula. Others, however, have argued that this cultural diversity is a stumbling block to the unification process, since the diversity of European culture will be an effective weapon in the hands of those who instead favour

European co-operation on an intergovernmental basis, and who want to prevent the transition of the Union into a supranational entity.

We shall first examine certain aspects of the history of the idea of European unity; then some theoretical issues concerning the idea of identity in general, and European identity in particular, will be considered. The question will be posed of whether one can indeed speak of a European identity, and if so, of what it might consist. The main evidence scrutinized to answer these questions is found in the international European treaties, which lie at the heart of the process of European integration.

The idea of European unity

Numerous studies have been written on the history of the idea of Europe, and many historians have discovered 'plurality of conflicting interpretations' of Europe.[1] Europe can have a geographical, an ethnographical, or a historical meaning, and be used in these contexts accordingly.[2] But even when used in a single context, there is no consensus on what it actually means. The question of where the borders of Europe end in the East is only one heavily debated example. Similarly, there are endless debates about the ethnographical and historical meanings of the word Europe. Given these disagreements, it is all the more surprising to read in the Treaty of Maastricht that the parties to this treaty reaffirm their commitment 'to continue the process of creating an ever closer union among the peoples of Europe'. It would seem that in the mind of the signatories this notion of the 'peoples of Europe' is a self-evident construction.

In his influential study, *L'idée d'Europe dans l'histoire*, the French historian Jean-Baptiste Duroselle brings his study to a close by grouping ideas of Europe in three categories.[3] The idea of European unity is one of them. Clearly the idea of European unity is not a novel one. The German historian Foerster, in his *Europa. Geschichte einer politischen Idee*, gives an insight into the scale of production in the field of schemes for European unity. He lists more than 300 plans to unify Europe from the Middle Ages up to 1945.[4] They disagree on the question of what exactly is meant by 'Europe', and therefore on what the basis of European unity should be. From these plans it becomes evident that the idea of European unity should be interpreted in the main as a desire to impose some order on a chaotic, restless, and above all warlike European continent.

None of these plans fell on fertile ground. The idea of European unity did not succeed in developing into an significant, cogent political concept; indeed, the idea has lived a marginal existence. In the nineteenth century for example, during the heyday of nationalism, the embryonic idea of European unity fought an uphill fight. First Italian and then German unification marginalized the idea of European unity, reducing it to little more than an obsolete theoretical notion. However, in the twentieth century, the majority of the proposals for European unity have not shared the almost absolute and obscure qualities of the

134

nineteenth-century plans.

Some of the twentieth-century proposals for some form of European unity associate the economic and political decline of Europe with a degeneration of European culture. The German Oswald Spengler and the Spaniard Ortega y Gasset provide clear examples of such an approach. Ortega, together with others, proposed the achievement of a federal unity to remedy this decline. The best-known example was of course Count Richard Coudenhove-Kalergi's proposal of the 1920s, which clearly contained a defensive element: he saw his Pan-European union as an answer to the rise of American economic world supremacy.

The idea of European unity also found advocates in Fascist and totalitarian political circles. Of course there is a major difference with the other initiatives: these Fascist ideas were not based on democratic views or on an organization of Europe on a voluntary basis. This is not to say, however, as some have argued, that these proposals are non-European or even anti-European.[5] The authoritarian-Fascist governments valued the idea of European unity differently. In principle the Italian leader Mussolini was not opposed to the idea of a Pan-European unity. However, his version of a unified Europe would be founded on different terms. Mussolini and Coudenhove-Kalergi did in fact meet three times to discuss the idea. Only one conclusion, however, may be drawn from these meetings: neither seems to have been able to convince his counterpart. The German Nazis showed less patience with Coudenhove-Kalergi's project. Hitler himself ignored both the man and his ideas. He showed no interest at all in any idea of a federal Europe. No federal plan could stand his test of criticism.[6] Only after 1943, when it became more and more apparent that Nazi Germany would not win the war by military means alone, proposals concerning a so-called 'New Order' and 'New Europe' were launched by the German Foreign Office.

The non-Communist parts of the resistance movement in occupied Europe, including the German and Italian ones, also contributed to plans based on the idea of European unity.[7] The Resistance Charter, their plan for setting up a European Federation, was published in Geneva in 1944. In this document the European war was seen as a failure of the sovereign nation-states in Europe to maintain democracy and to guarantee human rights for its citizens. According to the draft, the nation-states were to be replaced by a united federal Europe. Yet there were different opinions held on the form of government to be taken. Should a European constitution form the basis of this federation? Should the co-operation concern itself with all matters of policy, or should it in principle be limited? In addition to this discussion, some of those present in Geneva envisaged a Socialist future, while others argued for a Christian-Democrat united Europe. The Charter did not proceed beyond the drafting stage.

At the Congress of Europe, held in The Hague in 1948, federalists decided to combine their efforts for the political unification of Europe. Winston Churchill had already asked for a 'kind of United States of Europe' in his famous speech

135

in Zurich in 1946. But what kind of United States? A federation or a union? The final result of the meeting in The Hague was embodied in the Council of Europe in 1949. Whatever the merits of this body, it is not the kind of institution that many of the federalists had in mind. The dichotomy between intergovernmental and supranational co-operation would become - and still is - the central theme in the process of Western European co-operation in the period after the war.

After 1945 further plans for unification were formulated: there were at least fifty official and less official plans for some degree of organization of Western Europe.[8] All these post-war plans differ in approach and scope; some are aimed at a 'deepening' of the existent working situation. Such is the case with the Schaüble-Lamers plan of 1994, named after two German MPs, which proposes the formation of a leading group of countries in the field of monetary co-operation. This multi-speed approach would mean in practice that the principle of unanimity, which is the major stumbling block in the process of decision-making at top level in the European Council and the Council of Ministers, could be circumvented. Schäuble, together with much of the political elite in Germany, considers monetary union to be the key to a political union, and so the strong preference for such a construction is understandable.

Not all plans are based on multi-speed, variable speed, *géometrie variable*, concentric circles, or whatever label is put on it. Some simply aim for the overthrow of the existing structures of the European Union. An extreme example of such a plan is Paul Johnson's Northern European Protestant Union. He proposes first to 'clean Europe's Augean stables', and to deal once and for all with the spectre of corruption, which he identifies with Southern European political life, France included. After this, a Northern Block should be formed, consisting of Denmark, the Netherlands, Germany and Britain, all of which are 'EC states with traditionally high standards of public probity'.[9]

Perhaps we must conclude that the continuity in European history is formed by this kind of planning activity; after all, it has developed into a distinct historical tradition. One can argue that the idea of European unity is a remarkably resilient one; however, paradoxically, it has little popular political appeal.

Identity and the European treaties

A majority of the post-war plans mentioned have implicit or explicit views on the core or the essence of the proposed structure or framework for Europe. Accordingly, discussion here will focus on the essence or the *innere Substanz* of Europe.[10] Nowadays the word identity is used frequently for this concept, but the issue is by no means a new one. As early as 1935, the well known study by Paul Hazard, *La crise de la conscience Européenne*, tried to resolve the issue of the essence or nature of European civilization. Today his answer ('Une pensée qui ne se contente jamais') remains both articulated and compelling. Pope John Paul II showed how form and content cannot be separated when he made reference to De Gaulle's definition of Europe as stretching from the Atlantic to the Urals (that is, excluding the USA). The Pope's vision, in contrast, was of a *Christian* Europe, stretching from the Atlantic to the Urals.

The question arises of why this issue of identity attracts so much academic attention.[11] The notion of the identity of a nation or people goes back to nineteenth-century Romantic ideas about nations.[12] Nowadays, it would seem, it serves at least two purposes: it is either a rationalization of historical experience, and thus used in retrospect, or it serves as a legitimation for present and future political actions. The studies by Ernest Gellner, Anthony Smith, Benedict Anderson, Elie Kedourie, Eric Hobsbawm, and others have made lasting contributions to the debate on nationalism and national identity. Although the results of their studies are difficult to compare, because they address the issues from different perspectives, it has become obvious that objective standards with which to define 'national identity' do not exist. The concept is a subjective one, and often ideologically inspired. However, other academic disciplines such as sociology and cultural anthropology have shown more confidence in using the term.[13]

It is uncertain who first coined the phrase 'European identity', in its modern sense. It might have originated in the early 1960s, when the first conflicts were occurring within the Atlantic Alliance. President Kennedy recognized the differing interests of the USA and its European partners when, in July 1962, he proclaimed his 'Declaration of Interdependence between the USA and a United Europe'. 'Identity' emerged more explicitly in the 1970s. B. de Witte has pointed out that, some twenty years ago, due to a combination of pessimistic economic perspectives in Western Europe and the feeling of a lack of legitimacy among the political establishment in the European Community, a new recipe for popular support for Europe was attempted. It was christened 'identity'. The purpose was to create a common sense of loyalty among the citizens towards the European institutions and thus, in the words of De Witte, 'to remedy some very basic defects of the integration mechanism as it had been delineated in the Community treaties.'[14] He distinguishes between an internal and an external form of identity. Internal identity refers to that which is brought about from within the Community, while external identity, in contrast, is the outcome of external recognition of the EU as an entity.

In the remaining part of this article, both the internal and external types of identity will be examined. To that end a more 'philological' approach to the texts produced by the EU will be employed, looking at the main treaties concluded in the European unification process. What kind of Europe emerges from these texts? The treaty establishing the ECSC and the Treaties of Rome do not refer to a particular image of Europe (although 'Europe' is invariably used in the texts, instead of the more appropriate 'Western Europe'). As De Witte has rightly pointed out, there is a tension between the short-term and the long-term image, between the achievement of the goal of a common market and the long-term image of 'an ever closer union'.[15]

A much-disputed formulation of European identity began to take shape in the Copenhagen Declaration on European identity in 1973, which was an attempt to define the external identity of the Community. It gives a brief summary of the external relations of the Community with the rest of the world. Relations with the USA were portrayed in the Declaration as less important than, and were mentioned after those with Eastern Europe, the Middle East, and Africa. Politically and commercially this was an absurd view of the interests of the EU. The final paragraph of the Declaration refers to a spontaneous process which was to bring about an external identity. This is ambiguous: it may reflect a 'collective feeling of identity', but more probably its 'very object ... is to amend the functionalist view and to launch a policy of conscious promotion of identity.'[16]

Identity was further promoted in several official reports and above all in the concept of a Citizen's Europe, which aimed at bringing 'Europe' closer to its citizens. However, the results have been modest. The identity issue was relaunched in the 1980s with the Solemn Declaration on the European Union (1983). The most eye-catching phrase concerned the proposal that European co-operation should be extended to the field of culture 'in order to affirm the awareness of a common cultural heritage as an element in the European identity.'[17] Shortly afterwards the concept of a Citizen's Europe was replaced by that of a People's Europe, and preparations were made for the creation of European symbols such as a flag, emblem, and anthem.

The notion of European identity appears again in the Single European Act of 1987, which states (Title III, 30(6)) that 'The High Contracting Parties consider that closer co-operation on questions of European security would contribute in an essential way to the development of a European identity in external matters.' Here, for the first time in a treaty, we encounter the external meaning of identity in the shape of the *defence* identity of the Community.

The next important treaty is that of Maastricht in 1991. In the preamble we read: 'Resolved to implement a common foreign and security policy including the eventual framing of a common defence policy, which might in time lead to a common defence, thereby reinforcing the European identity and its independence in order to promote peace, security and progress in Europe and the world.' Thus, through the establishment of a common defence, the European identity, and in particular its external identity, will be reinforced. Another reference to the external identity of the Union is made in the section entitled Common Provisions. In Article B we read that the Union sets as an objective 'to assert its identity on the international scene, in particular through the implementation of a common foreign and security policy including the eventual framing of a common defence policy, which might in time lead to a common defence'. Up to this point, the Maastricht Treaty uses the notion of 'identity' in an entirely consistent way, referring to a common defence and security policy. When we move to Article F of the Common Provisions, however, we encounter a quite different meaning. Here it states that 'The Union shall respect the national identities of its Member States, whose systems of government are founded on the principles of democracy'. It is obvious that here identity does *not* refer to issues of security and defence. Here, apparently, something different is meant by national identity. Since it mentions the 'systems of government' (F(1), Common Provisions), it might mean the recognition of plurality of political institutions in the Community. But the term 'identity' may also refer to the internal identity of the member states, arguing that the Union's policies will be compatible with their national identities.

On reading the Maastricht Treaty, one might expect more on the subject of identity in Titles VII and IX, dealing with education, vocational training, youth, and culture. But here no references are made either to the reinforcement of the European identity or to the recognition of national identities. Instead we read in Article 126(2) that the 'Community action shall be aimed at: developing the European dimension in education'; and in Article 128(1) that 'The Community shall contribute to the flowering of the cultures of the member States, while respecting their national and regional diversity and at the same time bringing the common cultural heritage to the fore.' Article 138a (Title XVII, Development Co-operation) is a new provision. It recognizes that political parties at the European level are an important factor for integration within the Union: 'They contribute to forming a European awareness and to expressing the political will of the citizens of the Union'. It is further resolved 'to encourage greater involvement of national parliaments in the activities of the European Union.'

Clearly, the context in which 'identity' is used differs from article to article. The use of identity in its external meaning, that is, referring to a common security and defence policy, is easily recognizable, and is compatible with earlier examples. References to identity in the internal meaning, however, referring to the 'essence' or 'substance' of the Union, are not to be found. Instead, it seems as if the EU's civil servants have substituted such expressions as 'European dimension' and 'European awareness', almost as if taken from a thesaurus.

The use of European identity as a reference to a common security and defence policy is resumed in the Declaration of the Maastricht Treaty on 'The Role of the Western European Union and its Relations with the European Union and the Atlantic Alliance'. The formulation is that the objective is to develop the WEU as a means of strengthening the European pillar of the Atlantic Alliance. '[The] WEU will act in conformity with the positions adopted in the Atlantic Alliance.' The continuity in the use of identity in its external meaning, thus referring to defence and security matters, was further confirmed in the Copenhagen Declaration by NATO of June 1991, and at the Rome summit in November 1991. External identity is formulated as follows. In Copenhagen it was stated that 'the creation of a European identity in security and defence will underline the preparedness of the Europeans to take a greater share of responsibility for their security'. In Rome the statement runs, 'the development of a European security identity and defence role ... will reinforce the integrity and effectiveness of the Atlantic Alliance ... [We] further agree that ... we will develop practical arrangements to ensure the necessary transparency and complementarity between the European security and defence identity as it emerges in the Twelve and the WEU, and the Alliance.'

From these legal texts it may be concluded that the external meaning of European identity has been used most consistently. Its meaning refers to a common position or common policy in defence and security matters, something which Henry Kissinger had hoped for when he was in office. It seems that the European allies have finally made attempts 'to speak with one voice', as Kissinger put it.

Identity and unification in Europe

In the light of these texts, are European identity and European unification compatible notions? Are they, historically speaking, mututally exclusive? Or are they destined to contribute in a positive way to the construction of a new 'European' nation-state? From the findings of the studies of Gellner, Anderson, and others on national identity it is clear that the notion of identity is an artificial construction. It is no more and no less than a shared and usually artificially constructed historical experience, memory, or myth, or a combination of the three. It has been used in the past to build up the European national states. But a national identity as such does not exist: it is an image. The idea of a homogeneous national community, whether defined in religious, social, or linguistic terms, is a fallacy, as Charles Tilly has rightly argued.[18] This then applies *a fortiori* to Europe, since there is no such a thing as a European people. This is in fact what the Maastricht Treaty implies. Article 128(2) states that 'Action by the Community shall be aimed ... in the following areas: ... improvement of the knowledge and dissemination of the culture and history of the *European peoples*' [italics added].

When the results of these studies are applied to the question of the construction of a European identity, what then can be established? Obviously, this construction of a European identity will lead to an imagined entity, to borrow Anderson's words. Common traditions, such as the flag and an anthem, should support this, as has been the case with the European nation-states.[19] There are other inventions of tradition which may contribute to or reinforce the feeling of cohesion amongst the European peoples. Probably the most efficient way to reinforce a common feeling would be through the education systems of the EU. A standardized curriculum at primary school may be the key to this, and indeed was recommended by the European Parliament some ten years ago. The proposal, however, amounted to re-writing history. It suggested, for example, changing the names of main streets and railway stations which keep alive the memory of the major battlefields in European history. This would result in Waterloo Station in London being renamed, perhaps after a previous President of the Commission. It should be remembered that the practice of re-writing history in the Soviet Union did little to prevent its disintegration.

In the 1970s, the time of Euro-pessimism, identity was seen as a panacea for all problems in the EC. In the 1980s a new mood prevailed, that of Euro-optimism, due to more favourable economic prospects and a dynamic presidency of the European Commission. From the treaties it is clear that in the 1970s and 1980s identity was applied as a tool to bring some cohesion to the EC. Increasingly the essence of that *internal* identity was put forward in the formula of 'unity in diversity'. Its origins are obscure, but it is essentially a commonplace, little more than a rhetorical exercise. The forces for creating an internal European identity, such as language, history, political culture, and religion, do not add up to a solid basis. A single European language seems out of the question, although opinions do differ on the unity of European culture.[20] It makes more sense, as Alan Smith has argued, to speak of a European family of cultures,[21] a partial echo of De Gaulle's 'family of nations'.

The EU has made full use of the concept of identity in applying it to the field of external relations. In this sense, identity can be equated with security and foreign policy, and clearly a common position in such fields is of major importance to the Union. A stable international European order can be attained only if there is, in Kissinger's words, 'a generally accepted legitimacy'.[22] To date, however, the results of this common foreign policy have hardly been promising. The task of finding a common position has become more difficult in the absence of a potential enemy. Nor is it easy to define a unique destiny, since the Soviet bloc has ceased to serve as a viable counter-example, and all European countries now have adopted the principle of the market economy.

In the debate on the identity question, the national discourses prevail. In her widely reported speech at the Collège d'Europe in Bruges, Margaret Thatcher emphasized British commitment to the continent and made it clear that British history is part and parcel of European history. Typically for her view, she also incorporated into this British view on Europe the special relationship with the USA, which serves more as an illustration of the self-image of part of the British political establishment than as a realistic approach to American-British relations. In this context she fell back on the paradigm of Atlantic identity, giving a broad definition of Europe, defining it as 'that Europe on both sides of the Atlantic'.[23]

The definition of identity, then, is a hard issue to tackle. Its meaning depends on the self-image of the country and the image of Europe in the national historical and political discourse.[24] There does not exist one single image of Europe, but a variety of images, such as a German Europe, a French Europe, a British Europe. From this viewpoint it is clear that European identity and unification are hard to combine because of the lack of homogeneity both in European culture and in the definition of terms and images. Unification

141

supposes harmonization, in economics and law as well; after all, the origins of the EU are socio-economic. Yet it cannot be simply be imposed in all fields, in former Soviet style. Bureaucratic planning has its limitations, although this may be hard to accept for those who believe in the power of Brussels to forge a European nation-state from its present members.

Conclusion

From the investigation of the use of identity in the formal treaties of recent decades, the following conclusion may be drawn. Identity emerged in the 1970s to repair the deficiencies of the integration process. It was used in internal and external senses, in an attempt to bring about, respectively, more internal cohesion and a common foreign policy. In the 1980s the double meaning of 'identity' was continued. Projects such as a Citizens' Europe and a People's Europe signified, in theory, a vigorous policy aimed at strengthening the image of the Community by propagating elements of loyalty and symbols. With the end of the Cold War a setback occurred. The Maastricht Treaty is surprisingly modest in its use of the concept of internal identity. It even states explicitly that the national identities of the member states should be respected. This is a reversal of earlier policies, and may be due to the introduction of that theoretically vague but politically powerful concept of subsidiarity, which leaves more room for member-states to adopt an independent national stance on European policy issues, and thus weakens Brussels as a centre of policy-making.

The search for an external definition of identity, a common foreign and security policy, shows more continuity. Since the end of the Cold War the Europeans have been encouraged to take care of their own security interests, and to rely less on the American military deterrent which has operated since 1945. If the recent experiences in the former Yugoslavia can tell us anything, it is that there still is a long way to go in determining an external identity.

Of course one could ask whether the process of co-operation in Europe could not equally successfully be continued without an European identity. The demise of the Cold War has put an end to the Europe guided by the immediate post-war lessons of Monnet, Schuman, and Adenauer on the prevention of wars. The real problems of Europe today lie not in the search for an internal identity, but elsewhere. The end of the Cold War and of bipolarity liberated millions of people from oppressive regimes. There is a reverse side to this coin. While with the end of the Cold War, Europe's nations and nationalities now have more liberty to determine their own future than at any time since 1945, this new post-Cold War situation in Europe endangers the relative stability of the European continent. Also, due to the process of German unification, the position of France as well that of other countries has further been marginalized. Germany considers the European Monetary Union to be the cornerstone of the

142

Political Union. But what will happen if the Monetary Union is not established? Will the Bonn-Paris axis (soon to be Berlin-Paris) have outlived its usefulness? Will it be replaced by an equilibrium reminiscent of the nineteenth century? Or is this highly unlikely, given Germany's economic and political weight in Europe? It is this kind of material problem which really matters today.

Anthony Smith has argued that in the future people in the EU may experience double identities, or - more modestly - double loyalties. A double loyalty would consist of a national level, comprising a cultural dimension or orientation, and a supranational or European level, comprising a political dimension or orientation.[25] But he overlooks a fact of key importance: culture and politics can seldom be separated. Since the political cultures of the EU members differ a great deal (to say nothing of the future Eastern European members), it is hard to imagine how they could ever attain a common position. The differences in political culture contradict that official formula of 'unity in diversity'. Rather, a degree of unity can be obtained only if the variety of cultures is restricted dramatically. Since this would be an impossible policy, and counter-productive to boot, it is difficult to understand how unification and diversity can ever be reconciled.

Notes

1. Some key works: Duroselle, *L'idée d'Europe*; Hay, *Europe: the emergence of an idea*; Wilson & Van der Dussen, eds, *The history of the idea of Europe*.

2. Roobol, 'Europese identiteit', 6.

3. Duroselle, *L'idée d'Europe*, 316.

4. Foerster, *Europa*.

5. Cf. Salewski, 'Ideas of the National Socialist government and party', 54.

6. See Neulen, *Europa und das 3. Reich*.

7. See Lipgens, vol. II, p. 202ff.

8. Inventarized in a research project in the Department of European Studies, University of Amsterdam.

9. Johnson, 'Cleansing Europe's Augean stables'. Dr M. Spiering of the University of Amsterdam and contributor to this volume, collects anti-EC material from various countries, in particular from Britain, and brought this text to my attention.

10. See Roobol, 'What is Europe?'.

11. In France in particular. See e.g. *La conscience européenne*; Girault, ed., *Identité et conscience européennes*.

12. Cf. Mosse, *The culture of Western Europe*, part I, Chapters 1-6.

13. In particular, social scientists working on cross-cultural research in international management and business studies have used the concept of national identity. Some well-known researchers who work in this field include Nancy J. Adler, Charles Hampden-Turner, Geert Hofstede, and Fons Trompenaars.

14. De Witte, 'Building Europe's image', 134.

15. Ibid., 133. De Witte rightly assumes that the functionalist theory did not require a common political goal; there is considerable doubt, however, whether the founding fathers of the EEC were led by these theoretical reflections. See e.g. Duchêne, *Jean Monnet*.

16. De Witte, 'Building Europe's image', 135.

17. Ibid., 136.

18. Tilly, *Europese revoluties*, 54.

19. See Lager, 'Europe d'azur et d'or'.

20. Cf. Fuhrmann, 'L'Europe'; on the issue of language, see Fettes, 'Europe's Babylon'.

21. Smith, 'National identity'.

22. See the introduction to Kissinger, *A world restored*, 1.

23. See Roobol, 'In search of an Atlantic identity'.

24. Wilson & Van der Dussen, eds, *The history of the idea of Europe*, 181 ff.

25. Smith, 'National identity'.

References

Conscience européenne au XVe et au XVIe siecle, La [Actes du Colloque international organisé à l'Ecole Normale Supérieure des Jeunes Filles (30 September - 3 October 1980)] (Paris 1982).

Duchêne, F., *Jean Monnet: the first statesman of interdependence* (New York/London, 1994).

Duroselle, J.-B., *L'idée d'Europe dans l'histoire* (Paris, 1963).

Fettes, Mark, 'Europe's Babylon: towards a single European language', *History of European Ideas*, 13 no 3 (1991), 201-213.

Foerster, R.H., *Europa. Geschichte einer politischen Idee* (Munich, 1967).

Fuhrmann, Manfred, 'L'Europe - contribution à l'histoire d'une idée culturelle et politique', *History of European Ideas*, 4 no 1 (1983), 1-15.

Girault, R., ed., *Identité et conscience européennes au XXe siecle* (s.l., 1994).

Hay, D., *Europe: the emergence of an idea* (Edinburgh, 1957).

Johnson, Paul, 'Cleansing Europe's Augean stables', *The Sunday Telegraph* (20 October 1991).

Kissinger, H., *A world restored. Metternich, Castlereagh, and the problems of peace 1812-1822*, (Boston Mass., 1957).

Lager, Carole, 'Europe d'azur et d'or. Histoire et interprétation symbolique du drapeau européen', *Historiens de l'Europe Contemporaine*, 9, nos 1-2 (June 1994), 61-86.

Lipgens, W., ed., *Documents on the history of European integration*, 3 vols (Berlin, 1985-88).

Mosse, G.L., *The culture of Western Europe: the nineteenth and twentieth centuries*, third edition (Boulder & London, 1988).

Neulen, H. W., *Europa und das 3. Reich. Einigungsbestrebungen im deutschen Machtsbereich, 1939-1945* (Munich, 1987).

Roobol, W.H., 'What is Europe?', *Yearbook of European Studies*, 1(1988), 187-204.

Roobol, W.H., 'In search of an Atlantic identity', *Yearbook of European Studies*, 4 (1991), 1-14.

Roobol, W.H., 'Europese identiteit geen noodzaak voor politieke eenheid', *Staatscourant*, 38 (2 February 1995), 6.

Salewski, Michael, 'Ideas of the National Socialist government and party', in W. Lipgens, ed., *Documents on the history of European integration* (Berlin/New York), pp. 37-54.

Smith, Anthony D., 'National identity and the idea of European unity', *International Affairs*, 68 no 1 (1992), 55-76.

Tilly, Charles, *Europese revoluties 1492-1992* [translation of *European Revolutions 1492-1992*] (Amsterdam, 1993).

Wilson, Kevin & Jan van der Dussen, eds, *The history of the idea of Europe* (London, 1995).

Witte, B. de, 'Building Europe's image and identity', in A. Rijksbaron et al., eds, *Europe from a cultural perspective* (The Hague, 1987), pp. 132-139.

7 When East goes West: The political economy of European re-integration in the post-Cold War era

David Willis

This chapter considers the origins and effects on the development of East-West economic relations in the post-Cold War period of a belief that both Eastern and Western security interests are best served by the creation of an environment favourable to the development of a capitalist market economy. Although the creation of a 'market economy without epithets'[1] has been widely seen as a necessary condition for the reversal of the influence of the Communist hegemony in Eastern Europe, which will help these economies to 'return to the West', there has been growing evidence that the manner in which the reforms have been introduced, and the reliance on the state to dismantle itself, is contributing to a replication of many of the failings of the old system. Indeed, a reliance on market mechanisms *per se*, and the adoption of a 'big bang' competitive market remedy, has been increasingly viewed as giving rise to high political costs which threaten not only to undermine popular support for economic liberalization, but also the stability of the newly created democratic states, and as contributing at the very least to a reversal of the convergence on liberal democratic norms.

With the collapse of the bipolar system and Soviet hegemony in Eastern Europe, the security implications and dilemmas resulting from the emergence of new states, and the re-emergence or consolidation of old coalitions of states through regional economic co-operation and rivalries, have increasingly moved centre-stage in international relations. Thus the fragmentation of the global system, and Europe, into rival regions has been widely seen as a threat both to international security, and to the multilateral regimes established under US hegemony in the post-war period. The regionalization of the global and European economy has also been seen as a crucial change in the character of the international system. However, the political significance has been the subject of conflicting interpretations, which see regionalization either as a contribution to economic liberalization and the re-integration of the European economies, or as a renewal of trade-bloc rivalries.

European regional economic co-operation has been portrayed, within federalist theories, as offering a new paradigm and repertoire for the management both of regionally based conflict and of threats to international security. Regional co-operation, based on the recognition of economic interdependencies and the high costs of efforts to maintain territorial integrity and authority, has thus been viewed as having an application to problems of conflict management in a potentially wide variety of cases, where nationalistic and 'balance of power' solutions seem inappropriate or ineffectual. Examples include the problems of 'Balkanization' in Eastern Europe, the accommodation of nationalistic demands for greater autonomy from unitary states, the dilemmas of international responses to secessionist movements, and the need to create a system of European citizens' rights appropriate to the development of a 'Europe without frontiers'.

This chapter seeks to review the evidence on the political rationale for efforts to encourage the East to 'move West'. It focuses in particular on the arguments concerning the contribution of a 'Pax Europeana' to democratic transitions and stability in Eastern Europe. With the increasing complexity and institutionalization of transnational linkages, theories on the contribution of regional economic integration to peace have advanced beyond the simple Cobdenite theory that trade liberalization promotes peace. In particular, the high costs of inter-state conflicts arising from economic interdependencies, which have resulted from a more complex international division of labour, have been seen as making great-power conflict increasingly unlikely. Thus the observation of the effects of the liberalization of trade and financial markets on inter-state relations has led to a more positive view of the role of transnational and regionally based political authority and political movements, and of their role in shaping international society and international relations, in comparison with former theories of order enforced by gun-boat diplomacy.

The contribution of economic liberalization to more pacific economic relations is a long-standing theme in international relations, but its realism has been much disputed by neo-realist theorists. How plausible then is the claim of an increasingly protectionist EU as an agency for promotion of liberal values, and how far does the experience of regime transformation since the collapse of Cold War divisions support the claims frequently advanced for liberal economic and political systems in creating a basis for peace between rival states?[2]

At its most optimistic, in theories on the contribution of economic liberalization to the rise of cosmopolitan values and transnational political movements independent of the state, there appears to be an attractive alternative to post-modernist critiques of liberal ideology. Thus accounts of the EC integration and liberalization process in particular suggest the increasing detachment of liberal ideologies and institutions as instruments of hegemonic powers, and their importance in building up a European constitution on the basis of liberal economic principles - suggesting an impetus provided by common markets to the development and recognition of civil and economic rights independent of national identity. Indeed, at the extreme, the impetus given to the development of international rights by regional and global economic liberalization has been seen as representing a major challenge to the traditional system of states in which individual rights are defined solely by reference to state authority and territorial jurisdiction.[3]

Finally, the extent to which international diplomacy involving regional interests may depart from conventional models of international relations (which treat states as unitary actors, and negotiators as actors within a hierarchy of power) needs to be re-considered in the light of the increasing role of regional associations in international relations and conflict management. One extreme view of these developments is that regional economic integration is part of a much wider process of internationalization of the European economies, which is contributing to the break-down of the system of European nation-states, effectively undermining the traditional model of international order based on the sovereignty of the state.

The much looser (and often more informal) networks of international diplomacy and interaction resulting from regional economic co-operation, and the scope for the formation of coalitions of interest cutting across national boundaries, is thus seen as contributing to an increasing interpenetration of domestic and international politics, and to new areas of uncertainty in the conduct of international relations and enforcement of agreements between states, but also to a questioning of solutions to regional conflicts of interest which depend upon principles of territorial integrity, the sovereignty of nation states, and their ability to represent complex regional interests.

East moves West?

The claims of political groups to deep-rooted sources of cultural identity, particularly when linked to ethnicity, religion or language, has generally been treated with suspicion by political scientists and sociologists, who find good grounds for viewing such differences as politically constructed to serve the interests of political or economic elites. However, as Neumann notes in the case of the Central European debate, the importance of identity politics to more long-term strategic objectives has not been lost on the participants in the debate.[4] Peter Gklotz, a German Social Democrat, has argued for the use of the concept of Mitteleuropa, to be wielded 'as an instrument in a second phase of détente policy'.[5] However disingenuous this may appear to be at one level, given the connotations in some parts of Eastern Europe, the comment nevertheless reveals the extent to which politicians have sought consciously to exploit perceptions of cultural identity to further economic or political interests. It also highlights the extent to which such identities are subject to contention, thus raising fundamental questions about the reasons for one conception of collective or cultural identity prevailing over another. George Schöpflin, for example, has argued the merits of efforts to develop a Central European identity, seeing this as 'a viable way of re-Europeanizing the area ... of recovering some of the values, ideals, aspirations, solutions and practices that were eliminated by Soviet-type systems.'[6]

There are then, external (alliance building) implications of different nuances in claims to cultural and regional identity. A distinction has been drawn between Mitteleuropa, reflecting 'German interests and purposes', and Central Europe 'as discussed in Warsaw, Prague, Budapest and Vienna'. As Neumann puts it,

> Mitteleuropa and Central Europe are merely shorthand for conglomerates of loosely similar imagined communities, whose proponents try to convince a maximum number of other people to imagine them as they do.[7]

Neumann further argues that regional collective identity is thus not a question of a historical development of cultural identity, that is, of how a region can be defined, but rather, the political interests and context of particular actors seeking to develop a myth of regional identity: 'Why do certain people, at a certain point in history, within a certain political context, try to build a region?'[8]

One view that has emerged in the political science literature on regional economic integration is that the region is yet another 'site' of political conflict over identity and definition of interest. For Anderson, imagined national identities or cultural communities are a means of manipulating or building a sense of collective identity in support of often concealed political and economic interests.[9] A problem here is that a 'pre-history' and economic and political rationale can be found for almost any of the many conflicting conceptions of the European integration project or for the 'national' interest and identity. An alternative way of looking at the attempt of East European politicians to adopt liberal values is that this is a strategy of political elites to detach themselves from association with the 'East' and reattach themselves to the 'West'. This is to be viewed less as a political struggle than a diplomatic ploy to mobilize external and internal support for a system which gives greater freedom from the state as the definer of individual economic interests and preferences.

Historians emphasizing cultural and philosophical identities with Western liberal values have tended to reject a juxtaposition of 'Central' and 'Eastern' identities as inadequate, preferring (in Brzezinski's terms) a less relativistic, more diachronic conception.[10] Both Brzezinski and Bojtár have argued that Central Europe has been a cultural and philosophical identity for two hundred years or more, to which the term 'Eastern' would be misapplied.[11] Whilst this approach emphasizes the artificiality of the political and economic map created by the bipolar system and Russian hegemonic influence, there is a danger that such a formulation - based on notions of common identity, or shared European value systems - falls into the trap of seeking to impose identity on a culturally

149

heterogeneous society, contributing to the hegemony of a particular ethnic group. In other words, it contributes to a geopolitical conception which potentially negates the universality of market systems and associated political structures - the creation of a 'Europe without frontiers'.

Kristian Gerner has argued that the growing rivalry and lack of consensus between the central European states, which has emerged from the collapse of the Pax Sovietica in 1989-1990, gives the lie to aspirations to a collective European and particularly a Central European identity.[12] There is thus no such thing as Central Europe, and no reality in the different identities claimed, other than a conflict of identity and the attempt of politicians to use or even construct national mythologies in efforts to mobilize political support for their causes. There is, rather, a swing between Easternization and Westernization of the Central European states. Moreover, different intellectual traditions have surfaced. A common regional identity distinct from both East and West has been developed in particular by Hungarian proponents of the ideal of 'Central Europe'.[13] However, László Kis, speaking from a Hungarian perspective, develops a notion of a common European identity, and develops a notion of Europe as a 'common cultural homeland', arguing that, despite political divisions, Europe constitutes 'a single cultural whole, with a diversity of links that even the Cold War years could not dissever.'[14]

The Western orientation of the East European states, their association with Western values of liberal market capitalism and liberal democracy, and the re-awakening of the debate on the Central European identity distinctive from that of Russia or 'the East', have thus been reinforced by geopolitical and economic considerations, and have played on these in efforts to build Western support for market-oriented reforms and the right to self-determination.

Alternative, more geopolitical conceptions have been advanced which caution against the liberalization thesis. The novelist Danilo Kis has thus taken issue with the more symbolic formulations of Central European identity. Particular targets of criticism were Jacques Morin's notion of Europe as a 'concept without borders', and Bruno Bauwer's thesis that 'Europe is a community of destinies', formulations which Kis dismisses as almost meaningless in the light of the historical experiences of Central European states.[15] Garton Ash has similarly emphasized a geopolitical conception of Central Europe re-emerging well before the collapse of the Soviet Union. He thus refers to 'those countries that [before 1914] whilst subsumed in one of the three great multinational empires [Austro-Hungarian, Prussian German, and Russian], managed through these periods of imperial dominion to preserve major elements of Western traditions' (Western Christianity, the rule of law, separation of powers, constitutional government and civil society).[16]

Although these cultural identifications of the East European states with 'Western' traditions may be very real, it is the contribution made to the re-orientation towards the institutions and philosophies of liberal market economy which appears to be of significance, rather than the insistence on a geopolitical or national cultural identity, which has, for the most part, remained confined to an intelligentsia, and has proved inconclusive and at times incoherent and impractical as a guide to action.[17]

To summarize the argument so far, the notion of European regional identities has re-emerged with the collapse of the bipolar system, and, in Central Europe, has involved an effort of political elites to dissociate their national identity from that of 'Eastern Europe', especially Russia, and to associate more closely with the West, or an independent cultural and philosophical tradition (including market economy and liberal institutions), which links the Central European states more closely with the Western club of liberal economies. But has this been merely a symbolic device - a case of myth-making in the interests of reclaiming 'Western identity' - or has it contributed to a major shift in the centre of gravity in Europe and to new perspectives on European re-integration as a basis of European security and collective identity?

What the intellectual debate has brought forward is the idea of a regional alliance as a bridgehead to membership of the Western clubs of nation states, notably the EC and NATO. This appears to have been paramount in a number of Central European co-operative agreements, for example the Visegrad and Pentagonale initiatives.[18] The concessions to which these have led (notably the Association agreements between the Central European states and the EC) appear to have been won by the success of the diplomacy in establishing the importance to Western security of continuing support from the West for economic liberalization, rather than shared regional interests. That liberalization entails a liberal democracy underpinned by parliamentarianism, liberal market economy, and a subordination of the state to civil society.[19]

The role of the EU in constructing a 'Pax Europeana'

It has long been appreciated that regional economic co-operation, particularly the prominence of security concerns and the objective of regional conflict reduction in the federalist conception of the European Union, has provided the basis of an alternative paradigm of international relations and international conflict management in which the autonomous nation-state has a subordinate role.[20] A core assumption in theories of globalization and economic interdependence is that sensitivity of individual states to each others' economic and security interests will increase in proportion to the degree of economic interpenetration and interdependence. From both a federalist and a traditional liberal perspective, peace-inducing interdependencies can be accelerated by deliberate efforts to liberalize trade and abolish barriers to capital and labour mobility. Others have gone so far as to argue that the consequences of the internationalization of production, and of the penetration of domestic economies resulting from liberalization and the growth of foreign direct investment, is the collapse of the meaningfulness of distinctions between the

151

domestic and the international realms. Thus domestic security, traditionally the arena of domestic politics, and indeed national political agendas and structures, will be increasingly shaped by external factors and decision-makers. It can be argued that the nation-state is now essentially a permeable structure, a change which renders unworkable Keynesian systems of the management of demand and international regimes, in an increasingly turbulent international environment with little respect for national frontiers.

The importance of these problems in accounting for changes in approach to the management of international relations is well recognized in international regime theory concerned with the emergence of and limits to co-operative behaviour in the international system. The potential for conflict between the demands on national elites to maintain co-operative relationships and for 'regime compliance', particularly as a condition of multilateral aid, and the need to maintain domestic support, is also beginning to receive systematic attention, notably in 'omnibalancing theory'.[21]

The evidence of emerging tensions between EU Ostpolitik and, further afield, common policies towards aid to the economic development of the South (under the Lomé Conventions) has led many political scientists to question the ability of the EU to act as a pole for the re-integration of Europe, and to doubt its likely emergence as a 'liberal hegemon' with the ability to promote economic liberalization in the region, whether on an Atlanticist US/UK-dominated model of a free market, or along the lines of the German social market economy. Conflicts between internal pressures for protectionism and the economic gains from an 'outward orientation', to use IMF and World Bank language, seem already evident in the recognition of an emergent 'Fortress Europe' in response to Eastern pressures for economic liberalization and the extension of EU membership to encompass the former Socialist economies.

Such conflicts are likely to be particularly endemic to liberal democracies, and to members of common markets. Areas of policy-making in which tensions have become evident between considerations of external security and coalition maintenance on the one hand, and maintenance of domestic support on the other, include the impact of liberalization on the corporatist consensus, notably in disagreements between Britain and the eleven, and between representatives of labour and internationally oriented businesses on the completion of the 'social dimension' of the Single European Market. Another example is the growing political conflict associated with economic migration and minority-group rights, again exacerbated by the abolition of obstacles to labour and capital mobility; and yet another is the conflict in policies towards Eastern Europe between security considerations, which argue for further steps toward liberalization in support of East European economic and political reforms, and concerns with the maintenance of internal security, threatened by growing resentment of economic refugees and the downward pressures on labour markets resulting from liberalization of trade relations with the 'low wage' economies of Eastern Europe. The entry of both legal and illegal immigrants into the EEC (estimated at some 13m in 1992) has become a key focus of concern for negotiators and a major test of the ability of Common Market authorities to maintain the volition toward further liberalization. On the one hand, political pressures for more restrictive policies towards economic refugees constitute the true 'Fortress Europe', and are symptomatic of a retreat to nationalism. Thus the economic burdens threatened by mass economic migration are widely seen as a cause of the rise of the extreme right wing and xenophobic sentiments in Western Europe, and of the exacerbation of problems of accommodating non-citizen and minority-group rights in majoritarian systems. Similar problems have been experienced by Russia, with the break-up of the Soviet Union, which has increasingly looked to the international community to defend the rights of those expatriates in former republics of the Soviet Union. In the West, the paradoxical response to East-West liberalization has similarly been a growth of right-wing nationalism opposed to the development of 'a Europe without frontiers', in favour of a return to principles of national sovereignty and autarchy, and willing to use violence to defend the interests of nationals.

A consideration of domestic security suggests a nationalistic response, for example by a narrower definition of citizenship. However, a consideration of common security interests, together with the need for continuing support for liberalization in Eastern Europe and the internal logic of the Single Market (the extension of economic rights to ensure the freedom of movement of capital and labour), all suggest that major departures may be necessary from principles of nationally determined economic and political rights.

A significant contribution of common markets to the international management of tensions associated with economic migration is shown by the extent to which they have become forcing grounds for the development of political institutions expressing the rights of minorities, particularly those of immigrant or migrant workers. Given the long experience which the EEC and EFTA have had in dealing with the civil rights problems associated with political refugees, and more recently the development of transnational economic rights associated with the completion of the Single Market (the Social Chapter), the EEC may prove to be a model which might be followed by other states facing tensions between the freedom of movement associated with liberalization, and national identity. Thus whilst immigrants enjoy a limited right to vote (in local elections) in only a handful of countries (Ireland, Scandinavia, the Netherlands, the Jura and the Neuchatel Cantons in Switzerland), the legal systems generally allow immigrants to join secondary organizations such as trade unions, and to form their own organizations, including political parties. Empirical evidence concerning the involvement of such groups in transnational political organizations aimed at influencing both domestic and foreign policies appears to be consistent with the predictions of neo-functionalist groups on the impetus given by regional economic integration to the formation of transnational pressure groups. The concern of such groups

153

with the development of civil rights independent of national identity and residence, and to maintain freedom of movement, also suggests that common markets may play an important role in fostering transnational systems of rights, though recent critics of the Social Chapter have suggested that these are restricted to economic rights.

Finally, there are strong a priori grounds for expecting that the rise of ethnic nationalism, particularly separatist movements, may be best contained within a loose framework of regions with a stronger set of minority civil rights, rather than secessionist movements, or, as in the Bosnian crisis, efforts to make ethnic and national territorial boundaries contiguous. The emergence of a 'Europe of the Regions' and of concepts of minority-group rights therefore seems significant not only because of the implications for the dominance of the unitary state in the EU decision-making structures, with the opportunities provided for direct participation of representatives of the regions (for example the German Länder), but also because of the contribution of such developments to a looser and more informal and complex network for the conduct of international relations. This may be of particular importance in helping the non-unitary states deal with their own internal differences and regional cleavages. A wider regional context for foreign policy and the conduct of external economic relations therefore seems likely to be particularly attractive to countries which already have a federal structure (notably Belgium, Germany and Spain), a strong regional basis to economic policy (the Netherlands), or where strong regional identity and economic cleavages have contributed to pressures for independence of regional and local government from the centre (especially the Lombard League in Italy, and the Basque and Catalan greater regional autonomy in the new Spanish constitution).

The impetus given by the formation of common markets for a looser, less territorially bounded configuration of civil rights has potential implications for the management of national economic relations. The scope for resolving problems of 'Balkanization' through stronger protection for minority rights has received considerable attention in the response to the problems of minority-group repression in the former Yugoslavia. The Council of Europe, for example, has proposed a (Pan-) European Committee for the Protection of Minorities,[22] in which persecuted minority groups would have recourse to a transnational authority or to transnationally constituted mediation mechanisms. A similar proposal for the establishment of an arbitration mechanism has been made through the auspices of the CSCE European Committee for the protection of minorities, which would act as a last resort in the event of the failure of conflicting parties to nominate arbitrators, and which would also have the authority to draft procedural rules governing arbitration. Recent efforts to revive the institutions of international trusteeship, free from the connotation of neo-colonialism or the tutelage of hegemonic powers, is another instance.

Multilateral support for East European liberalization

The promotion of a convergence of the East European states and the successor states of the Soviet Union on Western economic values, broadly described as 'liberalization', but more accurately simply involving greater emphasis on market-based economic systems (marketization), has been widely viewed as entailing more than economic liberalization. The European Bank for Reconstruction and Development (EBRD), created within the framework of the Bretton Woods institutions and of the CSCE (aimed at promoting East-West economic co-operation and integration), regularly refers specifically to liberal economic objectives, like the private ownership of capital, but also to the development of political institutions characteristic of liberal democracies, making the development of these a condition of continuing economic aid. The element of political conditionality in the economic assistance of the World Bank and IMF has become increasingly explicit since the adoption of responsibilities for 'structural reforms' in the mid-1980s, whilst the policies of the European Community towards both financial aid, and possible enlargement, have included an explicit requirement for political as well as economic liberalization.

This heavy hand in dictating political reforms on a Western model might be regarded in some respects as essentially a hegemonic project, and has been cynically interpreted as laying down as a condition of either market entry or membership of the EU desiderata not even attained in the Western liberal democracies. However, there are several grounds for considering Western assistance as critical to democratic outcomes of the transitions occurring in Eastern Europe.

The most forceful claim on the virtues of economic liberalization from a democratic perspective involves assertions on the contribution which privatization can make to the dismantling of authoritarian states, and to the replacement of central 'command' by the more decentralized power structures of a market economy. This is seen, in turn, as essential to the separation of economy, civil society, and political society. Up until the revolutions of 1989, the conventional wisdom with respect to Mikhail Gorbachev's domestic reforms was that, whilst these might well enhance Western security, 'there was little the West could do to make the outcome more likely.'[23] Since the fall of the Soviet system, opinion on this score has changed, and talk has increasingly turned to the need for a new Marshall Plan to aid the process of economic and political reconstruction along liberal capitalist lines.

The major sources of leverage available to the EU are five. First, there is the use of trade-bloc relations, for example the exercise of the kind of 'imperial preference' associated with the Lomé Convention on EC-African economic relations. Second, the 'carrot' of membership of the EU can be used, principally through Association agreements which insist on policy reforms and economic convergence. Third, there is potential leverage (again carrot and stick) in the international financial institutions, notably the IMF, the World Bank and the newly created EBRD. Fourth, influence can be exerted by European multinationals and foreign direct investment in resourcing and directing economic modernization. Finally the 'West', and the EU in particular, can act as a role-model and reference group for reforming elites and electorates well placed in the new economic opportunity structures created by liberalization.

A major test of the theory of regional economic integration which favours both economic and political liberalization and the new 'Ostpolitik' must be the extent to which practical assistance or trade concessions have matched the shortfalls of East European economies resulting from the break-up of the CMEA and from the extent of their economic dependence on the Soviet Union. The symbolic gestures and rhetoric of the EU towards Eastern Europe have been clearly confident of the correctness of liberalization. The collapse of the Communist regimes in Eastern Europe was followed by a flurry of diplomatic activity and economic assistance to liberalization: the EC established the PHARE programme, pledging $1.3 billion for Polish and Hungarian reconstruction. The creation of the EBRD for Eastern Europe explicitly linked political and economic liberalization with Western security interests, and, both in its written constitution and membership (multilateral, serviced by bankers from the private sector), was liberal in the model of the IMF - with the possible exception of a slightly more democratic political constitution.

Yet the imposition of political and economic conditionality has itself been a contradictory process (as are those of the IMF and World Bank), in effect restructuring the political agendas of the newly autonomous states and new-found democracies according to liberal economic precepts, in particular extensive private ownership. Moreover, the extent of actual financial aid and tariff concession has fallen short of estimated requirements. Indeed, the financial agreements have increasingly been seen in Eastern Europe as a packaging of what is in effect a 'turnkey' operation on behalf of Western capital, leading to a domination of Eastern European companies by Western ones, and contributing to an adverse balance of trade with the EC.

The extent of bilateral aid, tying 'aid to trade', has been greater than that of multilateral aid. The 'Group of 24' pledged some $21 billion in 1991. Whist this was initially heralded as a new Marshall Plan for Eastern Europe, it has not been matched by the trade give-aways that were central to the US Marshall Plan for the reconstruction of Western Europe, and the initial result of asymmetrical liberalization (with the EU retaining protection of its 'sensitive' industries), coupled with the rush to import Western capital goods, was a catastrophic collapse in trade and GDP. Whilst more recent trade figures show a significant improvement in trade with the EU, there is increasing dependence of the East Europe economies on that trade. The trade figures alone look good, but critics have been quick to point out that these should be set against a background of a catastrophic collapse in output during the period of the CMEA's break-up, and have been confined to sectors not competitive with the West. The problem of convertibility of currency has meant that increased exports have generally also contributed to increased debt.[24] In short, there are all the symptoms of the emergence of a dependence relationship between the East and the EEC, characteristic of North-South economic relations - a parallel that has led some observers to see similarities with Third World experiences of liberalization.

A major problem in this respect, evident well before the moves to economic détente, is the asymmetry of trade between the two blocs. The volume of exports to the West looks large, as do Western exports to the East. However, they are small in volume terms in comparison with trade flows elsewhere and within the European Single Market. Put simply, the East needs the West more than the West needs the East, at least in economic terms, and this has contributed to major asymmetries in the bargaining power of the two blocs in negotiations on trade liberalization. This has been highlighted in the growing gap between the EU rhetoric of liberalization and economic support to Eastern Europe, and the political realities, with the EC continuing to respond more strongly to protectionist pressures within than to the logic of liberalization in support of the transformation. This is particularly evident in the apparent reluctance of the EC to lift restrictions on imports from Eastern Europe in the so-called 'sensitive' areas.[25]

The disjunction between the rhetoric of liberalization and the reality of protectionism has concealed even greater divisions within the Western bloc. As of May 1993, the European Community agreements on trade liberalization, which had been in effect in Poland and Hungary for over a year had been ratified by the UK, Ireland, Denmark, Luxembourg and Spain. Germany, Italy and the Netherlands were expected to ratify but were expressing doubts. France was experiencing 'legal problems', and Portugal floundered on 'translation difficulties', whilst Belgium had become bogged down on 'internal procedural problems'.[26] The emergent political realities thus look remarkably like a system of independent states, all calculating their own political interests and economic gains to be had for their national economies.

In March 1993, the European Commission became engaged in seeking to enlarge its mandate to partnership negotiations with Russia, with the eventual aim of free trade. It was under pressure from the looming Copenhagen Summit of June 1993, and was looking for a 'quick fix' to the embarrassments at the weakness of the response to the continuing deterioration of economic conditions associated with liberalization in the former Socialist economies (male life expectancy in Russia has actually fallen to 55). However, this was heavily qualified. Hans van den Broek, the External Affairs Commissioner, thus spoke of trade liberalization, 'provided political and economic circumstances allow this'. To some the formula appeared less symbolic than illusory: 'by expressing a willingness to go beyond traditional trade and co-operation and eventually achieve free trade with Russia, the Community would be sending an important signal to Moscow that it fully supported the reform process.' It was also clear that the 'safeguard clauses' - though linked to the contingency of 'serious injury' - held out few promises of a relaxation of a regime of 'managed trade'.[27]

In the West and the EU, therefore, the new 'Ostpolitik' has thus remained reminiscent of the characteristics of trade-bloc and power-bloc diplomacy associated with the bipolar system. Protection of state-based economic interests has remained central, and the EU is a means of securing bargaining power in the pursuit of these. The novelty has been the appeal to 'liberalization' as capable of bringing long-term gains to the new electorates of Eastern Europe and the successor states of the Soviet Union - an appeal which, at least initially, has made tolerance of the economic austerity associated with economic liberalization dependent on a belief in better things to come. What appears to be emerging is a new regional bloc system, in which the East European periphery has been re-incorporated into the Western sphere of interest and influence, but with the commitment to a liberal economy as the essence of the 'rules of the game' applied only to Eastern Europe, at least in the conduct of bloc relations.

A major weakness of the logic discerned by neo-functionalist theory is the circuitous nature of the explanation advanced for the 'ever-widening' circles which results in the increasing power of transnational authorities, and the increasing penetration of domestic politics by actors with an interest in transcending national boundaries. But why should these transnationally oriented actors, committed to a larger regional system, be more successful than nationally based economic groups whose interests lie in a more defensive national sphere and in the protection of the national prerogative in economic matters? For the neo-functionalist, the answer lies in the value of transnational authorities in helping transnational interests overcome national restrictions. The functional requirement of some interest groups for a legal and political authority which transcends the national authority is therefore given as the principal explanation for the emergence of a transnational authority.

The limits to a 'Pax Europeana': the emergence of Fortress Europe

Contrary to the neo-functionalist logic of economic liberalization promoting the development of transnational forms of political authority and concepts of European citizenship, political pressures at the level of the state have been in a more protectionist direction - in favour of strengthening of national borders, and provisions for tighter regulation of internal movements. A major feature of the debate on the re-integration of the Eastern and Western European economies has been the strain placed on the move towards political union by pressures for enlargement and more permeable borders. Whilst a flood of economic migrants from the East has contributed to galvanizing a common interest of EU members into the development of a common policy on immigration and the issues of state borders, this has increasingly focused on acceptance of the need for stronger control of immigration from Eastern Europe. Such developments contradict the political case for the development of a liberal constitution as the basis for the new architecture of regional economic co-operation, and have led to a contradictory situation of 'unrestrained capital, and political restraint'.[28]

Initially, most West European states adopted a positive response to economic refugees, and especially to political ones. However, legal distinctions have been introduced in a number of West European economies in response to conflicting pressures for liberalization and market co-ordination. This has been particularly controversial in Germany, committed by its constitution to generous asylum provisions, and with an economy built on the encouragement of immigrant labour. The compromise has aimed at only a partial opening of frontiers - a restraint which, as Rudolph notes in these cases of German policy towards foreign workers, has signalled the political resistance of a region with very high living standards to absorption into a global migration system which inevitably places a downward pressure on wages. Whilst this has been ameliorated by efforts to provide assistance to the economic modernization of the less privileged regions, the development has been seen as contradicting EU commitment to economic liberalization, and as a shift in favour of a strengthening of common borders, or the emergence, in effect, of a 'Fortress Europe'.[29]

Although the new polices are to some extent merely a modernization of existing migration regimes, rather than a radical departure, new expectations of freedom of movement under the European Single Market, and expectations of efforts to create a larger European 'economic space', have helped to highlight major problems in reconciling the commitment to a liberal constitutional state with a co-ordinated market economy. Whilst the former implies equality of citizenship, and legal protection of basic freedoms associated with free contract, the latter has encouraged the use of migrant labour to meet shortages in the labour market in the 1960s and 1970s. Over the last decade, and associated with the opening of borders with Eastern and Central Europe, there have been efforts to balance the interests of indigenous workers and business, in what has effectively turned an 'open-door' policy into a 'revolving-door' policy.[30]

If we are to question the unfolding story of European regional integration, what else follows from a replacement of 'history as myth' by 'history as science'? Or from the replacement of economics, supposedly divested of attention to political interest, by political economy? The argument is that, even were is possible to reconstruct a regional identity for Eastern Europe in the Western image of the liberal market economy, the EU, now nominated as the central agency for this project, is not the appropriate vehicle to achieve it.

The discussion so far focuses attention on the effect of the neglect of the power dimension in analysis of the problems of economic transition in Eastern Europe and its re-integration into the Western economic system. It is suggested that the potential for promoting security through economic means has been seriously overestimated, and the role of the former state structures in structuring economic relations, both domestic and international, neglected. One consequence of the neglect of power and its social context has been an underestimation of the influence of diverse political traditions of state-market relations in contemporary Europe on the political outcomes of economic liberalization. The proponents of a market-led reform (neo-liberal and anarcho-capitalist) have been especially prone to underestimating the continuities with the past regime, and its persistent influence on the transformation to market economy, which is leading from state dominance of production to state dominance of markets.

Path-dependent development

The failure of many of the newly industrializing economies to follow the path towards liberal democracy, according to the process of economic liberalization predicted by modernization theory and convergence theories of industrialization, has been attributed to many factors. They include the position of the newly industrializing economies in the international economy, and the absence of an economic structure capable of sustaining the development of capitalist institutions, which has meant that these economies have remained highly dependent on the state in providing the necessary concentrations of capital and in managing the interface with foreign capital and international markets. When state dependence has been combined with old colonial dependencies, for example, in the form of imperial preferences, it has been suggested that the strength of influence of past power structures in limiting the emergence of liberal democratic forms - which has been termed 'path-dependent development' - may be considerable. As a consequence of this, existing power structures embodied in the state are likely to be reinforced, and the economies, whilst converging on capitalist forms of economic development, diverge from the development of the pluralistic system of power associated with the West. The existence of a strong state structure (which in many cases, for example Poland, almost completely dominates the economy), coupled with a high level of dependence on external markets and finance (associated with trade imbalances and large accumulated debts), has led a number of observers to suggest that, far from converging on West European political norms, the East European pattern of development and East-West economic and political relations may well come to reflect the Third World experience of economic liberalization.[31]

There appear to be a number of factors potentially inhibiting the development of liberal political institutions in the East European economies in the process of market liberalization. These include the structural factors noted in theories of path-dependent development, the ideological vacuum arising from the collapse of the Communist ideal and the hazy notions of Western capitalism, the

160

'residues' of state Socialism in political culture, and the dependence of state privatization programmes on the state and on public officials with experience of economic management rooted in the Socialist state. On top of these institutional inertias, the high cost of economic liberalization and the unwillingness of Western institutions to shoulder it, and even the resurgence of protectionism in the West, have been seen as contributing to a failure of liberal reforms at the level of liberal democratic and citizen rights. However successful the reforming efforts of politicians in bringing about an economic convergence necessary to meet the conditions of the Association agreements for EU membership, the fractioning of the Western coalition in support of further movements towards closer political union, and the adverse effects of liberalization on organized interests in Western Europe, are seen as weakening the prospects for reciprocal economic liberalization. Although the gains to be had from a 'return to the West' in economic terms have been heavily endorsed both by Western multilateral financial agencies and by reforming political elites in Eastern Europe seeking Western assistance, the programmes of liberalization embarked upon so far have failed to bring the expected benefits in terms of re-integration into the economy of Western Europe and a re-balancing of trade exchanges to the benefit of the East. Indeed, for a variety of reasons, unequal terms of trade have persisted. Whilst, as Linden has noted, the movement against the Soviet Union economic system and the abandonment of the CMEA have been accompanied by a movement towards the 'European model', it has become increasingly evident that the conception of the Western system has been utopian in character, and has led not only to heightened expectations of the benefits to be had from the transformation to a liberal market economy, but also to an underestimation of the institutional and structural constraints and costs involved in aiding a transformation. Thus an actually existing Socialism in the East, built on a system of state-dominated privileges, has given way to a capitalist system that has become dominated by the state and the old nomenclature, in the absence of alternative institutions.[32]

The residues from the Socialist past

As Bunce and Csanadi have noted, the relatively peaceful nature of the revolutions in Eastern Europe has involved only a slow extrication from state Socialism, despite the rhetoric and advocacy of rapid transition to a competitive market economy and 'shock therapy'.[33] Though Thatcherism and the British privatization programmes have been highly regarded among reforming elites in Eastern Europe, there has been no equivalent to the London Stock exchange 'big bang' which opened the British economy almost overnight to competitive international forces. The East European transformations have thus involved much greater continuity with past regimes than has been characteristic of most revolutions. Indeed the revolutions were long in the making, and in some cases involved an informal redistribution of power in favour of a market economy long before the 1989 'revolutions', as for example in the Hungarian economic reforms of 1968. The dangers involved in these continuities with old regimes, in terms of both personnel and habits of thinking, have been stressed by a number of observers as likely to contribute to the persistence of the Socialist regimes.[34] Thus whilst the revolutions and elections for the most part ended the Communist monopoly of the state, it has not ended their power.[35] Indeed, a paradoxical outcome of the reforms has been to contribute to a fractioning of the opposition to the Communist party, which has generally retained its cohesion and has therefore been in a position both to increase and legitimate its power.

This continuity has been reinforced by the high degree of dependency of reformers in government on former state bureaucracies. Thus 'the revolutions left in place ... social systems that were structured on the principles of state Socialism, residues that were not liberal.'[36]

The political costs of economic liberalization

The high economic costs of the transformation to market economy, particularly those associated with the enforced dismantling of the 'social enterprise' (producing high levels of unemployment almost overnight), and the weakness of companies in the market place relative to Western producers, has already been noted and has been the subject of extensive economic analysis. However, the associated political costs have been less frequently considered. Indeed, a major criticism advanced very early of the faith being placed in economic liberalization was the likelihood of the high economic costs contributing to a retreat to the security of state protectionism.[37]

It is now well recognized that the emphasis placed by expert advisers in the West on 'shock therapy' may well have led to the undermining of political liberalism, due to contradictions between economic and political liberalization.[38] If this is the case, and the economic theory of politics (which holds that governments are judged mainly by economic performance and punished by electorates for their failure)[39] is true, the popular support for continuing economic reform might be expected to decline. In fact, this has not generally proved to be the case according to opinion poll evidence. Firstly, there has certainly been a growth of hostility towards parties in government. However, it has emerged that East European countries where economic liberalization has been economically less costly hold no less hostile views of government.[40] In Hungary, for example, politicians have been fairly circumspect in their approach to privatization, partly in response to public scandals associated with 'spontaneous privatization', as politicians in office sought to obtain personal benefits. However, whilst public opinion polls register considerable levels of discontent with politicians, including very low

162

levels of electoral turnout, support for economic liberalization has remained high.

One possible explanation for this, other than the continuing equation between economic liberalism and individual freedom of choice and absence of state repression, is the adoption of the West as a source of reference - however unattainable the life-style may be for the general population. Put concretely, whilst the Czech academic looking longingly at a highly priced Fiat in a newly opened showroom may be frustrated by his inability to afford the model, and resent the fact that the transformations have brought ownership no closer, he continues to aspire to the freedom to make such a purchase - a sense of disappointment and aroused expectations that has been noted as an endemic source of change in capitalist and commercialized economic systems. It is the dissatisfaction that is significant, which extends to the former regime that denied the possibility of contemplating choice, rather than the frustration.

Although this theory developed on the eve of the economic collapses in Eastern Europe seemed a little fanciful, recent evidence of the effects of the new economic opportunity structures arising with the market economy, and of patterns of political support for economic liberalization, seem to be broadly consistent with it.[41] For example, the cross-cutting pattern of support for economic liberalization includes those who are capable of identification and are 'economically mobile', some professional groups (such as lawyers), and the former *apparatchiks* turned *'entrepreneurchiks'*, who have been able to turn their privileges under the old system into economic advantage in the process of privatization.[42] This is also confirmed by the distribution of control and benefits of privatization through the emerging share economy.

Finally, theories which have emphasized the influence of state culture have tended to underestimate the extent to which state privilege can be readily converted to market-based privileges. Thus some recent accounts have emphasized the influence of 'bureaucratic residues' of the Socialist political culture in slowing the pace of reform, at odds with liberal economics. According to this theory, emphasizing the use of hegemonic control for political ends, the focus has been on certainty of outcome, even if the means of achieving it - bureaucratic bargaining for example - have often involved high levels of uncertainty.[43] In contrast, liberal systems are seen as uncertain in terms of outcome. This theory of a different political culture averse to entrepreneurship and risk-taking has been quite influential, for example on official policy involving a form of 'internal colonialism', or the replacement of Socialist elites by officials with a Western and capitalist orientation, as occurred in German unification. But the theory clearly underestimates the extent of the private economy in much of Eastern Europe, and also the degree of difference between entrepreneurship in the East (which is not so much of the competitive market in the Schumpeterian sense of a creative destruction, but of a bureaucratic form) and that in the centrally planned economies.

The strength of ethnic nationalism

Another challenge to the establishment of a 'Pax Europeana' built on an EU model of strong federalist states operating within a single 'economic space' has been the evidence on the resurgence of conceptions of the state based on ethnicity, a development attributed by many observers to the power vacuum left by the collapse of the Soviet Union - a vacuum inadequately filled by the market ideology and bloc diplomacy of the West European states.

The nostalgia for the predictabilities of the bipolar system has gained added force from the resurgence of ethnically based nationalistic conflict, and clearly rests on an ambiguous attitude in liberal theories of international economic and inter-state relations to the right to autonomy and self-determination of particular cultural groups. This has led some observers to predict that the end of the Cold War might lead to something rather worse. Ample fodder has been provided for the those who have wished to roll out the guns of states commanding super-power status in the interests of international order and European security.

A major problem highlighted by the resurgence of ethnic conflict and irredentist movements since the collapse of Soviet hegemony in Eastern Europe is the differing bases of sovereignty within a territory. Gerner, in a discussion of the threats posed to the European system of states by the claims for national self-determination based on ethnicity, suggests that the force of myth in the new ethnic claims should not be discounted, even if it may have little scientific status as 'history'. He thus distinguishes between mythology (tradition with plot) and history. He is not dismissive of mythology.

> The present European states often trace their origins back to a time when ethnic nationalism was not a state ideology. When political actors today define their states in ethnic terms and try to legitimize this by referring to historical entities with the same name, it is a case of mythologization of history. In political discourse there is an interplay of different modes of depicting the past: as history - *res gestae* - as tradition with a plot - *historia rerum gestarum* - and as myth. ... Historical science does not ... determine a society's view of its history and cultural identity. For this, myths are important.[44]

This recognition of the importance of ethnic identity as an alternative source of state identity, and as a motivating force behind both movements for secession and regional autonomy, and transnational movements in support of minority group interests, has attracted considerable attention in the literature, responding to the apparent resurgence of ethnically based conflict. To place the phenomenon in the context of myth building, rather than history, and to view these myths of ethnic identity as often the device of political elites seeking to mobilize support for particular interests (including their own interest in wielding power), is not to belittle either the force of such myths, or the historical experience in a more historical-scientific sense. The problem of national minorities has been dealt with severely in the past - with the forcible expulsion of German minorities from Poland, Czechoslovakia, Hungary, Romania and Yugoslavia, the exclusion of more than two million Poles from White Russia, and of over 60,000 Hungarians from Slovakia.[45]

Discussion

There can be no doubt of the momentous nature of the changes occurring in Eastern Europe and their effects both on the development of Europe, and on the international order. Eric Hobsbawm views the revolutions in Eastern Europe in 1989 alongside 1789 and 1917 in terms of historical significance, Eley sees the period 1989-1992 as one of the great moments of modern European History, and Fukuyama caught a mood in describing the fall of Communist ideology as the 'end of history'. But is the evidence of a shift towards managed trade, the creeping nostalgia for the stability and predictability of state behaviour afforded by the bipolar balance of power, and the 'path-dependent' development of the Eastern European economies consistent with the liberal and federalist visions of a European market-based order?

The creation of a European unity through the achievement of transnational orders has been a recurrent theme in European history, and has generally been either a cloak, or an instrument, for the achievement of hegemonic power, whether in the pursuit of religious, political, or cultural goals. Such efforts, in particular under the great empires established in European history, have had an important influence in shaping Europe's complex political culture and economic systems, whether through the enforced movement or assimilation of population to dominant cultural norms, or through their impact on national political and economic institutions. However, the hegemonic projects and the establishment of unity have invariably foundered on deeply seated nationalistic identities, to be viewed not as 'primordial' cultural differences, but as deliberately fostered alternative conceptions and mythologies of national identity which have been effective in mobilizing opposition to the hegemonic power, or which have achieved considerable concessions to autonomy within it.

In contrast to the politically and culturally based projects for European unity, the spread of liberal economic systems through market integration has been widely seen as contributing to unity, without the need for subordination of national differences to some central authority. This 'liberal mythology' has been questioned by historians and students of international relations, pointing to the importance of US hegemonic influence in post-war Europe in moving Western states in a liberal direction. The spread of a nationally defined social democracy in Western Europe, and the transcendental and transnational ideology of the Soviet economic system as a source of resistance to market values, have also been important. Nonetheless, it has generally been conceded that the emergence of the EC as a force for the spread of liberal market values through market integration has created a new powerful driving force for European unity under the liberal ideal, but one which is profoundly contradictory, in that it contains the seeds of a protectionist Europe.

There has been a resurgence of national protectionism in Western Europe, and of ethnically based state identity in Eastern Europe. There is an increasing perception of the threat posed to valued national difference by the process of economic integration or the Europeanization of the European economies. All these developments have brought again to the fore the question of whether even a 'unity in diversity', the slogan of a federalist Europe, may eventually fall with the reassertion of national identity.

Whilst economic liberalization in Europe generally has created new economic opportunity structures, and a growing constituency of interest in favour of more internationalist and cosmopolitan political values, it has also contributed to protectionist pressures and speculation that Europe may be on the brink of a regression to a system of competitive nation-states. Neither is the retreat to national protectionism, nor the inter-state rivalry associated with it, a novelty in European history. Indeed, the adverse effects of internationalization have been widely regarded as a contributive factor to beggar-thy-neighbour protectionist policies leading to international recession, and to the escalation of state conflict to the point of world war. On the basis of such a thesis, deliberate efforts to foster economic integration through trade, and the creation of economic interdependencies that dissolve the relevance of state frontiers, have become an important political 'sub-plot' in the agenda for the unification of Europe through market forces, albeit under a myth of market competition and collective European interests.

The theme of transnationalism has been central to the European federalist movement in the EU, and, more recently, in the political rhetoric and ideology in reaction to the creation of a larger European space and efforts to help the East European economies 'move West'. Whether this project turns out, in some respects, to depend on the emergence of a new hegemon and hegemonic project, has remained an open question. As Tarrow has noted, whilst the economics of 'Europeanization' and internationalization may be transnational, the political actions have tended to depend on the internal political authority and systems of interest representation of the nation-state, even when the origins of the politics they are opposed to are 'the state'.[46]

The resurgence of ethnically based nationalistic conflicts in Eastern Europe, and the apparent inability of the international community to manage this without recourse to state power, appears on the face of it to support the argument for a new Concert of Europe, or a new hegemon with the resources to compel economic liberalization. It may be an irony that the end of the Cold

War has contributed to a revival of neo-realism in international relations theory, rather than its demise, or to a system of managed trade and power-bloc relations, oscillating between protectionism and a more aggressive mercantilism. The American threat has been replaced by the European threat. Coupled with the increased domestic uncertainties associated with the prospects of competition from the low wage and relatively unregulated economies of the East, marketization as a strategy has contributed to the return of the Hobbesian state, and the reinstatement of the philosophy of Machievelli as the underpinning of the new *Realpolitik* of East-West relations. And East moves West, encouraged by the EU, but only so long as this remains orchestrated according to the interests of dominant states and their 'sensitive' or strategically important economic sectors.

So where does the experience of liberalization and marketization of East-West relations leave the viability of the EU's 'Pax Europeana' in replacing 'Pax Sovietica' in Eastern Europe as a project of security through means of a transnational liberal market ideology? The Socialist project of taming, controlling or replacing markets has long been challenged as unattainable by liberal economists, particularly the Austrian school, on the grounds that it is totalitarian in consequence.[47] However, despite the fears of the contribution of the Single Market to a process of competitive deregulation and 'social dumping', the central legal institutions of the EU appear to have been highly successful in building a European constitution on the basis of the direct effects of market principles in the Rome Treaty. However, this has been based on a relatively even balance of the powers of business and labour organizations, already destabilized by the Single Market, and appears also to have depended on a shared culture of civil society and the European 'welfare state', which are institutional and cultural elements that remain lacking in Eastern Europe. The absence of rigorous attention to the social dimension of market integration in Europe is reflected in the current disarray in the political responses to the Maastricht referendum on closer political union in the West, and, in the East, to the declining support for economic and political liberalization because of its high costs.

There have emerged at least two contradictory scenarios which closely link the changing power structure in the shift back to liberal market economy, the impact of internationalization and liberalization on domestic political structures, and the distribution of the costs of privatization. The first holds that democratization is a necessary foundation for the success of economic reforms - a theory that has generally favoured institutional change before the introduction of markets, in a gradualist fashion.[48] This lends some support to the potential importance of multilateral financial assistance to meet the costs of economic restructuring, and, internally, to a wider distribution of property rights (for example through share ownership schemes) in providing for some form of 'economic democracy' and to offset tendencies towards oligopoly and concentration of shares in the control of foreign companies.

A more pessimistic scenario regards the use of the word 'democracy' as exaggerated in the international context, and as dangerously obscuring more anarchic tendencies and preparing the ground for an authoritarian reaction. The liberalization process is thus seen as contributing, ironically, to an erosion of civil society, and an increasing concentration of control over resources. This is manifested in the emergence of repressive private oligarchies from the ranks of the old nomenclature, a growing threat of a shift to military dictatorship in the military states of the former Soviet Union, and in Western Europe, the rise of the monopolistic multinational corporation. Arato, for example, has argued that the economic transformation of Eastern Europe will only succeed in the form of an 'elite democracy' which effectively neutralizes civil society, because a politically mobilized society would be unwilling to bear the high costs of a liberal market economy.[49] Eckiert has gone even further, arguing that the emergence of a 'coercive politics' will be required to overcome political resistance to the economic dislocations resulting from liberalization.[50]

The ideological character of seemingly objective economic prescriptions associated with East European regime transformations, economic transformations in general, and privatization and liberalization policy in particular, has increasingly been identified in the more critical literature as a potential source of disaster. The inappropriateness of economic reforms 'imposed' by multilateral agencies on developing economies, and the serious neglect of the social, political, and cultural dimensions, have become a focus of attention in studies of the social and political impact of the economic impositions of the World Bank and IMF on countries seeking aid. More indirectly, such neglect is seen as central in conditioning the environment in which private sector financial institutions operate, which is their touchstone for establishing sound 'economic' criteria for capital transfer.[51] A similar demand to bring back consideration of the 'social' context and impact of market liberalization has also figured increasingly in response to the evident signs of the perverse outcomes and failures of reform efforts in Eastern Europe and the successor states of Soviet Union.[52]

A major problem that emerges, then, in the images of East-West convergence and economic re-integration through the adoption of liberal market economics, is the essentially utopian character of the theory of capitalism on which it is founded.[53] The political uses of ideological over-simplification should clearly not be discounted. The political success of American liberal ideals has been increasingly attributed to their heroic over-simplification and essentially mythical qualities, and they were, to a large extent, a deliberate and effective tool of foreign policy during the Cold War, including the use of film propaganda.[54] Notwithstanding these historical lessons, the crude logic of a two-world economic system, created in the bipolar balance of power, or efforts to establish a new 'Concert of Europe', have continued to structure East-West integration.

So what, then, are the economic consequences of the effort to regain the

168

cultures of capitalism? Hayek, writing in *The Road to Serfdom* (1944), lamented the

> abandoning of the views of Cobden and Bright, of Adam Smith and Hume, ...[of] one of the salient characteristics of Western civilization as it has grown from the foundations laid by Christianity and the Greeks and Romans. Not merely nineteenth and eighteenth-century liberalism, but the basic individualism inherited by us from Erasmus and Montaigne, from Cicero and Tacitus, Pericles and Thucydides.[55]

Hayek is pointing here to individual, rather than collective rationality and choice. Thus for him, the Socialist enterprises in both Eastern and Western Europe embarked on after the Second World War were bound to fail, because they took insufficient account of economic self-interest rationally determined. He felt it essential that the costs and benefits of making choices and taking risks fall on the individual, and are not externalized to some imagined collectivity. More than half a century on, some of the predictions have been confirmed. Yet the leaning of the lessons of history, and their application to the present, may need more careful reading.

Conclusions

The analysis presented here can only be treated as explorative and speculative. The author is not East European, and any views of reforms are prone to misinterpretation when the revolutions are viewed, and to a large extent being acted out, 'under Western eyes'. However, the East European economies' convergence on Western forms of capitalism, so long as they also retain competitive party systems, within a positivist theory of political economy, would lead to the expectation of a convergence on many of the features of Western political economies.

The notion that the strength of Western 'economic liberalism' and the associated political theories and institutions rests on their materialistic outlook is not particularly new. Whilst it has been appreciated by historians of state-building, and indeed has been the focus of post-modernist critiques of the liberal 'hegemonic' project and libertarian claims for the freedoms associated with capitalist market systems and liberal political institutions,[56] there is mounting empirical evidence to suggest that the tolerance of divergent cultural values in a materialist conception of the limits of state power is the basic source of its appeal. This would explain the emphasis in Western democracies on the structuring of the political game in such a way as to ensure a high degree of stability. Paradoxically, it is the 'materialist' basis of liberalism that has helped it to prevail internationally, due to its ability to accommodate rather than the requirement that it suppress a diversity of alternative sources of collective identity, including those of national culture.

This also defines the limits to a liberal free-market remedy which may also bring its own form of cultural domination. In the end, it seems, liberal reforms, and the international regimes which advance them, must be evolved through collective choice, and cannot be compelled from outside. To that extent liberal regimes remain unpredictable and possibly divergent in social outcomes. Market choices remain 'socially embedded' in a system that seeks to accommodate, rather than define, individual economic and political preferences. There can then be no expectation of convergence on a shared culture or collective identity, or of a social harmony based on some unifying vision of economy or society.

Notes

1. Havel, cited in Wolchick, *Czechoslovakia in transition*.

2. Hoole and Huang, 'The political economy of global conflict'; Joffe, 'Collective security'.

3. Tarrow, 'The Europeanization of conflict'.

4. Neumann, 'Russia as Central Europe's constituting other'.

5. Cited in Garton Ash, 'Mitteleuropa?'.

6. Cited in Neumann, 'Russia as Central Europe's constituting other', 354.

7. Ibid.

8. Ibid., 353.

9. Anderson, *Imagined communities*.

10. Cited in Neumann, 'Russia as Central Europe's constituting other', 351.

11. Cited in Bischof and Brix, 'The Central European perspective', 217.

12. Gerner, 'Ethnic rights as human rights', 146.

13. Agh, 'After the revolution', 84.

14. Kis, 'European security', 145; see also Neumann, 'Russia as Central Europe's constituting other', 358.

15. Kis, 'Variations on the theme'; Neumann, 'Russia as Central Europe's constituting other', 351.

16. Garton Ash, 'Reform or revolution?', 250.

17. Ibid.

18. For a detailed account of these, see Fitzmaurice, 'Regional co-operation'.

19. Another pointer to the importance of the CEI in working for a wider conception of European integration is in the involvement in outside agencies which operate on a more multilateral basis, including the World Bank and the EBRD, which has a special secretariat to deal with CEI projects.

20. See e.g. Lieber, *No common power*; Deutsch, *The analysis of international relations*.

21. See e.g. Önis, 'Privatization and the logic of coalition-building'.

22. 8 Feb. 1991. For the text, see *Human Rights Law Journal*, 12: 607 (12 July 1991), 270-3.

23. Snyder, 'Nationalism'.

24. According to GATT trade figures for 1993, the East European economies saw strong export gains with the EC of about 20% up to 1991. The strongest growth was by the Czech and Slovak republics (40% increase) and Bulgaria (24.5%). See 'Trade of Western Europe with Eastern Europe', *The Financial Times* (25 March 1993).

25. 40-50% of the exports of Central and Eastern Europe fall into the 'sensitive' category, and have therefore been liable to face EC import barriers and a reluctance to reduce tariffs. In the case of Hungary, these restrictions affect as much as 58% of exports, and in the case of Poland about 44%.

26. *The Financial Times* (10 May 1993).

27. 'Brussels explores trade plans for Moscow', *The Financial Times* (25 March 1993).

28. Rudolph, 'German Maquiladora?', 146.

29. Ireland, 'Facing the true Fortress Europe'.

30. Rudolph, 'German Maquiladora?', 137.

31. E.g. Nelson, 'The politics of economic transformation'.

32. Linden, 'The new international political economy', 7.

33. Bunce & Csanadi, 'Uncertainty in the transition'.

34. Bruszt & Stark, 'Remaking the political field'.

35. In Poland, the Communist party has remained the largest single group.

36. Bunce & Csanadi, 'Uncertainty in the transition', 243.

37. See Willis, 'Financial market liberalization'.

38. Bunce & Csanadi, 'Uncertainty in the transition', 254.

39. For a critique of this theory of electoral cycles of popularity, which seems to ignore the timing of elections and the ability of governments to shape electoral perceptions of the economy, see Willis, 'The political economy of post-war international economic security'.

40. Bunce & Csanadi, 'Uncertainty in the transition', 254.

41. Kitschelt, 'Political opportunity structures', 26-7.

42. Stark, 'Privatization in Hungary'.

43. McDonald, 'Transition to Utopia'; Bunce & Csanadi, 'Uncertainty in the transition', 244.

44. Gerner, 'From the Black Sea to the Adriatic', 56.

45. Bogdan, *Histoire des pays*.

46. Tarrow, 'The Europeanization of conflict', 233.

47. Hayek, *The road to serfdom*, 10.

48. Bartlett, 'The political economy of privatization'; and Bruszt, 'Transformative politics'.

49. Arato, 'Revolution, civil society and democracy'.

50. Ekiert, 'Democratic processes'.

51. For an account which favours this, see Llewelyn, 'Integration of European financial markets'; and for a critique of the implication of these principles when applied to the East European debt problem, see Willis, 'The political economy of post-war international economic security'.

52. See e.g. Bruszt, 'Transformative politics'.

53. On the utopian character of Hungarian transitions to market economy, see Kornai, 'The Hungarian reform process'.

54. See e.g. the account of US propaganda in support of 'productionism' in Italy under the Marshall Plan, in Stirk & Willis, eds, *Shaping post-war Europe*.

55. Hayek, *The road to serfdom*.

56. See for example Maier, 'The politics of productivity', 105, who argues on these grounds for a conception of Schuman's view of the 'New Deal' as a post-war imperial system writ large. A number of accounts of the international liberal order focusing on the role of state power have insisted that this was essentially an imperialist project.

References

Agh, Attila, 'After the revolution: a return to Europe', in Karl E. Birnbaum, Joseph B. Binter & Stephen K. Badzik, eds, *Towards a Future European Peace Order?* (London, 1991), 83-97.

Anderson, Benedict, *Imagined communities: reflections on the origin and spread of nationalism* (London, 1983).

Arato, Andrew, 'Revolution, civil society and democracy: paradoxes in the recent transition in Eastern Europe', Cornell Working papers on Transition from State Socialism, no 90.5 (New York, 1990).

Bartlett, D., 'The political economy of privatization: property reform and democracy in Hungary', *East European Politics and Society*, 6 no 1 (1992), 73-119.

Bischof, Guenter & Emil Brix, 'The Central European perspective', in Robert S. Jordan, ed., *Europe and the superpowers: essays on European international politics* (1991), 217-34.

Bogdan, Henry, *Histoire des pays de l'Est* (Paris, 1990).

Bruszt, László, 'Transformative politics: social costs and social peace in East Central Europe', *East European Politics and Societies*, 46(1992), 135-205.

Bruszt, László & David Stark, 'Remaking the political field in Hungary: from the politics of confrontation to the politics of competition', *East European Politics and Societies*, 45(1991), 210-45.

Bunce, Valerie & Mária Csanadi, 'Uncertainty in the transition: post-Communism in Hungary', *East European Politics and Society*, 7 no 2 (1993), 240-75.

Deutsch, K. W., *The analysis of international relations* (Eaglewood Cliffs N.J., 1988).

Ekiert, Grzegorz, 'Democratic processes in East-Central Europe: a theoretical reconsideration', *British Journal of Political Science*, 21 no 3 (1991), 485-513.

Fitzmaurice, J., 'Regional co-operation in Central Europe', *West European Politics*, 16 no 3 (1993), 380-400.

Garton Ash, Timothy, 'Reform or revolution?', in *The uses of adversity: essays on the fate of Central Europe* (New York, 1989), 242-303.

Garton Ash, Timothy, 'Mitteleuropa?', *Daedalus* 119 (1990), 1-21.

Gerner, Kristian, 'Ethnic rights as human rights: the case of the Baltic States and Hungary', in Vojtech Mastny Jan Zielonka, eds, *Human rights and security: Europe on the eve of a new era* (Boulder, Col., 1991), 159-176.

Gerner, Kristian, 'From the Black Sea to the Adriatic: ethnicity, territory and international security', *Security Dialogue*, 24 no 1 (1993), 55-68.

Hayek, Friedrich A., *The road to serfdom* (1979) [first published 1944].

Hoole, Francis W. & Chi Huang, 'The political economy of global conflict', *Journal of Politics*, 54 no 3 (1992), 835-56.

Ireland, P.R., 'Facing the true Fortress Europe: immigrants and politics in the EC', *Journal of Common Market Studies*, 29 no 5 (1991), 457-80.

Joffe, Joseph, 'Collective security and the future of Europe: failed dreams and dead ends', *Survival*, 34 no 1 (1992), 36-50.

Kis, Danilo, 'Variations on the theme of Central Europe', *Cross Currents: a Yearbook of Central European Culture*, 6(1987), 1-14.

Kis, László J., 'European security: Hungarian interpretations, perceptions, and foreign policy', in Ole Waver, Pierre Lemaitre and Elzbieta Tromer, eds, *European polyphony: perspectives beyond East-West co-operation* (London, 1989), 141-53.

Kitschelt, Herbert, 'Political opportunity structures and political protest', *British Journal of Political Science*, 16(1986), 57-85.

Kornai J., 'The Hungarian reform process: visions, hopes, and reality', *Journal of Economic Literature*, 24 no 4 (1989).

Kornai, J., 'Post-socialist transition', *European Review*, 1 no 1 (1989), 53-64.

Lieber, R.J., *No common power: understanding international relations* (London, 1991).

Linden, Ronald H., 'The new international political economy of Eastern Europe', *Studies in Comparative Communism*, 25 no 1 (1992), 3-21.

Llewellyn, D.T., 'Integration of European financial markets: implications for banking', *Review of Economic Conditions in Italy*, no. 3, *Internationalization of financial markets: recent evolution and new tendencies* (1989).

Maier, Charles C., 'The politics of productivity, foundation of American international economic policy after World War II', *International Organization*, 31(1977).

McDonald, Jason, 'Transition to Utopia: a reinterpretation of economics, ideas, and politics in Hungary 1984-1990', *East European Politics and Societies*, 7 no 2 (1993), 203-39.

Nelson, Joan M., 'The politics of economic transformation: is Third World experience relevant to Eastern Europe?', *World Politics*, 45(1993), 433-63.

Neumann, Iver B., 'Russia as Central Europe's constituting other', *East European Politics and Societies*, 7 no 2 (1993), 349-69.

Önis, Ziya, 'Privatization and the logic of coalition building: a comparative analysis of state divesture in Turkey and the United Kingdom', *Comparative Political Studies*, 24 no 2 (1991), 231-53.

Rudolph, Hedwig, 'German Maquiladora? Foreign workers in the process of regional economic restructuring', *Innovation*, 7 no 2 (1994), 137-49.

Snyder, Jack, 'Nationalism and the crisis of the post-Soviet state', *Survival*, 35 no 1 (1993), 5-26.

Stark, David, 'Privatization in Hungary: from plan to market or from plan to clan?', *East European Politics and Societies*, 34 no 3 (1990).

Stirk, P.R. & D. Willis, eds, *Shaping post-war Europe: European unity and disunity* (London, 1991).

Tarrow, Sidney, 'The Europeanization of conflict: reflections from a social movements perspective', *West European Politics*, 18 no 2 (1995), 223-51.

175

Willis, D., 'Financial market liberalization and the efficiency of capital transfer mechanisms: East-West-South perspectives', paper presented at the First International Conference of EACES, Verona, 27-29 September 1990.

Willis, D., 'The political economy of post-war international economic security: retrospect and prospects', in P.R. Stirk & D. Willis, eds, *Shaping post-war Europe: European unity and disunity* (London, 1991).

Wolchik, Sharon, *Czechoslovakia in transition: politics, economics and society* (London, 1991).

8 An identity for Europe? The role of the media

Vian Bakir

Since the project of European integration began, at issue has always been whether a European identity could develop to underpin political unification. The Treaty of Rome did not spell out the promotion of a European cultural identity, but it would have been considered integral to promoting an accelerated standard of living (an expressed aim of the Rome Treaty - Article 2). By 1974 the European Parliament was calling for the EC(EU) to become an active partner on the cultural stage.

A debate arose between anti- and pan-Europeans, centred on the possibility and desirability of creating a unified Europe 'from above' through economic and political institutions. Pan-Europeans acknowledged that there would be delays, but believed that European unity was imperative to prevent a recurrence of European civil war, to create a third power between East and West, and to secure a prosperous future for Europe's peoples. They also argued that the route of 'state-making' from above through bureaucratic incorporation and the building of institutions was the only way forward. Political union within Europe would forge a European consciousness in place of obsolete national identities.[1]

The debate about European cultural identity resurfaced in the middle of the 1980s due to widespread dissatisfaction with the faltering EC integration process, where the idea of Europe as a community of values had been subsumed in the scramble by nations and interest groups for economic gain. A further impetus to the process was the need to stabilize and deepen the Union as more countries were admitted. Thus the Maastricht Treaty of 1992 set out the EC's cultural policy (Articles 3(p) and 128), stipulating that cultural action should contribute to the flowering of national and regional cultural identities, whilst at the same time reinforcing the feeling that Europeans share a common cultural heritage and common values.[2]

The EC regarded the media as a crucial tool in this realization of a European identity. The audio-visual policy of the Commission was designed to sustain and develop a European identity, in the face of the onslaught from communication empires - in particular American, but also Japanese (such as Sony) and Australian (such as Murdoch). In the 1984 Green Paper, *Television Without Frontiers*, it was projected that television would play both an economic role (by opening up the advertising market and creating jobs in the television industry) and a cultural one (by fostering a European identity). The Green Paper argued that,

> European unification will only be achieved if Europeans want it. Europeans will only want it if there is such a thing as European identity. A European identity will only develop if Europeans are adequately informed. At present, information via the mass media is controlled at national level.[3]

Thus, unity is the goal, and information is the means of achieving it. This echoes Deutsch's thesis that the essential aspect of the unity of a people 'is the complementarity or relative efficiency of communication among individuals'. In other words, membership in a people consists of an 'ability to communicate more efficiently, and over a wider range of subjects, with members of one large group than with outsiders'.[4]

Do technologies have a decisive impact on cultural identities, as the EC here assumes? One way of answering this is to look at how the logic behind the EC's thinking fits in with models of mass communication. The EC appears to be subscribing both to a 'transmission' model of mass communication, and to an adulterated form of the 'ritual' model. Westley and MacLean's version of the transmission model portrays the media as relaying to a potential audience their own account (news) of a selection of events occurring in the environment, or giving access to the views and voices of some of those (such as advocates of opinions, advertisers, performers and writers) who want to reach a wider public.[5]

An immediately apparent problem with the transmission model is its limitation of communication to the matter of 'transmission'. This implies instrumentality, cause-and-effect relations and one-directional flow, all of which are refuted, or at least questioned by much subsequent research into media 'effects'. Indeed, the rejection by researchers of this notion of powerful direct effects is almost as old as the idea itself. The ritual, or 'expressive', model emphasizes the intrinsic satisfaction of the sender or receiver rather than assuming some instrumental purpose. Carey argues that, in the ritual model, communication is linked to such terms as sharing, participation, association, fellowship, and the possession of a common faith. A ritual view is not directed towards the extension of messages in space, but the maintenance of society in time; not the act of imparting information but the representation of shared beliefs. Although in natural conditions, ritual communication is not instrumental, it can be said to have consequences for society (such as increased integration) or for social relationships. In some planned communication campaigns - for instance in politics or advertising - the principles of ritual communication are sometimes taken over and exploited (with the use of potent symbols to make latent appeals to cultural values, togetherness and tradition). Examples of the ritual model can be found in the spheres of art, religion, public ceremonials and festivals.[6]

Thus the EC believes that the media can have a decisive impact on its audience, and that if the media is directed appropriately, this impact can be one of increased integration. Are these assumptions about the nature of media effects and the formation of collective identities justified? Schlesinger, drawing on Mackenzie, argues that the EC is addressing the wrong question. How collective identities are made and changed should be questioned before it can be seen how media technologies are implicated in their construction. This is examined in the next section.[7]

Following on is a case-study of the role of the media in fostering a British national identity. This exemplifies the issues inherent in any study of the construction of identities, as well as expounding problems of media constructions of national identities. The conclusion of the case-study is that national identity in the UK is weak, and that the media has been unable to strengthen it. The implications of this for using the media to forge a European identity will then be drawn.

How are collective identities forged?

The central question being addressed is whether an EU cultural identity can be created by the media. It is therefore instructive to look at whether national cultural identities can be so created, both for the purpose of analogy, and for the purpose of seeing whether the two forces (national identity and EU identity) conflict. This is particularly pertinent to the study, given the EU's cultural policy (as stated in the Maastricht Treaty) that regional, national and European identities should all be promoted and preserved.

It can be argued that 'national identity' is a concept different from and more questionable than cultural identity in general, and the notion of a European identity is even weaker since in the first place the EU consists of a collection of nations, each with their own cultural identities, and secondly, the notion of a European cultural identity is promoted for political reasons without a concomitant strongly felt emotional force. In order to test this argument, a closer look must be taken at the theories and actualities of cultural identities, national identities and European identities, and the relationships between the three.

Smith defines the concept of collective cultural identity as a sense of shared continuity on the part of successive generations of a given unit of population; shared memories of earlier periods, events and personages in the history of the unit; and the collective belief in a common destiny of that unit and its culture.

An important instance of a collective identity is the nation state. Smith defines a nation as a named human population sharing a historical territory, common memories and myths of origin, a mass standardized public culture, a common economy and territorial mobility, and common legal rights and duties for all members of the collectivity.[8]

There are those who point to the strength of national identities. For instance, Schlesinger asserts that the European space does not offer a cultural collage. Instead, there are many sharp assertions of national identity based upon divergences of interest, particularly in Central and Eastern Europe. Smith argues that a common European cultural identity does not yet have its counterpart on the political level because each member state has placed its perceived national interests and self-images above a concerted European policy based on a single presumed European interest and self-image.[9]

McQuail argues that there is a strong 'belief system', holding that cultures are both valuable collective properties of nations and places, and also very vulnerable to alien influences. The value attributed to a national culture is rooted in ideas developed during the nineteenth and twentieth centuries, when national independence movements were often intimately connected with the rediscovery of distinctive national cultural traditions (e.g. in Greece, Ireland and Finland). The frequent lack of correlation between newly established national boundaries (often invented) and 'natural' cultural divisions of peoples has done little to modify the rhetoric about the intrinsic value of a national culture. Conversely, Hall argues that a national identity cannot unify the various cultural identities in the nation, cancelling or subsuming cultural difference. This is because a national culture has never been simply a point of allegiance, bonding and symbolic identification, but is also a structure of cultural power. This disagreement at the theoretical level regarding the strength of national identities makes it difficult to determine the consequences for an EU identity. Are people capable of multiple identities?[10]

According to *The Economist*, the EU's own opinion polls show that half of the populations of Britain, Portugal and Greece, and a third of Germans, Spanish and Dutch, see themselves in purely national terms. Thus, a sizeable proportion of the EU's population has no concept of a European identity. However, against this, a quarter of Belgians, Germans, French, and Luxembourgers think of themselves as European first and their nationalities second, as do a sixth of the populations of Italy, Holland and the UK. The conclusion from these statistics is therefore ambiguous. Some people are aware of belonging to more than one collective identity, and some people are not. More positively, these figures show that the EU's cultural goal of fostering multiple identities is not unattainable, although they give no indication of whether it is something that can be engineered or must be left to evolve. The following analysis will attempt to shed some light on the matter.[11]

It is instructive to examine how 'the nation' arose in the first place. Primordialists argue that nations are natural units of history, based on primordial ties of language, religion, race, ethnicity and territory. In a similar vein, Perennialists believe that nations are simply larger, up-dated versions of pre-modern ties and sentiments arising from a human propensity to belong to a group. In these theories, there is little place for the media to have had a decisive impact. Such explanations of nationhood, however, are imperfect: the Primordialists because the mere existence of nations does not mean that they are necessarily natural, and the Perennialists because there is no necessary reason to link the need to belong to a group with the formation of nations and nationalism.[12]

A more plausible explanation of the rise of nations can be found in Modernists like Smith, Gellner, and Anderson, who argue that nations are a wholly modern phenomenon, although they differ over the mechanisms of nation formation. Smith emphasizes the importance of history by arguing that modern nations incorporate features of pre-modern *ethnie*. For instance, by the fourteenth century some of the processes that helped form the nation were discernible in England. These include well developed ethnic elements, a common name, a myth of ethnic descent, and historic memories and tradition fed by prolonged wars with Scotland, Wales and France.[13]

Gellner argues that nations and nationalism are the product of a growth-oriented industrial society. Its complexity and specialization required a large, uniformly literate, and technologically equipped workforce which could only be supplied by the modern state and its support for a compulsory and standardized education system. Gellner also refers to the need for a state communications system to maintain the nation's culture, although this is emphasized less than the role of state education.[14]

Anderson places greater emphasis on the role of the national media in stimulating a sense of national identity, by arguing that, with the decline of religion and the rise of global imperialism, it became possible and necessary to imagine the nation. Print capitalism and the media helped inculcate a sense of national identity by the creation of the daily ritual of newspaper reading in common with others in the country. Another factor was that newspapers needed a national market and hence created a universal print language for the nation: the fixity this gave to languages then helped to create the image of an ancient past - another idea central to the nation.[15]

A common element in the Modernists' approaches is the need for people to know about their history and culture - mythical or not - if they are to have a sense of national identity. This is particularly the case if one accepts the argument that nation-building is an activity that must be constantly renewed. Indeed, Hobsbawm argues that new 'traditions' must be invented to establish continuity with a suitable historic past, particularly when there is a rapid transformation of society.[16] If information is the key to the creation and maintenance of collective identities, this attributes a heavy burden of responsibility to the media.

How important is the media in forging collective identities?

We start from the assertion that there is no such thing as objective communication, since facts have to be both selected and situated within a framework of understanding before they 'speak for themselves'. The media defines things for us because we often have no first-hand experience of much of the external world. This is where its power lies. Thus, although the media may not be able to tell people what to think, it does tell them what to think about. The media performs this role not by analysing or arguing the merits of different issues, but in the manner in which they select and highlight certain issues: in other words, they set the political agenda. This selection process is both culturally encoded and socially determined.[17]

Beardsworth argues that the scale and complexity of modern society are regarded as factors which place upon the institutions and organs of mass communication the vital role of mediating between individuals, with their short range, personal knowledge of the social world, and those large-scale macro-processes which constrain them and impinge upon them, but which are by their very nature beyond their experience. Gerbner puts it thus:

> Publication is thus the basis of community consciousness ... among large groups of people too numerous or too dispersed to interact face-to-face or in any other personally mediated fashion. The truly revolutionary significance of modern mass communication is its 'public making' ability ... The terms of broadest interaction are those available in the most widely shared message systems of a culture. Increasingly these are mass-produced message systems. That is why mass media have been called the 'agenda setters' of modern society.[18]

McQuail cites Gerbner who argues that television is responsible for a major 'cultivating' and 'acculturing' process, according to which people are exposed systematically to a selective view of society on almost every aspect of life, a view which tends to shape their values and beliefs accordingly. The environment is so monopolized by television that its lessons are continually learned and relearned.[19]

These views all assume that by watching television, there is an assimilation of values. Rather than following the transmission model, recent Western media research shows that people are not passive media consumers, but interact with the media. They bring their own values to what they see, decoding the media according to their own culture. Corner argues that given that audiences are differentiated in the nature and use of knowledge they draw upon when making sense of television, it is likely that interpreted meanings and values will show variations too.[20]

Two strands therefore need to be examined. First, does the media produce symbols of national identity; and secondly, do these symbols have any impact on the population? Amongst those who argue that symbols of national identity are created is Hobsbawm, who states that the formation of national identities works partly through the creation of nationwide symbols and 'invented traditions'. Thus there is a discourse of the nation. Hall defines a nation as not only a political entity, but something which produces meanings - 'a system of cultural representation'.[21]

Many argue that the media plays an important role in the construction and dissemination of such symbolism. McQuail notes that a government-appointed committee on the BBC in Britain endorsed the view of the 'public service idea' as involving eight principles, one of which was having a concern for national identity and community. The other seven concerns could be said to help engender this goal by stipulating the inclusion of everyone, and the credibility of the accuracy and independence of BBC output (although this is not to suggest that this is the sole purpose of these other objectives). These other seven concerns are: geographical universality of provision and reception; the aim of providing for all tastes and interests; catering for minorities; keeping broadcasting independent from government and vested interests; having some element of direct funding by the public (thus not only from advertisers); encouraging competition in programmes and not just for audiences; and encouraging the freedom of broadcasters.[22]

The media, particularly the broadcast media, by its mode of operation, provides its audience with symbolic messages, summarizing and condensing information rather than explaining and expanding. Edelman, in describing symbolic meanings, explains that condensation symbols evoke the emotions associated with the situation. They condense into one symbolic event, sign, or act, such things as patriotic pride, anxieties, remembrances of past glories or humiliations, and promises of future greatness. It is very difficult, however, to create meaningful symbols out of thin air. It is generally argued that the most potent and relevant of symbols are those that have historical roots, and so are not totally artificial. There are a number of these to choose from, since there are certain processes occurring in societies that contribute to internal cohesion, giving it form and legitimacy. In Western democracies, one such process is that of politics. The political process is a nationally unifying force in that it is historically grounded, and in that it periodically brings the nation together at regular intervals in at least two ways.

The first is in the 'ceremony' of reading newspapers or watching the news, since these media are largely concerned with politics (the broadsheets and television at least, if only by token in the tabloids); and the ceremony is performed en masse on a daily basis. As far back as 1964, Edelman was asserting that for most people most of the time, politics is a series of pictures in the mind placed there by television news, newspapers, magazines and discussions. For much of the mass public, controversial political acts remote from individuals' immediate experience and which they cannot influence are bound to become condensation symbols, emotional in impact and calling for conformity to promote social harmony. Political news

> has everything: remoteness, the omnipotent state, crises and *détentes*. More than that, it has the blurring or absence of any realistic detail that might question or weaken the symbolic meanings we read into it.[23]

The second way in which the political process periodically brings the nation together is in the ceremony of voting. Edelman argues that election campaigns give people a chance to enjoy a sense of involvement. This is participation in a ritual act: only in a minor way is it participation in policy formation. Like all rituals, elections draw attention to common social ties and to the importance of accepting the public policies that are adopted. Some go even further in their claims about the symbiotic relationship between the media and politics. There is much research which shows that the media has become the central forum for political discourse.[24]

Either way, the media is important in producing some awareness of politics, whether superficial or meaningful. If it provides information on a meaningful level, it enables audience interaction and understanding. If it provides information on a superficial level, it reminds the audience that there is a political process, even if they do not know what it involves. Either process would act to symbolize politics as part of the culture of the nation.

It can therefore be argued that politics is one of the most appropriate facets of national life to choose as a symbol of the nation since it has real purchase on people's lives. People are affected by political decisions; they still largely take part in politics through elections (although there are concerns about the increase in of non-voters); and they are exposed to politics on a daily basis through the national print and broadcast media.

However, as a unifying symbol, even politics may be not particularly effective. Taking Britain as an example, the first-past-the-post system of electoral representation results in the over-representation of the Tory South at the expense of the rest of the nation, and totally disenfranchises minority parties (such as the Green Party, whose supporters are scattered around the country). In addition, ethnic minorities have always been under-represented in Parliament, leaving them to rely on extra-parliamentary pressure groups: indeed, Barry argues that it was only the race riots of the early 1980s which brought about positive representation of blacks on television.[25]

Case-study: national identity, the media, and the monarchy in the UK

This section looks in detail at what happens when a national symbol is made of a phenomenon that no longer has much purchase on people's lives. The

184

monarchy will be used to exemplify the argument that if a symbol is to have purchase on a nation's identity, then it must be relevant to the population at large.

During the inter-war years, the royal family was hugely popular. Partly as a result of the emergence of Empire from the 1880s onwards, the royal family moved out of and above political and class differences. The genuinely joyous national celebrations of King George V's Silver Jubilee in 1935 and George VI's coronation in 1937 were merely two of the many manifestations of this, with their official ceremonial and their unofficial communal gatherings in the form of street parties and outings. The Empire thus moved with the monarchy above the narrow connotation of class and sectional interest to be seen as a symbol of the nation and thus an object of general patriotism. Nairn argues that the British image of themselves today is inextricably bound up with this 'painted folklore' of the monarchy and Britain's past 'achievements': a grander past is constantly evoked in order to make Britain's present reduced and grey role in the world easier to bear.[26]

It is argued here, however, that since the 1980s the monarchy has decreased in relevance to large sections of the British public. Its status, role and privileges have been severely challenged by the public and MPs. An indication of the decreased relevance of the monarchy is a Gallup survey conducted in February 1993, which found that only 26 per cent of those polled considered the monarchy 'something to be proud of'.[27] Given this backdrop, can the monarchy usefully be used as a symbol of the nation?

This section's analysis will be limited to an investigation of the broadcast media, since most newspapers have a stated bias, which is more divisive than uniting. The BBC, on the other hand, has had a history of supporting national institutions, with its Reithian legacy (its mission being to inform, educate and entertain). Another reason is that television in general is the most trusted news medium in Britain. The 1986 IBA study stated that 'television is fair and unbiased in its coverage of news and current affairs, according to 74 per cent of the population'.[28]

In addition, the purpose of this analysis is to test the logic behind the European Commission's belief that television - especially European programmes - can play a major role in 'developing and nurturing awareness of the rich variety of Europe's common cultural and national heritage'.[29] It therefore makes sense to look at broadcasting in the UK, since broadcasting is what the Commission is focusing on. Indeed, since television is the prime medium of entertainment and information for most people, it is arguably the most potent when it comes to influencing 'the masses'.[30]

Problems encountered in constructing a national identity will be studied. Those first addressed will be the constraints on broadcasters due to the nature of their medium. The analysis will then progress to three main social forces which make it difficult to construct a British national identity. These forces are strong and disparate regional identities; the fact that Britain is a multicultural

185

state coupled with the legacy of colonialism; and the continuing existence of class divisions.

It is asserted by some that the national media is a major force in the process of nation-building. Cardiff and Scannell argue that as a result of BBC public-sector broadcasting, programmes designed to enhance a sense of national identity originally formed the backbone of British broadcasting. The feeling of a communal identity among dispersed audiences was fostered by linking them to the symbolic heartland of national life. This was achieved by regularly featuring public events, ceremonial services and festivals - particularly those on royalty. According to Cannadine, the monarchy has been part of an invented tradition of public splendour and popularity since 1870, examples being the royal Christmas broadcasts instituted in 1932, and the treatment of George the V's Silver Jubilee.[31] Hobsbawm sums up the treatment of the British monarchy as follows:

> Nothing appears more ancient and linked to an immemorial past, than the pageantry which surrounds British monarchy and its public ceremonial manifestations. Yet ... in its modern form it is the product of the late nineteenth and twentieth centuries.[32]

The rationale for such inventions was the need to provide a semblance of stability to combat social change - initially to appeal to the working-class as the electoral franchise was widened (thus checking the Socialist movement) - and to cope with a rapidly changing society after the two World Wars. Television made royal pageants accessible in a vivid and immediate manner not achievable by radio and newsreels, whilst the mystique and attraction of the royal family was bolstered by television's reverential attitude, exemplified by the broadcaster Richard Dimbleby's commentary.[33]

There is, however, a range of structural problems faced by broadcasters in creating symbols of national identity. Verma argues that, due to the nature of the medium, broadcasters over-simplify and trivialize complex social issues into stereotyped conflicts by means of the personification of nations and issues, with prominence given to violence rather than to underlying social and political conditions. Another problem is finding an image of national identity with legitimate historical roots.[34] For instance, according to Nairn there is no national dress, only an obscure and unresurrected folklore and a faltering iconography (such as 'John Bull').[35] Another problem is choosing an image of national identity that will work. Chaney argues that media organizations do not have time to consult the public on whose behalf they speak: public opinion is therefore taken as those attitudes that are available to producers. For instance, in covering the victory parade of 1946, the broadcasters presented an image at odds with the new post-war social-democratic consensus, because this mood in society was too recent to have imprinted itself as a permanent feature in the minds of the broadcasters.[36] Yet another problem is the expansion in the numbers of broadcast channels. When the BBC had a monopoly of the airwaves, the whole of the tuned-in nation would sit down to watch the same programme, and so a sizeable portion of the population would be exposed to the same cultural signs. This monopoly no longer exists, having been replaced by an unparalleled variety of sources and messages.

The next set of problems are the various social forces that militate against the construction of a national identity in Britain. The first is that, according to Hall, Britain is composed of disparate cultures, initially unified only by a lengthy process of violent conquest, and whose violent beginnings must be forgotten before an allegiance to national identity can be formed. This was unproblematic as long as the component cultures were happy to be part of Britain, for as Renan puts it, the nation arises out of a present-day desire or consent to live together - a 'daily plebiscite'. For instance, according to Smith, in the devolution debate of the 1970s, the Scots people realized the economic benefits of remaining in the UK and the difficulty of severing historical memories shared since their union.[37]

Problems arise, however, with the manifestation of separatist tendencies. The Scottish Nationalist Party, for example, desires outright independence, often harking back to the declaration of Arbroath (1320) in its claim to the long and distinctive history of their *ethnie*. Part of the problem, according to Hall, is that British culture still does not consist of an equal partnership between the component cultures of the UK, but of the effective hegemony of the English. It is therefore not surprising that the other cultures feel ill-treated and resentful. The argument that part of the process sustaining collective identities is that of exclusion, distinguishing 'us' from 'them', and the definition of 'the other' does not bode well for national identity when regional identities are strong.[38]

Such tensions, and the resulting separatist tendencies, make the construction of a cohesive, representative British national identity very difficult. For instance, Schlesinger argues that the BBC's reports on Northern Ireland ignored the Catholic community and accepted the status quo of a divided Ireland as an immutable truth. In such situations, the British monarchy with its imperial and hegemonic associations and its base firmly in London is more likely to antagonize unwilling subjects than unify them.[39]

A second problem in constructing a British national identity is the colonial legacy. According to Hall the fact that Britain exercised hegemony over the cultures of the colonized meant that many distinctive features of Englishness were first defined by a comparison of English virtues with the negative features of other cultures. As Said explains, the West's encounter with new different worlds reinforced western identity by promoting a sense of superiority and a Eurocentric world view, whilst stereotyping the Orient: this discourse he calls 'Orientalism'.[40]

Imperialist discourses in Britain are noted by Richards in his examination of feature films and imperialism in the 1930s. Similarly, in his examination of the

BBC between 1923 and 1953, MacKenzie found that the BBC had established flagship programmes marking days of national ritual, often involving members of the royal family and invoking imperial traditions. He notes that although in the early fifties there was an imperial re-evaluation, with the rise of nationalist revolt making it impossible to celebrate the image of an Empire of peace and prosperity, the coronation of a new monarch brought a fresh wave of national events centred on the monarchy. The coronation of 1953 was just as imperial an event as its predecessor in 1937, whilst extensive Commonwealth tours made good broadcasting for schools, and documentary and Christmas programmes.[41]

Although MacKenzie notes that in all of these, the BBC began to tread more warily, others argue that imperialist discourses are still to be found in the British national media, if less overtly than before World War II. Hall and Gieben argue that the media's transmission of the idea of the nation, and the language and style of transmission, is only understood by those included in the fold of the nation. Similarly, Gilroy proposes that race discourse, by focusing attention on the entry and exit of blacks, is concerned with the mechanics of exclusion and inclusion. Barry argues that from its inception, television constructed three myths regarding blacks based on Britain's colonial experience. The first was the myth of the black entertainer, personified in 'The Black and White Minstrel Show'. The second was the myth of black dependency, arising from the images of starving children in the 1967 Biafran war. The third myth was that of the black trouble-maker: the delinquent black youth was the folk-devil of the 1970s, conveniently fusing the three concerns of race, crime and youth. Barry argues that the white working class consented to these myths because by doing so they felt superior, and so were more able to bear their own exploitation. Such imagery may have real effects. Verma quotes national and local surveys of British prejudice which show that at least 20 per cent of the population are hard-line racialists; 60 per cent are assimilationists, accepting minorities only if they adopt British culture; and only 20 per cent are pluralists. It is therefore not surprising if emotional cues in programmes prompt negative responses to ethnic minorities.[42]

Given that imperialist discourses continue to affect the language, images, and assumptions of popular culture today, how can ethnic minorities feel included in a British national identity? The problem is reinforced by the argument previously referred to, that nations are defined as much by whom they exclude as by whom they include.

The image of the royal family is unlikely to engender a sense of British national identity among ethnic minorities. This is mainly because of its associations with the memory of the British empire, inextricably linked with Victoria - the 'Great White Queen' whose image had been carefully moulded into the shape of imperial firmness and enlightenment. Another negative connotation is the fact that the Queen is the head of the Commonwealth - an arrangement designed to help Britain maintain her sense of national greatness.

The Queen, as head, is meant to portray a benevolent figure, but this can all too easily be interpreted as patronizing.[43]

The fact that the nation is composed of different social classes is the third problem of constructing a British national identity. According to Hall, modern British nationalism arose from the effort in the late Victorian and high Imperial period to unify classes across social divisions by providing them with an alternative point of identification - common membership of the 'family of the nation'. Similarly, the BBC attached great importance to the 'family' as a symbol of national identity. For instance, the Christmas broadcasts (instituted in 1932) were immediately adopted as 'traditional' and enhanced the image of the monarch as the parent-figure speaking in people's homes. However, the credibility of this symbol is bound to have been diminished by the break-up of successive royal marriages after 1981, together with the increased media scrutiny of 'the royals' in the 1980s.[44]

Class divisions militate against the success of the BBC's ethos of public-sector broadcasting, which aims to produce programmes that act in the public interest. Barry poses the question of whose interest is being represented. It is unlikely to be that of the working class since the controlling voices of television organizations are mainly society's elite. Indeed, according to Cardiff and Scannell, this can be seen in Reith's desire for 'high culture' to be made accessible to the working class, whether they wanted it or not. The BBC is now shifting towards giving the public what they want rather than what would be good for them - in the climate of increased competition for viewers, and its need to justify licence fee increases to the government. This comparatively recent shift represents a recognition of the continued existence of class divisions, and the difficulty of producing popular cross-class programmes.[45]

Class conflict is often tied up with highly divisive and deeply felt regional interests: in such cases, it is unlikely that artificial, constructed images such as the royal family will have any unifying effect. Examples of class conflict in Britain which arose in the 1980s include the North-South divide, based on wealth, income and class differences; the coalminers' strike; and the ever-increasing gulf between top executives' pay and that of their workforce. Indeed, in such conflictual cases the image of the royal family may exacerbate the situation, due to their vast hereditary wealth and privileged lifestyle, despite their token attempts at easing the tax burden they impose on the nation. An indication of the popular rejection of the symbolic image of the monarch is the steep decline in the viewing figures for the 'traditional' Queen's Christmas broadcast - down from 17 million in the early 1980s to 10 million in 1991.[46]

To summarize, this analysis adopted the Modernists' viewpoint that the nation is a modern rather than a natural phenomenon (driven as a concept by information), and examined the role of the broadcast media in inculcating a sense of national identity (although this is not to reject the role of historical experience or mass education). It argued that the importance of the media in this respect is questionable since although the broadcast media - particularly the

BBC - aim to foster a sense of national identity, they are thwarted by an array of factors. The first set of factors arises from the structural limitations of television and radio, which lead to over-simplified and trivialized images. This is compounded by the fact that images of national identity are hard to find, and those chosen may be inappropriate since broadcasters may not be in tune with national feeling. The second set of difficulties in fostering a sense of national identity are real social forces of disparate regional cultures, the colonial legacy interacting with ethnic minorities, and class division. Such forces are strong, real and relevant to the public, unlike the more ephemeral loyalties associated with some symbols of national identity.

Implications for European identity and the media

The previous case-study shows that the media cannot create a meaningful symbol of national identity if there are not already many real sources of this identity on which to draw in society. For a cultural commodity to become popular it must be able to meet the various interests of the people amongst whom it is popular, as well as the interests of its producers. Popular culture must be relevant and responsive to needs, or else it will fail.[47]

This ties in with Schlesinger's conclusion that identity is not a static phenomenon - a 'prior condition of collective action' - but is a continually constituted and reconstructed category.[48] In its reconstruction, therefore, it must draw on symbols which are relevant to the present. If no such symbols exist, then no identity can be constructed or maintained. Several implications can be drawn from this.

Firstly, if national identities are weak, and the media cannot bolster or create them, then it will be all the harder to forge a European identity. This is particularly the case given that Smith argues that national identities possess distinct advantages over the idea of a unified European identity. They are more vivid, accessible, well established, long-popularized, and still widely believed, in broad outline at least. In each of these respects, 'Europe' is deficient both as an idea and as a process. It lacks a pre-modern past which can provide it with emotional sustenance and historical depth.

Smith argues that feeling European consists not of any single element - such as language, territorial symbolism, geography, religion, the sense of being distinct from outsiders, or shared history - since there are cleavages within Europe on each of these counts. Rather, there are shared traditions in which at one time or another, all Europe's communities have participated. These traditions include Roman law, political democracy, parliamentary institutions and Judaeo-Christian ethics, and cultural heritages like Renaissance Humanism, rationalism, empiricism, Romanticism and Classicism. However, together they constitute not a 'unity in diversity' - the official European cultural formula - but a 'family of cultures' made up of a syndrome of partially shared historical traditions and cultural heritages. It would therefore be very difficult to pick on a symbol that would mean something to everyone.[49]

It is questionable whether the reporting of politics (a symbol which has previously been referred to as one of the strongest in promoting a collective identity) can engender a specifically European identity. For a start, national news broadcasts will tend to focus on their own nation, in keeping with standard news values. Admittedly, Europe is now the largest producer and consumer of foreign news, and the 'strongest single news entity' in the world is the loose alliance of Reuters-Visnews-BBC, but this does not necessarily mean that they will supply Eurocentric, as opposed to nation-centric stories. Indeed, Boyd-Barrett argues that the international news agencies place a greater emphasis on their own domestic market interests, even when selling those stories to foreign clients.[50]

Added to the problem of choosing appropriate and relevant symbols is the lack of a guarantee that the audience will interpret any European message in the manner intended by the producers. It may be reinterpreted by audiences in ethnic and national terms, as is the case with so many cultural products. Secondly, the problems of creating a European identity are compounded by the non-integrated nature of the media in Europe, which is centred around the nation, or even around the region. News stories tend to be relayed, or at least interpreted, from a national standpoint, whilst drama, comedy, and the weather reports accord the national state and outlook first place.[51]

Heinderyckx argues that despite wishful thinking about merging identities in an ever more integrated European Union, cultural convergence has not yet affected the news media. There are a few interesting transnational experiences, but these are marginal (weeklies such as The European, dailies such as The International Herald Tribune or The Wall Street Journal Europe, and television stations like CNN or Euronews). In spite of the spectacular reduction of news sources (from news agency mergers and acquisitions) the news media reflect a fundamentally national or regional structure.[52]

Newspapers are unlikely to promote a European cultural identity. One reason is that they are culturally imbued with their own nation's practices. Kopper asserts that it is not rare for national daily newspapers to be synonymous with identity-endowing elements of the particular country's political and cultural development. For instance, he argues that, viewed from the outside, England is still today partially equated with what is on daily offer in The Times. Le Monde is likewise identified with France. Fletcher goes further than this, arguing that Le Monde, as France's leading quality national daily, transmits the cultural values of the elite by reinforcement: it sets a standard of literacy and assumes a level of seriousness and sophistication in its readers that automatically defines them as an educated elite and locates them securely within the establishment. Official figures show that Le Monde is the newspaper which France's decision-makers and opinion-formers are most likely to buy.[53]

Hemels argues that the press and broadcasting have a long tradition of playing an important role in the social and personal life of Dutch people. In the Netherlands, the press is not only oriented to the expression of opinion, but is a subscription press, and at the same time, a family press. A principle valued on a par with freedom of the press has been 'pluriformity' - essentially the diversity of press structure and content, as manifested in alternative opinions and outlooks which reflect key differences in the national society.[54]

Another reason why newspapers are unlikely to promote a European identity is that the consumption of daily newspapers across Europe is extremely diverse. For instance, the total circulation varied from 21,447 in the UK to 2,696 in Spain in 1990.[55] Kuhn records that the French in general are poor consumers of daily newspapers compared with the British, Americans, Japanese, Scandinavians, and most North Europeans, although they do come ahead of the Spanish, Greeks, Italians, and Portuguese. The national dailies have a much greater share of the market in Britain (70.1 per cent) than in Germany (34.4 per cent), where the regional and local papers dominate (taking 65.6 per cent of the market). These variations in the number of people reading national newspapers mean that newspapers are likely to vary in their importance as cultural disseminators and national unifiers (following Anderson's description of the role of the media).[56]

Broadcasting fares no better as a disseminator of an EU identity, despite being a more integrated and hence controllable medium. McQuail and Siune assert that the pursuit of national self-interest remains the predominant tendency on the part of politicians and governments of small as well as large countries, and neither large broadcasting organizations nor media businesses are likely to be any more altruistic. They argue that an illustration of non-altruism is the lukewarm support for the pan-European television service sponsored by the European Broadcasting Union, or the tendency of the BBC and ITV in the UK to seek maximum advantage from their large accumulated programme archive. Both failed to co-operate effectively with each other and with other firms in the British satellite television venture which the government wanted to encourage.[57]

Even in nations with an avowed aim of creating a European identity, national considerations are paramount. An example is France under the Socialists' regime from the 1980s, whose desire for a European identity is partly to protect French culture from perceived American hegemony, and partly to incorporate the previously illegitimate popular culture. However, these aims were contradicted by the desire of French policy-makers to maintain their tradition of viewing broadcasting as a forum for the dissemination of 'high culture' to all (dating back to the creation of the French Ministry of Culture in 1959), rather than an economic enterprise. They therefore did not wish to relinquish the marks of distinction of official culture, nor the privileged status of the French intelligentsia as mediators of patrimony and creativity.[58]

Kleinsteuber et al. give a further example of the regionalism/nationalism of the media in relation to cultural identity. They argue that the (now foundered)

Scandinavian jointly run satellite network NORDSAT was aimed at the Scandinavian cultural area, and therefore showed itself to be contrary to ideas of pan-European cultural identity. Only Luxembourg demonstrates a pan-European media policy. They suggest that as a classic 'spill-over' country, and the home of an internationally operating media concern (CLT), Luxembourg's media policy has from the start been transnational and pan-European.[59]

To summarize, the obstacles to using the media to create a European identity are that there are few EU symbols to choose from which are relevant to all people; that whatever symbol is chosen, the audience may interpret its meaning differently from what the producers intended; and that the mechanisms for producing a unified media output either do not exist (as shown by the diversity of the press, most of which is firmly rooted in the nation or the region), or are not used (as in the case of broadcasting, where national self-interest wins over promoting a European image). Added to this, there are real social forces which militate against a European identity emerging naturally, and which feed back into the first problem identified - namely the problem of choosing relevant symbols. These social forces are the trends towards both globalization and regionalization.

Globalization refers to those processes operating on a global scale which cut across national boundaries, integrating and connecting communities and organizations in new space-time combinations. Smith points out the existence of a globalizing culture, as witnessed by the rise of multinational corporations, economic interdependence, and the rise of the communications industry. Although Moores argues that the spread of satellite television helps people re-imagine the boundaries of their community, making them feel more European, it could be that globalization trends may by-pass or subsume Europe, an example being the world-wide spread of American culture.[60]

McQuail and Siune argue that even if cultural policy is possible at the level of the European region, the fear is widespread that Europeanization will mainly mean either more commercialization in the form of European multimedia transnationals or greater American penetration by way of satellite television services. They argue that it is mainly smaller countries which have the most to fear from these developments, since they probably have less to gain from Europe-level industrial policy and more to lose in terms of loss of national control over their own cultural environment.[61]

A final problem with creating an EU identity is the trend of regionalization. Some argue that this is a by-product of EU integration. Smith asserts that there has been a conscious rediscovery and revival of indigenous styles and cultures. He argues that we are witnessing an ethnic revival today, which is challenging the accepted frameworks of the national state. One reason for this is that since 1945 the state has become much more powerful, both as an international actor, and regarding society within its boundaries: hence its more obvious presence is more likely to provoke resentment among the disaffected elements of its population. A second reason is that the spread of literacy and the mass media to the remotest hinterlands of European and other states has raised the level of consciousness and expectations of minority peoples, who witness national protests and movements in neighbouring territories almost as soon as they occur. Thirdly, the impact of public, mass education systems, while uniting a national population into a single civic culture, also creates divisions along pre-existing ethnic lines. This is because in preaching a single civic language and symbolism, the state's elites may stir up resentment at the neglect or suppression of minority cultures.[62]

Given that it is extremely difficult for the media to create meaningful EU symbols, and to disseminate these over the EU region, it must be concluded that the media will fail in this mission unless there are strong social forces in the real world that are already working towards this goal. In other words, if a European identity is to emerge, it must do so in an evolutionary manner. It is not something that can be constructed. However, in view of the existence of the social forces of globalization and regionalization, it seems that we may be in for a long wait.

Notes

1. Bidwell, *Help from Brussels*; Smith, 'National identity and the idea of European unity', 55, 67.

2. Kleinsteuber, et al., 'The mass media'; Bidwell, *Help from Brussels*.

3. CEC, *Television without frontiers*, 2.

4. Deutsch, *Nationalism and social communication*, 188 & 97, cited in Schlesinger, *Media, state and nations*, 139, 157.

5. Cited in McQuail, *Mass communication theory*, 50.

6. Ibid., 45, 51.

7. Schlesinger, *Media, state and nations*, 150; MacKenzie, *Political identity*.

8. Smith, 'National identity and the idea of European unity', 58, 60.

9. Ibid.; Schlesinger, *Media, state and nations*, 179.

10. McQuail, *Mass communication theory*, 114; Hall, 'The question of cultural identity', 296.

11. 'More-or-less European Union', 40.

12. Smith, *The ethnic origins of nations*, 23.

13. Smith, *National identity*.

14. Gellner, *Nations and nationalism*, 48, 50, 52.

15. Anderson, *Imagined communities*.

16. Hobsbawm, 'Mass-producing traditions', 263.

17. Boyd-Barrett, *The international news agencies*; & Bennett, 'Theories of the media'.

18. Cited in Beardsworth, 'Analysing press content', 371.

19. McQuail, *Mass communication theory*, 111.

20. See e.g. Ang, *Watching 'Dallas'*, for various audience readings of the soap; Corner, 'Meaning, genre and context'.

21. Hobsbawm, 'Introduction: inventing traditions', 7; Hall, 'The question of cultural identity', 292.

22. McQuail, *Mass communication theory*, 126-7; Peacock, *Report of the Committee on financing the BBC*.

23. Edelman, *The symbolic use of politics*, 8-9; see also Smith, 'National identity and the idea of European unity'.

24. Edelman, *The symbolic use of politics*; see also e.g. Seymour-Ure, *The political impact of mass media*; Patterson, 'The press and candidate images'; Patterson, 'More style than substance'; Manning, 'The mass media and pressure politics'; and Mazzoleni, 'Emergence of the candidate and political marketing'.

25. Barry, 'Black mythologies', 97.

26. Richards, 'Boys Own empire', 161; Nairn, *The enchanted glass*.

27. Haseler, *The end of the House of Windsor*, 3.

28. McQuail, *Mass communication theory*, 15; McNair, *Images of the enemy*, 4.

29. CEC, *Television without frontiers*, 28, cited in Schlesinger, *Media, state and nations*, 140.

30. Verma, 'Attitudes, race relations and television'.

31. Cardiff & Scannell, 'Broadcasting and national unity'; Cannadine, 'The context, performance and meaning of ritual', 104.

32. Hobsbawm, 'Introduction: inventing traditions', 1.

33. Cannadine, 'The context, performance and meaning of ritual', 158.

34. Verma, 'Attitudes, race relations and television'.

35. Nairn, *The break-up of Britain*.

36. Chaney, 'A symbolic mirror of ourselves'.

37. Hall, 'The question of cultural identity', 296; Renan, 'What is a nation?', 19; Smith, *National identity*, 139.

38. Ibid., 51; Hall, 'The question of cultural identity', 297; Schlesinger, *Media, state and nations*.

39. Schlesinger, *Putting reality together*.

40. Hall, 'The question of cultural identity', 297; Said, *Culture and imperialism*.

41. Richards, 'Boys Own empire', 184; MacKenzie, '"In touch with the infinite"', 167, 184, 186.

42. Hall & Gieben, eds, *Formations of modernity*; Gilroy, 'There ain't no black in the Union Jack'; Barry, 'Black mythologies', 86-92; Verma, 'Attitudes, race relations and television'.

43.   Haseler, *The end of the House of Windsor*, 143.

44. Hall, 'The question of cultural identity', 297.

45. Barry, 'Black mythologies', 92; Cardiff & Scannell, 'Broadcasting and national unity'.

46. Gilroy, 'There ain't no black in the Union Jack'; Haseler, *The end of the House of Windsor*, 39.

196

47. Fiske, *Television culture*, 310.

48. Schlesinger, *Media, state and nations*, 173.

49. Smith, 'National identity and the idea of European unity', 62, 70.

50. Galtung & Ruge, 'The structure of foreign news'; McQuail, *Mass communication theory*, 178; Boyd-Barrett, *The international news agencies*.

51. Smith, 'National identity and the idea of European unity', 72.

52. Heinderyckx, 'Quality and business dailies in Europe'

53. Kopper, 'Press markets in Europe'; Fletcher, 'Le Monde'.

54. Hemels, 'The development of the press in the Netherlands'.

55. Palmer, 'Daily newspapers and news values in Europe'.

56. Ibid.; Kuhn, 'Do French newspapers have a future?'; Anderson, *Imagined communities*.

57. McQuail & Siune, eds, *New media politics*, 205.

58. Moores, 'The big issue in France'; Emanuel, 'Culture in space', 283.

59. Kleinsteuber, et al., 'The mass media'.

60. Smith, 'National identity and the idea of European unity', 64; Emanuel, 'Culture in space', 283; Moores, 'Satellite TV as cultural sign'.

61. McQuail & Siune, eds, *New media politics*.

62. Smith, 'National identity and the idea of European unity', 63, 66.

References

Anderson, B., *Imagined communities* (London, Verso, 1983).

Ang, I., *Watching 'Dallas': soap opera and the melodramatic imagination* (London, Methuen, 1985).

Barry, A., 'Black mythologies: representation of black people on British television', in J. Twitchin, ed., *The black and white media book* (Stoke on Trent, Trentham Books, 1988), 83-102.

Beardsworth, A., 'Analysing press content: some technical and methodological issues', in H. Christian, ed., *The sociology of journalism and the press*, Sociological Review Monograph 29 (University of Keele, 1980), 371-95.

Bennett, T., 'Theories of the media, theories of society', in M. Gurevitch, et al., eds, *Culture, society and the media* (London, Methuen, 1992), 30-55.

Bidwell, C., *Help from Brussels* (Oxford, Public Affairs Consultants Europe Ltd., 1994).

Boyd-Barrett, O., *The international news agencies* (London, Constable, 1981).

Cannadine, D., 'The context, performance and meaning of ritual: the British monarchy and the "invention of tradition", c. 1820-1977', in E. Hobsbawm & T. Ranger, eds, *The invention of tradition* (Cambridge, Cambridge Univesity Press, 1983), 101-64.

Cardiff, D. & P. Scannell, 'Broadcasting and national unity', in J. Curran, et al., eds, *Impacts and influences* (London, Methuen, 1987), 157-73.

Chaney, D., 'A symbolic mirror of ourselves: civic ritual in a mass society', in R. Collins, ed., *Media, culture and society: a critical reader* (London, Sage, 1986), 247-63.

Commission of the European Communities, *Television without frontiers: Green Paper on the establishment of the Common Market for Broadcasting, especially by satellite and cable*, COM, 84, 300 final (Brussels, CEC, 1984).

Corner, J., 'Meaning, genre and context: the problematic of "public knowledge" in the new audience research', in J. Curran & M. Gurevitch, eds, *Mass media and society* (London, Edward Arnold, 1991), 267-84.

Deutsch, K.W., *Nationalism and social communication: an inquiry into the foundations of nationality*, second edition (Cambridge & London, MIT Press, 1966).

Edelman, M., *The symbolic use of politics* (Urbana, University of Illinois Press, 1964).

Emanuel, S., 'Culture in space: the European Cultural Channel', *Media, Culture and Society*, 14(1992), 281-99.

Fiske, J., *Television culture* (London, Routledge, 1987).

Fletcher, J., 'Le Monde, past, present and future: a vehicle for the transmission of the cultural values of the French elite', paper prepared for the Second Conference on the Press, 'The Press in Europe - Past, Present and Future', City University of London, 4 February 1995.

Galtung, J. & Ruge, M., 'The structure of foreign news', *Journal of Peace Research*, 1(1965), 64-90.

Gellner, E., *Nations and nationalism* (Oxford, Blackwell, 1983).

Gilroy, P., *'There ain't no black in the Union Jack': the cultural politics of race and nation* (London, Hutchinson, 1987).

Hall, S. & B. Gieben, eds, *Formations of modernity* (Cambridge, Polity Press, 1991).

Hall, S., 'The question of cultural identity', in S. Hall, et al., eds, *Modernity and its futures* (Cambridge, Polity Press 1992), 274-323.

Haseler, S., *The end of the House of Windsor: birth of a British Republic* (London, Tauris, 1993).

Heinderyckx, F., 'Quality and business dailies in Europe: a comparative study', paper prepared for the Second Conference on the Press, 'The Press in Europe - Past, Present and Future', City University of London, 4 February 1995.

Hemels, J., 'The development of the press in the Netherlands', paper prepared for the Second Conference on the Press, 'The Press in Europe - Past, Present and Future', City University of London, 4 February 1995.

Hobsbawm, E., 'Introduction: inventing traditions', in E. Hobsbawm & T. Ranger, eds, *The invention of tradition* (Cambridge, Cambridge Univesity Press, 1983), 1-14.

Hobsbawm, E., 'Mass-producing traditions: Europe 1870-1914', in E. Hobsbawm & T. Ranger, eds, *The invention of tradition* (Cambridge, Cambridge Univesity Press, 1983), 263-308.

Kleinsteuber, H.J., et al., 'The mass media', in M. Shelley, ed., *Aspects of European cultural diversity* (London, Routledge, 1994).

Kopper, G.G., 'Press markets in Europe. Avenues towards analysis', paper prepared for the Second Conference on the Press, 'The Press in Europe - Past, Present and Future', City University of London, 4 February 1995.

Kuhn, R., 'Do French newspapers have a future?', paper prepared for the Second Conference on the Press, 'The Press in Europe - Past, Present and Future', City University of London, 4 February 1995.

MacKenzie, J.M., '"In touch with the infinite": the BBC and the Empire, 1923-53', in J. MacKenzie, ed., *Imperialism and popular culture* (Manchester, Manchester University Press, 1986), 165-91.

MacKenzie, W.J.M., *Political identity* (Manchester, Manchester University Press, 1978).

Manning, P., 'The mass media and pressure politics', *Social Studies Review*, 6 no 4 (1991), 159-63.

Mazzoleni, G., 'Emergence of the candidate and political marketing: television and election campaigns in Italy in the 1980s', *Political Communication and Persuasion*, 8 no 3 (1991), 201-12.

McNair, B., *Images of the enemy* (London, Routledge, 1988).

McQuail, D. & K. Siune, eds, *New media politics* (London, Sage, 1986).

McQuail, D., *Mass communication theory*, third edition (London, Sage, 1994).

Moores, P.M., 'The big issue in France: voice of an underclass or commercial hijack?', paper prepared for the Second Conference on the Press, 'The Press in Europe - Past, Present and Future', City University of London, 4 February 1995.

Moores, S., 'Satellite TV as cultural sign: consumption, embedding and articulation', *Media, Culture and Society*, 15(1993), 621-39.

'More-or-less European Union', *The Economist*, 336 no 7929 (26 August 1995), 40.

Nairn, T., *The break-up of Britain; crisis and neo-nationalism* (London, NLB, 1977).

Nairn, T., *The enchanted glass: Britain and its monarchy* (London, Radius, 1988).

Palmer, M., 'Daily newspapers and news values in Europe: a north/south divide and "western" norms. A view from France', paper prepared for the Second Conference on the Press, 'The Press in Europe - Past, Present and Future', City University of London, 4 February 1995.

Patterson, T.E., 'The press and candidate images', *International Journal of Public Opinion Research*, 1 no 2 (1989), 123-35.

Patterson, T.E., 'More style than substance: television news in US national elections', *Political Communication and Persuasion*, 8 no 3 (1991), 141-61.

Peacock, A., *Report of the Committee on financing the BBC*, cmnd 9824 (London, HMSO, 1986).

Renan, P., 'What is a nation?', in H. Bhabha, ed., *Narrating the nation* (London, Routledge, 1990).

Richards, J., 'Boys Own empire: feature films and imperialism in the 1930s', in J. MacKenzie, ed., *Imperialism and popular culture* (Manchester, Manchester University Press, 1986), 140-64.

Said, E., *Culture and imperialism* (London, Chatto & Windus, 1993).

Schlesinger, P., *Putting reality together: BBC news* (London, Methuen, 1987).

Schlesinger, P., *Media, state and nations* (London, Sage, 1991).

Seymour-Ure, C., *The political impact of mass media* (London, Constable, 1974).

Smith, A.D., *The ethnic origins of nations* (Oxford, Blackwell, 1989).

Smith, A.D., *National identity* (London, Penguin, 1991).

Smith, A.D., 'National identity and the idea of European unity', *International Affairs*, 68(1992), 55-76.

Verma, G., 'Attitudes, race relations and television', in J. Twitchin, ed., *The black and white media book* (Stoke on Trent, Trentham Books, 1988), 123-9.

9 Technical convergence and policy divergence in the European information society: The case of new TV systems

Xiudian Dai

Since the mid-1980s Europe has been witnessing a substantial move in terms of policy-making power, shifting from the national government level to the European Union (EU) level. It is certainly the case that large-scale research and development (R&D) projects have been targeted as one of the most important areas, in which the EU authorities, in particular the European Commission, find a role to play. In this respect, there are two important factors, in the mind of pro-European politicians, leading to the argument for a European policy approach. Firstly, the pressure of increased international competition from the leading economic blocs including the US, Japan, and newly industrialized countries in the Asia-Pacific region has made a singular or unified European policy solution a pre-requisite for Europe to sustain its industrial competitiveness. Compared to the geographical, cultural, political and social diversity in Europe, the US and Japan are said to be more capable of innovation in some key technological areas due to their more effective policy-making process and homogeneous home market.

Secondly, it is believed that the trend of rapid technological convergence is opening a window of opportunity for Europe to catch up with its counterparts - in particular the US and Japan - in the newly emergent information society. This convergence process mainly involves consumer electronics, computing, and telecommunications, which have traditionally been separate technological, industrial, and business domains. Nowadays the on-going process of technical convergence between these three areas has led to the emergence of the information and communications technology (ICT) sector. Technically speaking, convergence is based on digitalization - a process or technique that translates all kinds of analogue source materials into a series of '1s' and '0s', which can be easily understood and manipulated by the computer. Having identified ICT as a strategic industrial sector, as the Clinton Administration has done in the US, the EU has been making political efforts to promote the development of ICT to help re-draw the economic map of the future global information society.

The National Information Infrastructure (NII) initiative, launched by the

American government to construct a nationwide optical fibre cable network to provide broadband interactive multimedia services, has had a great impact on national technological and industrial policy in many other developed and developing countries. For example, Japan has started to investigate the possibility of building a national optical fibre cable network through its underground water system. The Singaporean government has launched the 'Intelligent Island' programme to build its own version of the information superhighway. The Danish government has launched the 'Info-2000' programme with the objective of laying down a optical fibre network linking all the country's municipalities by the year 2000. China, as a newly emergent economic power, has launched the 'Three Golden Projects'[1] with the intention of leap-frogging the traditional industrialization process and building an 'informationized national economy'. In the UK, disagreement between the ruling Conservative Party and the opposition Labour Party about ways of developing a British information superhighway has been news since the early 1990s. The Conservative Party emphasizes the possibility of distorted competition if the government were to relax the rules prohibiting British Telecom (BT) from entering television entertainment broadcasting services; the Labour Party puts at the top of its political agenda that BT should be allowed to provide new services including TV entertainment broadcasting, which would give the company the incentive to provide a nationwide optical fibre cable network.[2]

The impact of the NII initiative is also seen in many interesting projects at the municipality level in the Western world. With financial support from both the Dutch central government and the Amsterdam City Council, 'De Digitale Stad' (Digital City) has been in operation since the beginning of 1994 in Amsterdam. Using currently available technologies provided by the Internet,[3] the Digital City project enables citizens of Amsterdam and people living outside the city to have immediate access to the locally managed computer network, and to participate in local politics and cultural events. The local government in Amsterdam uses this digital network to disseminate various information among the citizens. In Kingston-upon-Hull in the UK, sponsored by the City Council and Kingston Communications, the 'Virtual City' project is now being viewed as a key initiative in the city's regeneration programme. Similar to the Digital City project in Amsterdam, Hull's Virtual City project is proposed to develop applications based on the Internet.

At the EU level, the much publicized Bangemann Report was an immediate response to the new challenges from the US and other countries. It is highlighted in this Report that a telecommunications and audio-visual policy reflecting the trend of technical convergence and new development in ICT would be critical to the rapidly emergent 'European information society'. In other words, the Bangemann Report acknowledged the gap between two parallel tracks: on the one hand, traditional industrial borders between consumer electronics, computing, and telecommunications are disappearing due to technical convergence; on the other hand, conventional regulatory regimes governing each sector are still in force and they are increasingly becoming a barrier to the exploitation of benefits to be offered by technical convergence. This raises a range of important issues. Would the EU be able to facilitate the process of technical convergence within the ICT sector? Are the diversified regulatory regimes adopted in different European countries going to be harmonized by or replaced with a unified EU technology policy with regard to the development of the European information society? In other words, would there be a policy identity emerging from a European information society and, if so, what are the costs of creating such an 'identity'?

Bearing in mind the multiple factors associated with the concept of technical change and the complexity of the European information society, this chapter sets out to analyse the policy-making process in the EU and to assess the effectiveness of European policy implementation through the case of the development of new TV broadcasting systems, which include high definition television (HDTV) and digital TV systems. Both the transmission of new TV programmes via a new TV broadcasting system and the display of these programmes on a new TV set will certainly be an important aspect of the future information society. An analysis of the European HDTV strategy from the mid-1980s will assist an understanding of the issues and challenges related to regulating the European ICT sector, and the future of the European information society as a whole.

Innovation and international competition for HDTV

Research and development for HDTV started in Japan in the 1960s. By the mid-1980s NHK (Nippon Hoso Kyokai, or the Japan Broadcasting Corporation), the state-owned public broadcaster, with support from the Japanese consumer electronics industry led by Sony, had successfully developed a high definition TV system called Hi-Vision with MUSE (Multiple Sub-nyquist Sampling Encoding) as the transmission standard. With no competition whatsoever from other parts of the industrialized world, the Japanese industry was confident that Hi-Vision and the MUSE transmission standard would become a world standard for the next generation of TV broadcasting. The Japanese proposal for a world HDTV standard was presented for approval to the CCIR (Consultative Committee for International Radio) conference held in Dubrovnik, from 12 to 23 May 1986.

Contrary to the expectation of the Japanese government and Japanese industry, the Dubrovnik CCIR conference ended up with severe disagreement over HDTV. The European governments, as well as the European Commission, joined forces to block the Japanese proposal on the grounds that the Japanese system was not compatible with all current colour TV broadcasting standards including PAL, SECAM and NTSC.[4] This would inevitably make all current TV sets obsolete and consumers would have to buy a new one if they wished to watch TV programmes. Among other European countries, the French government was the most determined force against the Japanese proposal, as they had been with colour TV standardization in Europe. When the PAL system was developed and adopted in the UK and Germany in the 1960s, the French government was loath to become a technology follower of fellow European states, in the fear that the French culture might lose its prestige if TV programmes from other countries were allowed to be broadcast in France. Instead, France developed its own SECAM standard which completely blocked PAL, and certainly NTSC, TV programmes at its borders. Reminiscent of this French-style cultural protectionism, the allied European political powers firmly rejected the Japanese innovation of HDTV.

Behind the technical reason there were other considerations in the minds of European politicians of why a Japanese standard could not be accepted. By the mid-1980s, the world consumer electronics industry had already been conquered by Japanese companies. In Europe, Philips and Thomson were the only remaining big companies competing against the Japanese. If a Japanese HDTV standard were adopted all over the world including Europe, future TV transmission and receiving equipment would have to be manufactured to the Japanese standard. In other words, the Japanese domination in consumer electronics would be extended to the next generation of TV products in the 1990s and beyond.

Many industrialists and politicians believe that HDTV is a strategic technology. Strategic technologists claim that HDTV is the most important element in the new consumer electronics products, and that firms in this industry would treat it as an important part of their strategic planning. HDTV is also strategic because it is a generic technology and is likely to have an impact in many other technology domains of the ICT sector, such as computing and communications.[5]

HDTV appeared to be the most important technical breakthrough in television technology since the introduction of colour TV in the 1950s in the US and 1960s in Europe. Compared to conventional colour TV, HDTV has a number of distinctive features. First, it offers high picture resolution with horizontal scanning lines of above 1000 (compared to 525 lines for NTSC and 625 for PAL). Second, HDTV sets will be built with a wide screen (i.e. the aspect ratio of the screen is 16X9 rather than 4X3 for conventional TV sets used today). Third, genuine HDTV will have a 'hung on the wall' flat screen, instead of the traditional CRT (Cathode Ray Tube) display technology.[6] Fourth, all audio channels of HDTV transmission will use digital technology, and so digital sound of up to compact disc quality is promised by HDTV.[7] In short, as a new generation of audio-visual system, HDTV will create the so-called 'home cinema' type of entertainment for the consumer. Optimistic forecasts claim that, by the year 2000, the number of HDTV receivers sold in the market will account for 50 per cent of total TV sales in the three most important economic blocs including Japan, the US and Western Europe, as shown in Table 9.1. It is hoped by leading manufacturers that the introduction of HDTV service would create new demand for advanced gadgets, and therefore revive the currently saturated consumer electronics market in most industrialized countries.

Table 9.1

Forecast Demand for CTV and HDTV Receivers in 2000 (mn receivers)

Region	Colour TV Receivers	HDTV Receivers	HDTV % Share
Japan	11.0	5.5	50
USA	24.0	12.0	50
Western Europe	25.0	12.5	50
Eastern Europe and USSR	15.0	1.5	10
China	25.0	-	-
Other Asia, Africa and Latin America	40.0	-	-
World Total	**140.0**	-	-

Source: EIU, *High definition television progress and prospects*, 104.

In addition to the perceived importance of HDTV to the consumer electronics industry, HDTV will also create huge demand for a number of hi-tech components. For instance, the manufacture of HDTV broadcasting and receiving equipment would need a large number of advanced memory and processing chips, in order to encode and decode the programme signals. This would have a positive impact on the advanced semi-conductors market. The ideal of building a genuine HDTV with a flat screen of more than 36" is also speeding up the R&D process for FPDs (Flat Panel Displays) in many parts of the world. In addition, the high volume of information needed for high resolution pictures can not be transmitted via the normal bandwidth (e.g. 6MHz in the US). To solve this problem, digital compression techniques are used. Undoubtedly, the development of HDTV would boost the improvement of digital compression techniques which are also critical to the development of other ICT technology areas. To a great extent, HDTV is a strategic technology not only because of the perceived size of the future market for the next generation of TV sets; rather, the spill-over effects which HDTV would have on a number of key hi-tech components (e.g. FDP and advanced semi-conductors as well as digital compression techniques), as viewed by strategic trade theorists, are believed to have more industrial implications than consumer electronics itself. Certainly, the competitiveness of a future European information society would be contingent upon the European industry's market share in new technologies such as HDTV and those strategic components and techniques immediately related to it.

In the light of this view of HDTV, European politicians, particularly those from the French government and the European Commission, quickly mobilized the European industry to act and take on the Japanese competition. Shortly after the CCIR Dubrovnik conference, Philips of the Netherlands, Thomson of France, Thorn EMI of the UK, and Bosch of Germany formed a research consortium to develop a European version of the HDTV standard by 1990. The European consortium submitted their proposal to the Eureka Secretariat and, subsequently, the European HDTV proposal was accepted as Eureka 95 Project (EU95). The Eureka Programme was launched by the former French President François Mitterand in 1985 as a direct response to the US SDI (Strategic Defence Initiative, otherwise known as Star Wars). It was agreed that companies involved in Eureka, the pan-European R&D programme, could get direct subsidy from their national governments. It is not difficult to understand the reason why the four European electronics firms acted promptly to submit their HDTV proposal to Eureka: they would immediately get government financing for their R&D activities. For Philips and Thomson, two leading European firms struggling to survive the fierce competition in the consumer electronics industry, the EU95 HDTV project would entirely suit their long-term competitive strategy, which is to use public resources and political backing to help the fight against the Japanese in Europe and to expand their own presence in the new business markets elsewhere. On the EU side, the long-expected collaboration between Philips and Thomson would help realise the political ambition of some parts of the European Commission of upgrading the national industrial champions to Euro-champions, with the Commission gaining more power in the process of making and implementing industrial policies at the European level, superceding the national level.

The proposed European HDTV system was HD-MAC (High Definition-Multiplexed Analogue Component). HD-MAC was proposed on the basis of the then available MAC standard family used for DBS (Direct Broadcast by Satellite) colour TV transmission in Europe. In other words, HD-MAC was not defined from scratch; on the contrary, it was a technical extension of the MAC/packet family. There are similarities between HD-MAC and MUSE: both systems are largely analogue (for TV picture transmission) but with digital elements (e.g. digital audio channels); both are intended as DBS transmission standards, rather than terrestrial transmission; 16X9 widescreen format is common to both systems. There are also technical differences between the European and Japanese systems: HD-MAC adopted 1250 horizontal scanning lines which exactly doubles that for the PAL standard, whilst MUSE was defined with 1125 lines (more than doubling that for NTSC, 525, and less than doubling that for PAL). As a result, MUSE was said to be a 'revolutionary' approach, incompatible with any of the current colour TV transmission standards, while HD-MAC was claimed to be an evolutionary approach, which would not make the current TV sets obsolete. However, this European claim is misleading: although MAC uses 625 horizontal scanning lines as PAL does, the newly proposed HD-MAC system was only compatible with PAL if a MAC decoder was installed. Compared to the PAL/SECAM terrestrial transmission standard in Europe, the subscription rate amongst Europeans to MAC transmission is relatively insignificant. It was hoped or, more precisely, argued by the EU95 consortium and some European Commission officials that MAC would be the stepping-stone to the success of HD-MAC.

The attitude of the American government towards the issue of HDTV was more complicated. Prior to the CCIR conference in 1986, Sony managed, via CBS, successfully to lobby the State Department to support the Japanese system as the single world standard. This decision was partly prompted by the fact that all the indigenous American consumer electronics firms, apart from Zenith, had left the industry, and a protectionist policy measure for HDTV was not at the top of the US government's agenda. Now that the Japanese HDTV proposal was blocked by the allied European government representatives at the CCIR conference in Dubrovnik, with the Europeans deciding to develop a rival system, the American government asked the FCC (Federal Communications Committee) to work out a new policy on HDTV development in the US.

Instead of following either the Japanese or the European proposal, the FCC ruled in the late 1980s that the US should have an independent system for HDTV broadcasting. The future HDTV system in the US, as stipulated by the FCC, would have to comply with the following aspects:

1. Future HDTV should use a terrestrial transmission standard, rather than a DBS as proposed by the Japanese and the Europeans.
2. Simulcast (simultaneous broadcast). All HDTV programmes should be made available to the conventional NTSC transmission so that consumers who cannot afford or do not want to buy a new HDTV set would not be excluded from receiving new TV programmes, although with an unavoidable degradation of picture quality in terms of resolution and aspect ratio.
3. Any proposed HDTV system would have to be able to transmit high definition programmes via the currently available channel of 6MHz bandwidth.

Another important point of the FCC policy for HDTV in the late 1980s was that foreign companies, including Sony from Japan and Philips and Thomson from Europe, were allowed to participate in the bidding process for the future American system with their own technical expertise and capital investment. In sharp contrast, foreign firms were excluded from the HDTV R&D process in Japan and Europe.

It seems that the FCC ruling, compared to both European and Japanese HDTV technology policy, was less protectionist but also more capable of facilitating the process of technical change without sacrificing market competition.

By the mid-1990s, the scenario of international competition for HDTV had become substantially different from what it used to be ten years previously. With rapid progress in digital compression technology led by General Instrument (GI), which succeeded in digitally compressing HDTV signals into a normal transmission channel of 6MHz bandwidth, the FCC decided that the future American HDTV should be a fully digital system. In response to this new policy, the bidding industrial consortia, including one led by Philips and Thomson, either withdrew their analogue systems (as Sony and NHK did with their Narrow-MUSE) or changed their proposals from analogue to digital. At that point the competing consortia in the US agreed to pool their technical expertise, and formed the 'Grand Alliance', to establish a single fully digital standard. This digital revolution in the US had tremendous impact on the rest of the world. In Europe, Philips, the leading manufacturer in the EU95 consortium, decided to suspend its planned manufacturing of receivers to the HD-MAC standard in January 1993. This led the European Commission to give up HD-MAC as the proposed official standard. After the collapse of HD-MAC, the European Commission also decided to foster R&D activities dedicated to fully digital TV systems. Among others, the Digital Video Broadcasting (DVB) group is gathering momentum and getting support from the European Commission. The Japanese government officials responsible for HDTV policy, particularly those from the Ministry of Posts and Telecommunications (MPT), are well aware that analogue HDTV systems will be replaced with fully digital ones, but the Japanese consumer electronics industry has been lobbying hard against any substantial change to the already fully established MUSE standard. Consequently, Japan is still maintaining its daily MUSE broadcasting in the hope that this analogue HDTV system will be accepted by the consumer. Now the Japanese government has decided that the MUSE transmission system will be kept until the year 2003, when a fully digital ultra-high definition TV system will be adopted.

It is estimated that the cost of developing the HD-MAC system was as high as 2bn ECUs (roughly one half from the companies involved and the other half from public, mainly EU, subsidies). But why did HD-MAC fail? There were technical reasons, such as the rapid progress in digital compression techniques which might have been difficult to foresee in the mid-1980s. However, the most fundamental factor contributing to the collapse of the European HDTV system, HD-MAC, lies in the policy-making process and the policy itself, both at EU and national level.

EU technology policy for HDTV

The process of public policy-making in Europe since the mid-1980s is, in many cases, much more complicated than that in the US or Japan, where one constitution rules the whole country and one government manages the national economy; this also applies to HDTV. The European Commission has been trying to make itself the 'government' for a 'united Europe'. However, first of all, there is still a long way before we see the end of the social, political, economic, and market integration process. Despite the everyday use of concepts such as 'the European Community' (before the Maastricht . Treaty) and 'European Union' (thereafter), Europe is not united at all in many aspects. For the time being, the Council of Ministers, in which ministerial-level government officials of all member countries sit, is the ultimate body deciding on most aspects of European policy and regulatory change. In other words, it is the national governments who jointly make decisions on EU laws, either unanimously or by majority voting. In the meantime, regulatory and policy differences between member states still have a strong influence on the efficiency and effectiveness of the policy-making process at the EU level.

Secondly, vested interests of member countries sometimes evoke disagreement among member states within the Council of Ministers. When the EU was deciding a subsidy package for the further promotion of the HD-MAC standard, the French and Dutch governments showed more enthusiasm than others such as the UK. This is not surprising simply because Thomson and Philips, the major companies leading the R&D consortium for HD-MAC, are from France and the Netherlands respectively. Thorn EMI, the UK firm, participated in EU95 via its Ferguson branch but Ferguson was taken over by Thomson in 1987. The UK government saw little benefit in further supporting and financing EU95. In this respect, it is the national economic interest rather than the common European interest which has been given priority consideration by the EU member states.

Thirdly, EU technology policy for HDTV was also made less effective due to institutional failure. It is an open secret that EU trade policy, including technology policy, often runs into conflict with EU competition policy. Different power domains within the European Commission sometimes hold conflicting attitudes towards the same matter. Although Eureka is a pan-European R&D programme, the European Commission, in particular DGXIII, saw EU95 and HD-MAC as its own special affair. DGXIII hoped very much to make HD-MAC a success in order to establish a flagship for its technology policy towards the ICT sector. However, other parts of the Commission did not necessarily share DGXIII's view and, therefore, some of them refused to be co-operative. Shortly after the collapse of HD-MAC, DGXIII was reshuffled and the responsibility for

HDTV was taken away from it. Now DGIII and DGX have principal charge, respectively, of the HDTV matter and broadcasting programme-making.

It seems that a smooth process of policy-making for new technology within the EU is difficult to achieve. The HDTV experience shows the EU has suffered from the opposite as far as technology policy is concerned.

Formal regulation for the next generation of television broadcasting at the EU level began with the MAC Directive of 1986.[8] The MAC Directive stipulates that:

1. The MAC/packet family, including C-MAC, D-MAC and D2-MAC, is adopted as the official standard for DBS television transmission in the channels defined by the WARC BS-77 and RARC SAT-83 documents throughout all member countries of the EU.
2. As an extension of the MAC family, the newly proposed HD-MAC system would be adopted as the official transmission standard for high definition TV transmission via satellite, when it has been fully established.
3. All EU member countries should give full legal backing and support to the HD-MAC standard, due to the strategic importance of HDTV.

To be sure, the MAC Directive was an important regulatory foundation for the technical progress achieved by the EU95 consortium in developing HD-MAC within the next few years. By September 1990, major European consumer electronics firms such as Philips, Thomson, and Nokia were already able to present their HD-MAC broadcasting equipment and receivers at the International Broadcasting Convention in Brighton. In other words, the EU95 consortium had spent four years developing a fully working HDTV system, which took the Japanese industry more than fifteen years to do. However, as it is argued, MAC is an isolationist technology designed for the main purpose of keeping the Japanese out of Europe.[9]

The EU technology policy, and the MAC Directive for HDTV in particular, suffered a number of setbacks and uncertainties, which eventually led to the defeat of this policy. Among others, the launch of Rupert Murdoch's DBS service, Sky Television, and its subsequent takeover of BSB (British Satellite Broadcasting), the impact of digital TV development in the US and Europe, and the British government's long-standing objection to a proposed EU subsidy package were the main factors which contributed to the eventual failure of the EU's HDTV strategy in the early 1990s.

The BSkyB Affair

As discussed above, the EU initially intended to create a regional monopoly for new TV broadcasting technology, the MAC/packet standard family, for the EU95 European consortium led by Philips and Thomson. Instead of fostering market competition, the EU passed legislation, the MAC Directive, to secure the success of its new technology. As the MAC Directive stipulated, all member countries of the European Union were required to ensure legal backing to MAC and HD-MAC as official DBS standards in each country. It is in this circumstance that BSB was launched in the UK in May 1990 and transmitted via the Marco Polo satellite. BSB was the only satellite TV service using the MAC transmission standard.[10] It was hoped that the launch of BSB would kick-start a new market for the MAC technology and, naturally, that the UK would in the future provide an important number of consumers who might wish to upgrade their subscription from MAC to HD-MAC.

In 1989, shortly before the launch of BSB, Rupert Murdoch launched his Sky Television, another DBS service using the conventional PAL transmission standard in the UK with the permission of the British government. Many European organizations believed that the adoption of the PAL standard for DBS was contravening the European MAC legislation. As a counter-argument, Rupert Murdoch and the British government, under the Prime Minister of the day Margaret Thatcher, insisted that the EU MAC Directive had been framed to apply only to high-power DBS broadcasting as defined at the World Administrative Radio Conference (WARC) in 1977.[11] Technological advances since the mid-1980s in satellite broadcasting transmission had substantially changed the circumstances of the 1970s when the WARC documents were drafted. By taking the advantage of new technologies, Rupert Murdoch managed to launch Sky Television using the Luxembourg-based Astra satellite, which is a low-power communications satellite.

The European Commission and European industry, represented by the EU95 consortium, were not at all content with the launch of Sky Television. However, with strong political backing from the Thatcher government and the widely believed 'loophole' in the MAC Directive, the European Commission appeared to be powerless to prevent Sky Television. When the EU's MAC strategy started crumbling in 1993, Philips criticized the Commission for its failure to defend European legislation with respect to Sky Television in the UK.[12] In the meantime, the Commission complained about the inadequate political power it had been granted to implement EU policy.

The political fuss became worse when BSB fell into trouble. Due to the high running costs incurred in buying more expensive decoders and receiving dishes and, ultimately, the low service-subscription rate, BSB ran into financial crisis. In November 1990, merely six months after its commercial launch, BSB was going bankrupt, and had to merge with Rupert Murdoch's Sky Television to form a combined company BSkyB (British Sky Broadcasting) in order best to serve the investors' interests. It seems that the merger between BSB and Sky Television was more like a takeover of the former by the latter. Although the original channels of BSB were retained after the merger, all programmes under the new management of BSkyB were broadcast in the PAL format and the European DBS standard MAC used by BSB was immediately scrapped.

The death of BSB and the MAC transmission technology in the UK had a tremendous impact on the EU's HDTV strategy. Reminiscent of the VCR (Video Cassette Recorder) format battle in the early 1980s, when the technically superior Philips technology (V2000 format) was defeated by the Japanese VHS system, the asserted better technology (MAC) lost the brief format battle to the old but more popular standard (PAL) in the UK DBS market. Politicians and public bureaucrats may feel it necessary to pick winners among competing companies or technologies, but they cannot guarantee which will be the eventual winning party in the market-place, where volatile consumer choice may not always be predictable. In addition, the collapse of BSB was a great setback to the already politically controversial European HDTV policy. The failure of the MAC technology in the UK meant that HD-MAC lost a potentially significant stepping-stone in one of the most important European consumer markets. Politically, the BSkyB affair appears to be another example demonstrating the policy conflicts between Brussels and the national capitals of EU member countries in the early 1990s.

The politics of '1s' and '0s': implications of the digital revolution

The EU's technology policy for HDTV has suffered further blows from the rapid progress of digital technology in the US and Europe since the beginning of the 1990s. More specifically, the news that General Instrument of the US had found a way of digitally compressing HDTV broadcasting programmes into a 6MHz channel suddenly changed the entire course of HDTV development all over the world. Digital compression had been the bottle-neck which prevented the Japanese and European as well as, initially, American companies from adopting a fully digital approach for HDTV in the first place. Now that digital technology was available, the FCC swiftly announced that the future HDTV standard in the US would have to be a fully digital system, and that analogue or hybrid (comprising both analogue and digital techniques) proposals would not be considered.

Companies, indigenous and foreign, tendering for the American HDTV standard were quick to adjust their strategies and changed their proposals into fully digital systems. Among others, the Philips/Thomson-led ATRC (Advanced Television Research Consortium) group abandoned their previously proposed hybrid system and started concentrating on fully digital TV R&D in the US. NHK and Sony subsequently withdrew their Narrow-MUSE, a revised version of the MUSE system used in Japan, from the bidding process without making any further application to the FCC. In the early 1990s, there were three big consortia left in the US with fully digital proposals lodged with the FCC. These were:

1. the American Consortium (AC) comprising Zenith and AT&T;

2. the American Alliance (AA) comprising GI and MIT;
3. the Advanced Television Research Consortium (ATRC) comprising Philips, Thomson, David Sarnoff Research Centre, Compression Labs and NBC.

The FCC received four fully digital HDTV proposals: one from the AC group, one from the ATRC consortium, and two from the AA group. After initial technical tests, the FCC was advised by its appointed testing centre that the four proposals had achieved similar or equivalent technical parameters. Under this circumstance, the FCC suggested to all parties that it would be an optimal solution if the three tendering consortia could co-operate and put their proposals together to establish a single standard for digital HDTV. There would be a number of positive points worth considering as far as the FCC suggestion was concerned:

1. By putting the four competing standards together, the future common standard would benefit from the best elements of each proposal;
2. The joining of forces by the three competing groups would substantially speed up the standardization process of digital HDTV development in the US;
3. The co-operation would avoid the huge financial loss (i.e. the costs of R&D) to be associated with the two consortia whose proposals would be rejected by the FCC, simply because only one system would be accepted under previous FCC policy; moreover,
4. The FCC suggestion, if accepted, would also make room for every participating organization to share the royalties to be paid by future licensees, whoever won the competition.

As a matter of fact, the FCC suggestion ensured that every organization would be a winner by contributing to the process of digital HDTV standardization during the last stage. It is also true that any consortium would like to win the competition by themselves without sharing the royalties with competitors. However, with equivalent technical and financial capacities, this would appear to be a typical prisoner's dilemma: nobody can afford losing the competitive game. In response to the FCC suggestion, the three competing consortia, later joined by East Asian firms including Toshiba and Samsung, agreed to form a 'Grand Alliance' and establish a single standard for future digital HDTV. The Grand Alliance obviously pre-empted any competition between the industrial groups concerned and has left hardly any room for future competitors - one would find it hard if not impossible to test the HDTV water against the allied forces, given the latter's unprecedented and almost insurmountable combined technical and financial capacities. It seems unusual that the State Justice Department did not see the Grand Alliance as a case for anti-trust investigation. Once again, for people following the HDTV debate it might be worthwhile to recall the concept of so-called 'strategic technology'. With hindsight, a fully defined digital HDTV system ahead of the Japanese and Europeans could possibly give the US the lucrative 'first mover advantage' in the process of global competition for the next generation of TV technologies. But it is not clear at all what exactly are the reasons why the FCC and the Grand Alliance have managed to avoid any intervention from the anti-trust authorities, for investigation would normally have occurred with other similar co-operative arrangements between industrial organizations in the US in recent years.

Digital HDTV development was not confined to the US. At the International Broadcasting Convention held in Amsterdam in 1992, a group of Scandinavian broadcasting and telecommunications organizations[13] successfully demonstrated a fully digital HDTV system, called HD-Divine (High Definition-Digital Video Narrowband Emission). To the surprise of the European Commission, the HD-Divine group announced a launching date for digital HDTV service no later than the previous scheduled launch for HD-MAC services in Europe by the EU95 consortium. This was another substantial development in digital HDTV almost in parallel with R&D activities led by members of the Grand Alliance in the US. In parallel with HD-Divine, in April 1991, the VADIS (Video Digital Interactive System) consortium was launched under the umbrella of the Eureka 625 Project, with a total budget of $24 million. The VADIS consortium was joined by thirty-three companies from thirteen European countries in order to develop digital HDTV in Europe by the year 1994. Furthermore, the EU also sponsored another research proposal, the digital terrestrial broadcasting (dTTb) project, under the Community's RACE (Research for Advanced Communications for Europe) programme.

It seems, therefore, that there were a number of research projects dedicated to developing digital HDTV technologies in Europe in the early 1990s. However, compared to the status of HD-MAC, these projects appeared to be Cinderella schemes in the agenda of European technology policy-makers. Nonetheless, the progress in digital HDTV research within and outside Europe seemed to have gathered enough momentum to shake the EU's entire technology policy for new TV systems.

Arguments across the English Channel

EU technology policy for HDTV, as embodied in the MAC Directive of 1986, had been controversial since the early days, despite the fact that it was approved by the Council of Ministers and adopted as the top-level regulatory document over new DBS TV technologies. On the one hand, it suits the interests of some member countries (i.e. France and the Netherlands) and the indigenous European consumer electronics manufacturing industry (led by Philips and Thomson). Some domains (e.g. DGXIII) of the European Commission believed HDTV was a window of opportunity to boost their political influence on technology policy-making within the EU. On the other side, certain political factions within the EU were not at all happy with the HD-MAC strategy. For instance, the competition policy (the responsibility of DGIV) side of the European Commission, and some member countries represented by the UK, had their reservations about, and sometimes objections to, the EU's HDTV policy.

On the continent, the French government, joined by DGXIII, had led a remarkable campaign against the Japanese HDTV competition since the mid-1980s. The pro-MAC political force was reinforced by support from the manufacturing industry in arguing that the consumer electronics industry in the 1990s and beyond would be continuously dominated by the Japanese if the MUSE system became the single world standard for HDTV; and that fully digital HDTV technology would not become a reality until the beginning of the twenty-first century.

The interplay of corporate strategies and public policy for new TV technologies in Europe merits attention. It seems that European technology policy was undertaken to assist the execution of the global strategy of leading European firms. In the case of HDTV, Philips and Thomson made clear to EU policy-makers that they were committed to HD-MAC. These two companies never supported in public the argument that digital HDTV might be available sooner than expected. On the contrary, they lobbied the Commission to the effect that HD-MAC would hold the future for Europe until at least the turn of the century. The Commission, in the form of DGXIII, was firmly convinced of the perceived potential of HD-MAC and, accordingly, a series of policies including the MAC Directive were drafted in favour of the equipment manufacturers.[14] However, as mentioned earlier, Philips and Thomson were jointly leading a private research consortium, the ATRC group, to develop a fully digital HDTV system in the US without government subsidy at all. The two companies, and the ATRC group, have also been included in the Grand Alliance. It is highly likely that the expertise gained through their R&D activities in the US will be used by the two companies to manufacture and supply digital TV equipment to the European market, once the digital era comes. In short, industrial lobbying for gaining political and financial support for HD-MAC (mainly an analogue system with digital audio channels) by Philips and Thomson does seem to ontradict these two firms' wholehearted commitment to digital TV R&D activities in the US.

Across the English Channel the UK government had made counter-arguments on many occasions before the collapse of HD-MAC. As discussed above, the Thatcher government had given permission to Rupert Murdoch to launch Sky Television, broadcast to the old PAL standard, which subsequently merged with BSB to terminate the life of MAC as the European DBS standard in the UK. More importantly, the UK government was not even entirely convinced of the technical and market potential of HD-MAC claimed by supporters of this system.

The MAC Directive was due to be renewed by the end of 1991. Due to disagreement about the MAC strategy, the renewal of the Directive was not issued until 11 May 1992. Despite the political difficulties, the Council of Ministers approved the renewed version of the MAC Directive but has left room in the wording of the regulatory text for alternative technologies, such as digital TV, to develop. Compared to the original version of the MAC Directive, the new version emphasizes that European R&D efforts 'must remain the forefront of all new significant developments, such as a trend towards digital television broadcasting emissions', rather than just making MAC and HD-MAC exclusively the official standards for DBS under any circumstance; the new version of the Directive describes MAC and HD-MAC as 'not completely digital transmission standards'.[15] The new version of the MAC Directive is obviously a retreat from the position adopted by the EU in the previous version, on taking into account digital TV development. Unlike the US and Japan, where (respectively) fully digital HDTV and hybrid MUSE systems were firmly supported by government, now the EU's official strategy over HDTV has become obscuring and confusing.

The European Commission led the EU's HDTV policy into deeper political difficulties when it proposed in 1992 another financial subsidy package of 850 million ECUs, called the 'Action Plan', towards MAC and HD-MAC programme-making. The Action Plan, if approved by the Council of Ministers, was intended to run for a five year period from 1992 to 1996 (see Table 9.2). The UK government, via the DTI (Department of Trade and Industry), immediately objected to the Action Plan on the ground that EU taxpayers should not subsidize a technology such as MAC that would soon become obsolete due to the development of digital TV technologies in the US and Europe. The disagreement over the Action Plan between the UK and the other member states became more confrontational in the wake of the EU Edinburgh summit in December 1992. The UK had continuously used its veto power to block the approval of the Action Plan until an acceptable compromise was reached. In order to satisfy the UK government, the Commission cut down its subsidy proposal first to 500 million ECUs, and then to a mere 228 million ECUs from the originally planned 850 million ECUs. In addition to the cut in the amount of subsidy, the technology focus contained in the Action Play was also lost: the finally approved amount of 228 million ECUs was not solely dedicated to helping programme-making to the MAC and HD-MAC standards; on the contrary, the EU subsidy would be made available to the production of advanced TV programmes to any technical standard, so long as the programmes are made with a widescreen format, i.e. the 16X9 picture frame aspect ratio. One may still claim that the Action Plan was part of the EU's technology strategy for HDTV; but it seems to be a strategy without a focus at all.

Table 9.2

Action Plan for the Introduction of Advanced Television Services in Europe (1992-1996), MECU

	1992	1993	1994	1995	1996	**TOTAL**
Broadcasting - Transmission	25	90	100	125	120	**460**
Studio upgrades	-	24	30	6	-	**60**
Production - Production of programmes - Conversion of programmes	4	32.5	70	59.5	54	**220**
Retransmission - Cable networks	4	30	45	19	12	**110**
TOTAL	33	176.5	245	209.5	186	**850**

Source: adapted from CEC, *Proposal for a Council decision on an action plan.*

The declining commitment of the EU to HD-MAC started worrying the manufacturers, particularly Philips, who have already developed prototypes of fully working systems to the European HDTV standard. In January 1993, Philips first announced that the company was to suspend its planned production of HD-MAC receivers. Subsequently, in the following month, Martin Bangemann, the then EU technology commissioner, had to admit in public that the EU might consider adopting the forthcoming American standard for fully digital HDTV in order to foster a global standard for the next generation of TV broadcasting. This announcement has effectively pronounced the total failure of the EU's technology policy for HDTV since the mid-1980s. In the meantime, the same announcement has also spelt out the coming of another era for new TV technologies: digital TV development was to win back the blessing of European policy-makers from analogue or hybrid systems.

Regulating new technologies in an information society

The end of HD-MAC heralded the beginning of a new march towards digital TV broadcasting in Europe. At the top of the list of digital TV research activities at the moment is the formation of the Digital Video Broadcasting (DVB) group in September 1993 with support from the German government and the EBU (European Broadcasting Union). Now the DVB group has been joined by 120 European broadcasting organizations, and it supports the MPEG-2 standard of the ISO (International Standard Organization) for video compression. It seems that the DVB group's approach is winning increased support from the television broadcasting industry and policy-makers in Europe. Instead of regulating the newly emergent digital broadcasting initiatives, the Council of Ministers has now adopted a 'softer' but more flexible policy approach: it has assigned the European Commission the task of monitoring digital TV development and facilitating the co-operative activities within the DVB group so that a common technical solution for digital TV broadcasting can be agreed by members involved. To a certain extent, the EU's new policy stance resembles the FCC's approach since the late 1980s in co-ordinating the process of HDTV development in the US.

In the meantime, the UK government has already made an early move in launching a digital TV broadcasting programme in the autumn 1995. Under the UK government's recent proposal, public organizations (like the BBC) and private companies may apply for the digital channels either independently or in consortium. This government proposal would allow for up to eighteen new digital channels in addition to the four existing analogue ones. If other member states follow suit, digital TV services might see a start in Europe earlier than expected. However, the UK government's digital TV channel allocation plan is being severely challenged by regulatory issues. The ITC (Independent Television Commission) insists that it should be responsible for the allocation of the newly proposed digital channels, whilst the OFTEL argues it is up to them to manage the bidding process. The ITC is currently in charge of independent broadcasting organizations and the OFTEL is a quasi-governmental agency responsible for telecommunications policies. Would these two organizations be merged into a single regulatory body or completely replaced with a new authority in charge of regulating all branches of the ICT sector? It is unlikely that the independent existence of the ITC and OFTEL will last for ever, taking into account the process of convergence led by digitalization.

The change-over from analogue HDTV to digital TV development is another great step towards the formation of an integrated information and communications sector. Now that the telecommunications industry is also being transformed from the traditional analogue transmission (based on the copper wire networks) to digital services with international standards such as the ISDN (Integrated Services Digital Network) and ATM (Asynchronous Transfer Mode) (based on the ever-expanding optical fibre cable networks), consumer electronics, TV broadcasting, and the computer industry are converging into a single ICT sector based on the same digital technology comprising '1s' and '0s'. This in part forms the backbone of the future information society, as far as technology is concerned.

However, the technology convergence process has not been met by a unified body of policies or regulatory regimes at either a national or European level, not to mention a global level. In other words, the disappearance of traditional industry borders within the ICT sector has not been followed by the demise of differentiation between the conventional regulations governing different domains of the same sector.

To be sure, there are attempts by the EU authorities to make policy changes reflect the fast-changing technical circumstances. Among other measures, the European Commission has proposed a deadline of 1 January 1998 for most EU member states to open their telecommunications market to access and more competition within Europe. As the deadline approaches, it seems increasing difficult, if not impossible, for every member state to meet it. In most European countries, the domestic market for telecommunications is still being firmly controlled by the formidable national operators, who own the infrastructures, despite signs of privatization and deregulation efforts made by some member countries.

In June 1993, the Council of Ministers requested a communication from the European Commission on the potential of digital TV broadcasting technology and its implications for the information and communications technology sector as a whole. This in part shows the eagerness of the Council of Ministers to understand and grasp the on-going digital revolution. The Bangemann Report on the European Information Society does seem to be another effort by the European Commission in putting the digitalized ICT jigsaw pieces together. Whilst most member states and many public and commercial organizations have started to respond to the Bangemann Report with great enthusiasm, it is worth recalling the process and result of regulating technical change in ICT by the EU.

The EU's strong interventionist technology policy in picking winners at the early stages of technical change in HDTV, and the inability of public authorities to understand, and reflect accordingly, the development of new technology, led to the eventual failure of the European HD-MAC technology. In contrast, the more open and flexible policy approach adopted by the FCC did help establish the single digital HDTV system. The case of HDTV development in Europe and abroad seems to have important implications for the rest of the ICT sector and, more broadly, for the future European information society. Referring to the questions raised at the beginning of this chapter, it is not my intention to suggest a hands-off approach to public policy makers. Indeed, market failure seems to exist in certain domains of ICT, such as the telecommunications industry and the TV broadcasting industry, where public regulatory authorities may not and should not avoid holding responsibilities. The standardization process of these ICT branches is so complicated that not regulation, nor deregulation, nor the market in its own right would solve the difficulties. Most importantly, when there exists an interplay between corporate strategies and public policy, the risk and consequence of being unable to make a balance between private and public interests seems to be high and serious, as the case of HDTV has shown. Finally, despite the importance of the ICT sector to the future European information society, the costs of creating a parochialist European policy response to external competition, regardless of the process of digitalization and global standardization, are likely to be high; this is because the European information society will exist only when it is a part of a broader global information society.

Notes

1. The original 'Three Golden Projects' started in 1993, including the Golden Bridge, Golden Customs and Golden Card projects. Several other projects have been subsequently added to the 'Golden Projects' lists. These are Golden Tax, Golden Agriculture, Golden Enterprises, Golden Intelligence, Golden Education and Golden Macroscopic. It is hoped that the completion of these 'Golden Projects' will lead to an early stage of an information society in China characterized by digital ISDN and broadband multimedia communications and services all over the country.

2. BT estimates that to lay a nationwide optical fibre network would cost about £15bn.

3. Internet is the largest computer network in the world. Started as a military, and then a research and academic, computer network in the US in the 1960s, the Internet now reaches most parts of the world. To a certain extent, the Internet is an early version of the future global information superhighway. Free access to the Internet is now being seriously challenged by commercialized information provision from a range of private companies such as CompuServe, Delphi, and the newly launched Microsoft Network.

4. PAL (Phase Alteration by Line) is adopted in most European countries such as the UK and Germany; SECAM (Séquence à Memoire) is the TV standard in France; NTSC (National Television Systems Committee) is used in the US and Japan. Now that PAL and SECAM have already been made compatible with each other, standard difference between European countries for colour TV broadcasting has now disappeared. However, the two European standards remain incompatible with the American standard (note that

NTSC was developed in the US and subsequently adopted in Japan).

5. On HDTV as a strategic technology, see Dai, Cawson, & Holmes, *Competition, collaboration and public policy.*

6. All the HDTV sets currently available in Japan have been built with traditional CRTs, rather than flat screens. This is because the electronics companies are unable to bring out a flat panel display large enough for being used as a 'home cinema' screen.

7. Note that digital stereo sound effect is also realized on today's conventional colour TV sets built with NICAM technology.

8. The MAC Directive refers to the EC Council Directive, *On the adoption of common technical specifications.*

9. See *The Financial Times*, 29 April 1995.

10. More precisely, BSB used the D-MAC version of the MAC/packet standard family.

11. See Cawson, 'High definition television', 163.

12. See Dai, 'Corporate strategies and public policy', Chapter 6.

13. Members of this group include the Swedish Broadcasting Corporation, Telia Research, Teracom, Telecom Denmark and Telecom Norway.

14. For instance, in the text of the 1986 MAC Directive it was made clear that the implementation of common technical specifications for the MAC and HD-MAC 'leads to the creation of a large unified market, on which products will be freely exchanged without any technical barriers, which will be of great economic benefit for the European electronics industry as regards its competitiveness.' It is obvious that priority consideration was given to the European manufacturing industry in the MAC Directive, rather than any other interested group such as the private broadcasting industry or European consumers.

15. See EC Directive, 'On the adoption of standards'.

References

Bangemann, M., *Meeting the challenges: establishing a successful European industrial policy* (London, Kogan Page, 1993).

Bangemann, M. [on behalf of the European Commission], *Europe and the global information society: recommendations to the European Council* (Corfu, 24-25 June 1994) ['The Bangemann Report'].

Cawson, A., 'High definition television in Europe', *The Political Quarterly* (April-June 1995), 157-73.

Commission of the European Communities, *Improving the functioning of consumer electronics markets* (Brussels, 1991).

Commission of the European Communities, *Proposal for a Council decision on an action plan for the introduction of advanced television services in Europe,* COM(92) 154 final (Brussels, 5 May 1992).

Commission of the European Communities, *Digital video broadcasting: a framework for Community policy: communications from the Commission and draft Council resolution,* EC/6 COM(93)557 (Brussels, 1993).

Commission of the European Communities, *Strategy options to strengthen the European programme industry in the context of the audiovisual policy of the European Union,* Green Paper, COM(94) 96 final (Brussels, 1994).

Dai, X., 'Corporate strategies and public policy in the European consumer electronics industry: a case study of Philips', unpublished PhD thesis, University of Sussex (Brighton, 1994).

Dai, X., *Corporate strategy, public policy and new technologies: Philips and the European consumer electronics industry* (Oxford, Elesevier, 1996).

Dai, X, A. Cawson, & P. Holmes, *Competition, collaboration and public policy: a case study of the European HDTV strategy,* Working Papers in Contemporary European Studies 3 (Brighton, Sussex European Institute, February 1994).

Dai, X, A. Cawson, & P. Holmes, 'The rise and fall of high definition television: the impact of European technology policy', *Journal of Common Market Studies* (forthcoming, June 1996).

EIU (The Economist Intelligence Unit), *High definition television progress and prospects: a maturing technology in search of a market*, Special Report No. 2189 (London, Business International Ltd, 1991).

EU95 Directorate, *Progressing towards HDTV* (Brussels, Eureka 95 HDTV Directorate, June 1991).

European Community Council Directive, *On the adoption of common technical specifications of the MAC/packet family of standards for direct satellite television broadcasting,* 86/529/EEC (Brussels, 3 November 1986).

European Community Council Directive, 'On the adoption of standards for satellite broadcasting of television signals', 11 May 1992, *Official Journal of the European Communities,* L 137 (20 May 1992).

Evans, B., *Digital HDTV: the way forward* (London, IBC Technical Services Ltd., 1992).

Farrell, J. & C. Shapiro, 'Standard setting in high-definition television', *Brookings Papers on Economic Activity: Microeconomics* (Washington D.C., The Brookings Institution, 1992), 1-93.

Krugman, P.R., ed., *Strategic trade policy and the new international economics* (Cambridge Mass., MIT Press, 1986).

Lang, Y.H., *Dianshi zai Germing: Mingri de Dianshi Shijie* [TV revolution: tomorrow's world of television] (Taiwan, Cheng Chung Book Co., 1990).

Tyson, L. d'A., *Who's bashing whom? Trade conflicts in high-technology industries* (Washington DC, Institute for International Economics, 1992).

Watson-Brown, A., 'The campaign for high definition television: a case study in triad power', *Euro-Asia Business Review*, 6 no 2 (April 1987), 3-11.

Index

European Bank for Reconstruction and Development (EBRD) 155-156
European Broadcasting Union (EBU) 192, 218
European Coal and Steel Community (ECSC) 9, 11, 33, 46-49, 98, 102, 137
European Cultural Foundation 101
European Defence Community (EDC) 47-48
European Monetary Union (EMU) 136, 142-143
European Movement 49, 100-101, 103
European Parliament 14, 38, 140, 177
Federal Communications Committee (FCC) 207-208, 212-214, 218-219
First World War 33, 40, 56, 79, 87, 113
Francken, Frans 82
Franks 22, 54, 57
Gasperi, Alcide de 102
Grotius, Hugo 14
Habermas, Jürgen 110, 126
Hecataeus 65, 68
High Definition Television (HDTV) 203-220
Hippocrates 15, 59
Hitler, Adolf 24, 135
Homer 11
Hondius, Jodocus 73
Hugo, Victor Marie 55
Humanism
    Classical 12
    Renaissance 11, 190
Imperialism 2, 15, 56, 85, 87-88, 181, 187
Industrialization 1, 13-15, 39, 108-110, 124, 160, 202

Integrated Services Digital Network (ISDN) 218
International Monetary Fund (IMF) 152, 168
Isidore, Bishop of Seville 68, 80
Islam 20, 54-55, 57
Jerome, St. 79
Josephus 79
Keulen, Gerard van 84-85
League of Nations 40, 42, 44-45
MAC (Multiplexed Analogue Component) Directive 210-211, 214-216
Machiavelli, Niccolò 16
Magellan, Ferdinand 72
Marshall Plan 46, 155-156
Martel, Charles 54
Mazzini, Guiseppe 40, 55, 106
Mercator, Gerard 73
Messina Declaration 48
Modernism 10-11
Monnet, Jean 47, 49, 102, 142
Montesquieu, Charles de Secondat 16, 38, 115-116
Multiplexed Analogue Component (MAC) 206-219
Münster, Sebastian 16, 82
Mussolini, Benito 135
Napoleon I (Bonaparte) 38, 57-58, 62-63, 125
National Information Infrastructure (NII) initiative 201-202
Nationalism 2-4, 23, 56, 85, 87-89, 99, 103-105, 108-109, 111, 118, 124-125, 134, 137, 153-154, 164, 166, 181, 189, 192
Nazism 23, 58, 79, 116
NORDSAT 193
Organization for European Economic Cooperation (OEEC) 46
Ortelius 60, 82
Ostpolitik 152, 156, 158